strange foods

bush meat, bats, and butterflies
an epicurean adventure around the world

strange foods

**bush meat, bats,
and butterflies**
an epicurean adventure
around the world

by jerry hopkins
photography by michael freeman

PERIPLUS

Published by Periplus Editions (HK) Ltd.
Text copyright© 1999 Haku 'Olelo Inc
Photos copyright© 1999 Michael Freeman
ISBN 962-593-154-6

Hopkins, Jerry.
  Strange foods: bush meats, bats and
butterflies
by Jerry Hopkins: with photographs by
Michael Freeman. -- 1st. ed.
    p. cm.
  ISBN 9625931546 (pb)
  1. Gastronomy. 2. Cookery. I. Title.
TX631.H56   1999
641'.01'3--dc21   98-56158
                                             CIP

Publisher: Eric Oey
Associate Publisher: Christina Ong
Designer: William Atyeo

Distributed by:
USA: Tuttle Publishing, Airport Industrial
Park, PR1 Box 231-5, North Clarendon,
Vermont 05759-9700

Japan: Tuttle Publishing, R K Building,
2nd Floor 2-13-10, Shimo-Meguro,
Meguro-ku, Tokyo 1530064.

Asia Pacific: Berkeley Books Pte. Ltd.,
5 Little Road, #08-01 Singapore 536983

Endpaper front: The preparation of cassava
bread from poisonous manioc in a
Wapisana village in the interior of today's
Guyana is shown in this 1840 print. Two
women grate the tubers to a pulp, which
will then be squeezed in the long woven
tube hanging behind them. The resulting
paste, in the tray in the foreground, is then
formed into flat, thin cakes, which another
woman cooks on a large hotplate. The
finished bread is stored on the roof thatch.
Endpaper back: Cricket Lick-It lollipops:
candy with a crunchy center.
Endpaper verso: The agave "worm" at the
end of a bottle of Mexican mezcal is in fact
a moth pupa.
Title page: Tibetan pilgrims halt on the
arduous circuit around Mount Kailash –
Asia's most sacred mountain – to eat yak
meat and brew yak butter tea.
This page: One of the oldest Eskimo
groups, the Ostiaks, are pictured here eating
raw reindeer meat off the bone, a delicacy
not usually enjoyed by these people.

Photographer's Note

My secret training began as a child, at
an English boarding school. I realise that
few readers will truly appreciate the
significance of this, but survival depended
heavily on being able to eat, for weeks at
a time, a food regime that was modelled
loosely on that of Victorian prisons.
A cartoonist called Ronald Searle once
produced a book about these very English
institutions, and to my mind no-one has
bettered his description of school dinner
as "the piece of cod which passeth all
understanding." There can no finer
education of the palate to accept the
impossible than the one I and my fellow
inmates received, and for that I am, as
was intoned before each meal, "truly
grateful."

　　As a photographer, I put my catholic
tastes to work and began, many years ago,
shooting the weird culinary habits that I
came across. Much of this was in Asia,
not only because the region became
something of a speciality of mine, but
because the southern Chinese and their
neighbours, particularly in Thailand, Laos
and Vietnam, have a greater fascination
with unusual foods than any other culture
I know. So where more appropriate should
I meet Jerry for the first time than in
Bangkok, where we found that we shared
many of the same tastes.

　　With very few exceptions, I ate what
you see photographed here. Keeping or
consuming the props, I should explain, is
considered one of the perks of
photography, and where a fashion
photographer might get the clothes at the
end of the shoot (or the model if lucky), I
would be left with the gooey parts. Yes,
that includes the rats and the bats and the
buffalo's penis—two-and-a-half feet, by
the way, when flaccid. My only regret is
that the publisher excised some of the best
bits on the grounds of common decency.
Surely you wouldn't have been offended
by the breakfast of raw chopped dog,
flavoured with its bile? On second
thought, perhaps you would.

reptiles & water creatures 70

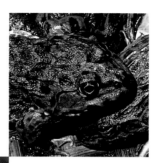

72   snake
78   lizards
84   alligator & crocodile
90   frog & toad
94   shark
98   fugu
104   jellyfish
106   snails & slugs
110   worms
112   fish eggs

viii   one man's meat...another's poison

mammals 2

4   dogs & cats
10   horse
14   rat & mouse
20   bats
26   primates & other bush meat
36   bison, water buffalo, & yak
42   whale
46   guts
50   ears, eyes, noses, lungs, tongues,
      lips, gums, glands, & feet
56   genitilia
60   urine
62   human flesh

contents

insects, spiders, & scorpions 142

144 grasshoppers
148 ants & termites
154 spiders & scorpions
158 beetles
164 crickets & cicadas
168 butterflies & moths
172 flies

plants 178

180 poisonous plants
186 flowers
190 cactus
194 durian

leftovers 202

birds 118

120 ostrich & emu
124 song birds, pigeons, & doves
128 birds' nest
136 balut

204 blood
208 live & almost live
212 fermented food
216 fake food
222 gold, silver, & pearls
226 dirt
230 selected bibliography
232 acknowledgments

one man's meat...another's poison

He was a
bold man
who first
swallowed
an oyster.

—Jonathan Swift

About 150 years ago, an eccentric English gentle-man named Francis Trevelyan Buckland invited a group of influential Earls and Viscounts and Marquis to dinner and in an attempt to expand their dietary horizons placed the freshly-killed haunch of an African beast on the table at London's famed Aldersgate Tavern. It was, he said, eland, a large ante-lope, and he thought they should be imported and bred on the green meadows of Great Britain, to the gustatory delight and nutritional benefit of all its citi-zens. The crusade that followed the dinner attracted considerable attention in the daily press, but no one seemed much interested in taking it any further, and the eland remained in Africa.

Buckland was not discouraged. He was raised by eccentric and imaginative parents, and as a child he had eaten dog, crocodile, and garden snails, a habit he kept for life. To a fellow undergraduate at Oxford he confessed that earwigs were "horribly bitter," although the worst-tasting thing was the mole, until he ate a bluebottle fly. Later, guests at his London home were served panther, elephant trunk soup, and roast giraffe, and it was reliably reported that whenever an animal died at the London Zoo, the curator called the Buckland home.

Buckland pressed on, forming, in 1860, the Acclimatisation Society of the United Kingdom, followed by sister societies in Scotland, the Channel Islands, France, Russia, the United States, the Hawaiian Islands, Australia, and New Zealand. His goal was the same: to introduce new food sources worldwide. In the end, his efforts failed. The world's dinner table did not welcome Tibetan yak, Eurasian beaver, parrots and parakeets, the Japanese sea slug, steamed kangaroo, seaweed jelly, silkworms, bird's nest soup, or sinews of the Axis deer, and Buckland died in 1880 in relative obscurity, where he remains today.

Since Buckland's failed effort, there have been several campaigns, both public and private, under-written by the United Nations and individual countries as well as by ranchers, academics, and businessmen, to introduce "exotic" foods to the closed diet of what generally is called the "west," but in fact is epitomized by the gastronomical habits of Europe and North America. (And hereafter will be called Euro-America.) Nearly all have been unsuccessful and many were opposed vehemently.

Then, in 1996, came "mad cow disease," and when British beef was banned by the European Union, the media published and broadcast stories about ostrich and kangaroo and other beef substitutes. As British Airways added ostrich medallions to its first-class menu and other unusual protein sources appeared in European supermarkets and more wild game became available in North America, a growing number started taking "strange foods" seriously. In Southeast Asia, Australia, and the United States, struggling alligator and crocodile farms found new markets, domestic and foreign. In Singapore, an established investment ser-vice began offering ostrich "futures": invest in a pair of breeders and reap the profits in the sale of their offspring, ranging from twenty to forty a year. From Sydney to Nairobi to Los Angeles, "jungle" restau-rants, where game and other exotic dishes were served, became an overpriced trend. At the same time, a few naturalists made an interesting pitch to envi-ronmentalists, arguing that the way to save threatened species was to give them commercial value: guarantee their survival by eating them. Once there was a mar-ket for these beasts as a food, they suggested, people would start breeding endangered species instead of killing them.

"There are no more than one dozen species of domestic animals which are major food producers around the world," Russell Kyle argued logically in *A Feast in the Wild*, a book published in 1987. "If one adds the species with limited, local importance, such as the yak in the Himalayas, or the alpaca in the Andes, there are still fewer than twenty domestic species altogether with a major role as food producers. And yet the world as a whole contains over 200 species of herbivorous animals from the size of a hare upwards. Why have men apparently never considered making more deliberate use of so many wild animals for food production?"

Through history and around the world, what is eaten has varied greatly from time to time and place to place, from one culture to another. Much of the dietary change has resulted from history's "natural" development—for example, the Portuguese introduced Brazilian chili peppers to Asian cuisine when they started trading there and Marco Polo packed spices and teas back to Europe following his first journeys to China. Similar change continues today as modern travelers return home with a newfound taste for foods experienced abroad, and as more migrants from one part of the world to another take their distinctive cuisines along with them; thus, most if not all Euro-American cities now have sushi bars and Thai restaurants (to name just two examples), unknown only a few years ago. Over the centuries, many other factors have influenced diet, from religious beliefs to hunger to flavor to status to medicinal (and, some insist, aphrodisiacal) properties and more.

What it all comes down to was stated simply and eloquently by M.F.K. Fisher, arguably the best writer about food in the twentieth century, who wrote in a book aptly titled *How to Cook a Wolf* (1942). "Why," she asked, "is it worse, in the end, to see an animal's head cooked and prepared for our pleasure than a thigh or a tail or a rib? If we are going to live on other inhabitants of this world we must not bind ourselves with illogical prejudices, but savor to the fullest the beasts we have killed.

"People who feel that a lamb's cheek is gross and vulgar when a chop is not are like the medieval philosophers who argued about such hair-splitting

problems as how many angels could dance on the head of a pin. If you have these prejudices, ask yourself if they are not built on what you may have been taught when you were young and unthinking, and then if you can, teach yourself to enjoy some of the parts of an animal that are not commonly prepared."

Calf brains, sheep tongues, chicken feet, pig entrails, fish heads, the list goes on and on. Add "unusual" species such as ants and termites, beetles, bats, water buffalo, algae, cactus, rats and mice, flowers, elephants, whales, grubs, and earthworms, the start of another long list. And, yes, add all those protein sources that so many regard only as pets: cats and dogs, hamsters and gerbils, horses, exotic birds and fish. How many of us would push ourselves away from the table when such dishes were served, as the late Ms. Fisher said, because of what we learned when we were young?

All that said, much regional individuality remains in the world. In Taiwan, serpent blood is a tonic. Many in the southwestern part of the United States swear by rattlesnake steak, just as kangaroo meat is a principal part of the diet for many Australian aborigines and appears on restaurant menus in dozens of Aussie restaurants. A small neighborhood in Hanoi and several in Seoul specialize in dog dishes (not to be confused with dishes from which dogs eat). Bulls' and sheep's testicles called Rocky Mountain Oysters are accepted in the American west, while in China, pigs' ears, fish eyes, and rooster wattle are chopsticked up with gusto. In Southeast Asia, fried locusts are regarded as tasty snacks, just as monkey stew is a staple in parts of Africa and the Amazon, guinea pig is an essential protein source in Peru. Ants and termites are cherished in Africa and South America, yak milk is made

Above: In the November 22, 1890 issue of the French publication *Le Don Quichotte*, the French deride acts of cannibalism allegedly taking place in the British colonies of Africa.

into butter in Tibet and then added to tea, and horse-meat has an avid, centuries-old following in France, with another market expanding in Japan. These foods, accepted in one region, are rejected by diners in others. What is considered repulsive to someone in one part of the world, in another part of the world is simply considered lunch.

I've followed Ms. Fisher's lead and tried to make this book a guide to how the other half dines and why. I'm no Frank Buckland, but over a period of twenty-five years I have rejected my meat-and-potatoes upbringing in the United States frequently to try a wide variety of regional specialties, from steamed water beetles, fried grasshoppers and ants, to sparrow, bison and crocodile, the latter three served en casserole, grilled, and in a curry, respectively. I have eaten deep-fried bull's testicles in Mexico, live shrimp sushi in Hawaii, mice cooked over an open wood fire in

Thailand, pig stomach soup in Singapore, minced water buffalo and yak butter tea in Nepal, stir-fried dog and "five penis wine" in China, and the boiled blood of a variety of animals in Vietnam. This list, too, goes on, and I share some of these experiences in the chapters following, along with some recipes. After all, no matter what humans eat, by choice or circumstance, the one thing all the dishes have in common is that they must be prepared properly. Of course, there are some people who oppose such exploration. Conservationists are concerned, correctly, about the disappearance of endangered species. Others worry about animal rights, objecting to the manner in which even non-threatened species are penned or caged and slaughtered. A third group—called "bunny-huggers" in wildlife circles—cries out when people eat animals that they, the protestors, call pets, reminding me of Alice at the banquet in *Through the Looking Glass*, who turned away the mutton because it was impolite to eat food you'd been introduced to.

I will not engage animal rights people in debate. Their point of view is valid and, in fact, carries incalculable weight in a world where resources and environment are being threatened in a manner that is as alarming as it is unrelenting. Many argue that this alone will expand our gastronomical frontiers, whether we like it or not. As Mr. Kyle wrote, cattle are notoriously unkind to the earth and in time there won't be enough pasture to accommodate the world demand, forcing us to dine on alternate protein sources. The one mentioned most often? Insects.

I don't insist that you to add ostrich or dog or grasshopper to your menu, although I do suggest that you consider expanding your diet to include something outside the ordinary. However, as a frequent traveler, I do urge anyone who shares my passion for new places and peoples to heed that old but good advice about "when in Rome, do as the Romans do." Try some of the local food; I believe that it's a path to understanding the culture better than any other outside learning the language, marrying a native, or con-

Below: The ingredients for a special Balinese version of *pepes,* a dish cooked in banana leaf packets over an open grill. Garlic, ginger, lime, chillies, fish paste, tamarind paste, monosodium glutamate, coconut paste, and freshly caught dragonflies (less wings).
Opposite, above: The appeal of raw seafood—here abalone, sea squirt and octopus—lies as much in the interesting, often rubbery, textures as in the delicate flavour.
Opposite, below: What could be stranger than Space Shuttle food? A dinner of marinated shrimp, noodles, peas, sliced fruit, and candies would make anyone long for comfort food.

verting to the local religion.

Of course, species on the endangered list are not recommended, except under special circumstances. (There are sections on elephants and whales.) There is no need. There are too many other tasty choices.

There also is the matter of curiosity and the pleasant surprise that frequently follows it. "I have always believed, perhaps too optimistically," Ms. Fisher wrote in a book called *An Alphabet for Gourmets* (1949), "that I would like to taste everything once, never from such hunger as made friends of mine in France in 1942 eat guinea-pig ragout, but from pure gourmandism."

Remember the person who first tasted the oyster. It's not just dinner, it's an adventure.

mammals

mammals

Previous: Irula rat catchers in southern India fill their sack with the day's haul of animals caught from their nests and tunnels under the rice fields.
Below: The embryo of a calf on sale at a meat stall in the morning market of Phayao in northern Thailand.
Opposite: Held in the soil-encrusted fingers of a south Indian rat-catcher, a newly born mole-rat, found in a nest under a rice field, will be a part of the evening meal for the family. Rats threaten the country's rice crop, and the catchers are non-caste tribal peoples who eke out a living by selling the animals, which are also an essential part of their diet.

No one is sure what the first humans ate. In Neanderthal times, the mammoth played a large role in human life: courageously brought down by hunters with spears, a mammoth could feed, say, a dozen or more caves full of people for a week or more. Many drawings found in such caves in Europe, North America, and elsewhere show men hunting great hairy beasts. Archeological digs have uncovered the well-chewed bones of dozens of animals.

Since then, of course, the number of mammal species consumed throughout the world has multiplied quickly as hunting, transport, and marketing advances have enabled all types of meat to reach a larger audience, and in smaller, more manageable portions. It is not necessary nowadays to deal with a dead mammoth outside the cave when there are steaks in the freezer and quarter-pounders at the fast-food outlet.

That said, despite these advances and a current upward trend in the consumption of certain exotic foods, it can be argued that the number of protein sources for a growing world population is shrinking rather than expanding, at least proportionately. Through history, humans have eaten virtually everything that walked, including each other. However, the consumption of the four herbivorous mammals that provide eighty percent of the world's protein—cattle, pigs, sheep, and goats—has become more prevalent. Thus, as the number of species being added to the menu goes up, the proportions, worldwide, are running the other way.

Some chapters here include animals found on endangered-species lists. I am not advocating irresponsible or illegal hunting activities. These species have a long history as food that continues to the present time, so they cannot be denied from any survey that has any pretensions to historical accuracy. More importantly, *some of these animals are not always threatened* in every location and circumstance. That many mammals have disappeared from the menu can be explained in part by the unfortunate number of species added to the endangered lists, and their removal from the approved diet may be applauded. At the same time, the Gang of Four—beef, pork, lamb, and goat—has gained ground because of fashion and the outside influence that accompanies the press of history. In Japan, for example, meat was virtually untouched before the country opened up to the West in the mid-nineteenth century, and in China, where tofu was first produced some two thousand years ago McDonald's outlets now rival

the number of vegetarian restaurants in Beijing.

Notions of class and caste exerted other forces. Some animal foods, such as possum in the United States, became associated with the poor, the "lower class," and thus were not accepted at "better" tables, just as what is called "bush meat" in Africa and "bush tucker" in Australia traditionally was consumed by indigenous peoples, and thus shunned by those who fancied themselves fancier. At the same time, a number of specific mammal parts—blood, brains, certain innards, and sexual organs, for example—were disdained because they were not considered a "proper" food for the proper lady and gentleman.

Certain religions also played and continue to play a role. Hindus do not eat beef, Muslims and Orthodox Jews do not eat pork, and even today many Catholics eat only fish on Fridays. Some of these guidelines and taboos have their origins in practicality. Pork has been banned for thousands of years in the Middle East and remains on the taboo list for many hundreds of millions today because it is an unclean animal and spoils quickly; modern refrigeration has eliminated most of the threat, but the belief remains in force. It may also be argued that beef in modern India is an inefficient food source because grazing cattle would take away land required by more productive crops such as rice and vegetables; before 800 B.C., however, when India was lightly populated, beef was welcome at mealtimes.

In the chapters that follow, I talk about mammals ranging in size from the mouse and the bat to the elephant and the whale, including animals both domesticated and wild. I've also selected foods from all corners of the earth, from horse tartare in France to dog soup in Korea.

Some the chapters may offend some Euro-Americans because the animals they regard as pets or partners are eaten elsewhere in the world. Perhaps with no other food is the "gastronomical

gap" made more clear than with the dog, welcome on laps by Euro-Americans, and on plates in China and Southeast Asia, where it is ordinary fare. Second to the dog comes the horse as man's closest companion and helper through history. Yet, horses are regarded highly at mealtime in many countries, from France and Belgium to Japan, where horse is cherished by many as a delicacy. A recent Indian prime minister began each day with a glass of his own urine, and on a program produced by the BBC in London in 1997, human placenta was blended into a delicious paté.

dogs & cats

In most Euro-American countries (except in some immigrant communities, of course), dog is man's best friend, or so they say. That explains why so many North Americans and Europeans get so upset when this animal is eaten so matter-of-factly in many Asian and Latin American countries, and why one-time movie sex goddess in France, Brigitte Bardot, is campaigning so vigorously to get the government of South Korea to ban the eating of dog—a cherished staple in that country—in advance of soccer's 2002 World Cup tourney.

Ms. Bardot speaks for an animal-rights foundation bearing her name that is telling soccer fans not to attend the games if eating dogs is not outlawed and all the restaurants in Seoul offering dog on the menu aren't closed. While hers is a valid point of view shared by many Euro-Americans, in other parts of the world—especially in numerous Asian countries—it is incomprehensible. Dog is an affordable protein source not only Korea, but in most of southern China (including Hong Kong) and much of Southeast Asia, as well as in parts of Latin America.

There are precedents for Ms. Bardot's proposed ban, however. In 1988, the South Korean government ruled that restaurants serving dog soup, or *poshintang*, be closed to present a better image for foreigners attending the Olympic Games. Ten years later, in 1998, Philippine President Fidel Ramos signed into law a statute banning the killing of dogs for food, although its extreme popularity in the north made success of enforcement questionable.

Similar action has been taken elsewhere. In 1989, two Cambodian refugees living in Southern California were charged with animal cruelty for eating a German Shepherd puppy. The charges eventually were dropped when a judge ruled that the dog was killed by the acceptable practices of slaughtering agricultural livestock. That did not satisfy activists who later the same year convinced the California legislature into passing a law making it a misdemeanor to eat a dog or a cat, punishable by up to six months in jail and a fine of $1,000. Later still, the law was amended to include any animal traditionally kept as a pet or companion. Presumably, those charged with enforcing this law were expected to look the other way when 4-H Club members led their prize cattle and pigs to slaughter, animals they had raised from birth and for whom they frequently developed great affection. Furthermore, rabbits could still be killed and eaten and so could tropical fish, because they were legally categorized as livestock and fish, not pets.

There is no mystery why so many Euro-Americans oppose the eating of dog. There have been too many

How Much Is That Doggie in the Paddy?

"The Lao [residents of Laos and northeastern Thailand] say eel is the best water meat and that dog is the best land meat," Chavalit Phorak, a man in the dog-slaughtering business in Thailand told *The Nation*, a Bangkok newspaper, in 1997. "It's much tastier than beef and not as tough. In the past, families used to kill a dog to eat each week. People liked the meat, but they had to be careful not to exhaust their supply. After all, there's not much meat on a big dog, let alone a pup, and a dog takes time to grow, so farming them is still impractical."

In most countries where dog is eaten, farming is not necessary, as strays and other unwanted canines are plentiful. For this reason, there are men like Chavalit, who travels the back roads and barters for village dogs, then sells the meat, entrails, and skins. "My truck has a loudspeaker," he said. "Everywhere I go I tell people that I will give them pails for their naughty or lazy dogs."

A healthy dog, in 1997, was worth two buckets. It took Chavalit three or four days to collect a hundred dogs, the number at which he broke even and possibly earned a small profit, as each trip cost as much as US$400 for petrol and pails. He then returned to the slaughterhouse, where butchers were paid twelve cents for every dog they killed, with a blow to the head with a hammer so as not to damage the skin.

Another twelve cents was paid for skinning the dogs, plus sixteen cents for butchering the meat. The meat was then sold for up to $2 a kilo, with each dog contributing about three kilos, and the skins were sold for between $1 and $2 to factories in Thailand, Taiwan, and Japan, where they were turned into golf gloves. (Think about that next time you step up to the tee.) The genitals were also sold, for about forty cents, and used in soup and wine, mainly in China, Korea, Vietnam, and Japan.

dog heroes in literature, TV, and film—in stories by Jack London and dozens more, in movies like *Rin Tin Tin, Lassie, Benji,* and Disney's enduring *101 Dalmatians,* in virtually everything writ large in popular culture, from the heroic K-9 Corps in the U.S. military to the Saint Bernard who carries a flask of life-saving grog to humans lost in the Alps. In addition, the dog—believed to be a domestication of a Neolithic Asiatic wolf—through the years has proven useful to man because of its speed, hearing, sense of smell, hunting instinct, herding abilities, and companionship. So even for those who enjoy snails and octopus and may even be so brave as to try rattlesnake chili and shark's fin soup, the line is drawn when it comes to man's canine friend.

All that said, dog has been a welcome dish across much of the world's history and geography. The recorded eating of dog goes back to Confucius's time in China, circa 500 B.C., when the *Li chi,* a handbook of ancient ritual translated in 1885, offered recipes for delicacies prepared on ceremonial occasions. One of the dishes was canine, fried rice with crispy chunks cut from a wolf's breast, served with dog liver basted in its own fat, roasted and seared over charcoal. During the same period, an emperor who wanted more warriors encouraged childbirth by awarding what was described in the literature of the time as a succulent puppy to any woman bearing a boy.

The Chinese (and other Asians) regarded dog meat as more than a culinary treat. It was considered to be very good for the *yang,* the male, hot, extroverted part of human nature, as opposed to the female, cool, introverted *yin.* It was believed to "warm" the blood and thus was consumed in greatest frequency during the winter months. As early as the fourth century B.C., a Chinese philosopher named Mencius praised dog meat for its pharmaceutical properties, recommending it for liver ailments, malaria, and jaundice. Along with many other foods, it also was believed to enhance virility. The Chinese also served a sort of dog wine, believed to be a remedy for weariness.

Later, the Manchu Dynasty that ruled China from the seventeenth century A.D. banned dog meat, declaring its consumption barbarian. However, southern Chinese continued to eat it and Sun Yat-sen's opposition Kuomintang followers began their meetings by cooking dog, believing the act symbolized their anti-Manchu revolution. The code name was "Three-Six Meat," a play on the Chinese word for the number nine, which rhymed with the word for dog. Even today in Hong Kong, where since 1950 it has been illegal to catch or kill dogs or to possess their meat, butchers and customers use the expression "Three-Six Meat" when selling and buying it. Because Hong Kong Chinese are from southern China, where dog is still regarded as a staple, enforcement of the law has been negligible: punishment (up to six months in prison and a fine of US$125) has been lax, and the law is widely ignored, especially during the winter months when demand is greatest.

It is well-known that the American Indian originated in what is now Mongolia, and it's believed that they brought the dog with them when they crossed the Bering Sea and eventually settled the wilderness that became North America. When European explorers and settlers arrived in the New World, they counted seventeen dog varieties, many of them raised specifically as food, although it was noted that not all tribes indulged. Those that did included the Iroquois and several Algonquin tribes of the central and eastern woodlands and the Utes of Utah, who cooked and ate dog meat before performing sacred ceremonial dances. While the very name of the Arapahoe means "dog-eater." David Comfort writes in *The First Pet History of the World* (1994) that puppies were generally preferred because of their tenderness: "They were fattened with a special mixture of pemmican and dried fruit. After harvest with a tomahawk, the puppy was suspended upside down from a lodge pole, and the carcass hand-marinated with buffalo fat. Then it was skewered."

Many of the early European arrivals contentedly, or at least circumstantially, joined in. According to Mr.

Dog Capital of the World

Guangzhou, about two hours from Hong Kong, is regarded as the "dog capital" of the gastronomical world. I stayed on Shamian Island, a onetime sandspit in the Pearl River that was ceded to the British and French following the Opium Wars of the 18th century, now a European-styled neighborhood with gardens and colonial buildings, as well as several tourist-class hotels. Across the canal separating Shamian Island from what is otherwise an undistinguished Chinese city is the Qingping Market, one of the late Premier Deng Xiaoping's most radical innovations, a street market operated by entrepreneurs, a concept that subsequently spread throughout much of China. The market in Guangzhou is different from the others, however.

Once past two city blocks of stalls selling traditional medicine—beetles,

lizards, starfish, seahorses, deer antlers, flowers and the like, all dried— I came to a cross street where the goods were all alive. Hundreds of frogs hopped in wire cages and eels and large water bugs swarmed in plastic tanks of aerated water. More tubs offered crawling crabs, crayfish, worms, and scorpions. There were turtles from one inch across to the size of a small beer keg. In metal cages stacked head-high were dogs, cats, small deer, pigeons, peacocks, guinea pigs, rabbits, and a number of dog-sized rodents called coypu. Everything was butchered on the spot on request or shoved into a sack for home preparation if the buyer wished to keep the dinner fresh.

In a phrase: a take-away zoo. Best to arrive before 10:00 am for the widest choice.

Comfort's text, Cabeza de Vaca, the Spanish explorer, was shipwrecked in the Gulf of Mexico and wandered for eight years on foot throughout the American Southwest, eating canine regularly. In Christopher Columbus's time, Mexico's only domesticated livestock were the turkey and the dog and according to a history written in the sixteenth century, the two meats were served in a single dish. Meriwether Lewis, leader of the Lewis and Clark Expedition that opened the American Northwest, wrote in his journal in 1804, "Having been so long accustomed to live on the flesh of dogs, the greater part of us have acquired a fondness for it, and our original aversion for it overcome by reflecting that while we subsisted on that food we were fatter, stronger, and in general enjoyed better health than at any period since leaving buffalo country." As recently as 1928, the Norwegian explorer Roald Amundsen ate his sled dogs in the Arctic in his attempt to reach the North Pole, although that was, admittedly, for reasons of survival and not by choice.

Nor was canine cuisine limited to Asia and North America. For at least a thousand years, Polynesians cherished the *poi* dog, so called because the animal's diet was vegetarian, consisting largely of *poi*, or cooked taro root. This was one of the food animals taken to what is now Hawaii on primitive sailing ships from Tahiti and the Marquesas (along with the pig). At large feasts in Hawaii in the early 1800s, hosted by local royalty and attended by sailors from England and the United States, as many as two hundred to four hundred dogs were served at a single sitting.

In 1870, a cookbook was published in France with recipes for dozens of dishes based on the meat of dogs. Across the English Channel, however, the British typically rejected anything enjoyed by the French and in the 1890s *Punch*, the humor magazine, published several cartoons demonstrating their disapproval. The same magazine also satirically described an anonymous Englishman's encounter with a canine meal:

...he brightened up
And thought himself in luck
When close before him what he saw
Looked something like a duck!

Still cautious grown, but, to be sure,
His brain he set to rack;
At length he turned to one behind,
And, pointing, cried, 'Quack, quack?'

The Chinese gravely shook his head,
Next made a reverent bow;
And then expressed what dish it was,
By uttering, 'Bow-wow-wow!'

Today, dog remains popular in southern China, Hong Kong, parts of Japan, Korea, much of Southeast Asia, and to a lesser degree in Mexico, Central and South America, but not without controversy. For years, organizers of the world's most famous dog show, in England, welcomed sponsorship from the Korean electronics giant Samsung, until the International Fund for Animal Welfare protested in 1995, claiming that up to two million dogs were processed for the Korean food industry annually.

When such protests earned worldwide media attention, drawing attention to the slaughter of dog for meat in Thailand, Britain's National Canine Defense League complained. It was no crime to kill and eat dogs in Thailand, so there was little the government could do to satisfy anyone at the league. Still, when Queen Elizabeth II and Prince Philip visited Bangkok in 1996, officials in Sakon Nakhon—the province where most of the dogs were killed—vowed to enact measures to try to keep any dogs from being butchered during the five-day visit so as not to offend Britain's royalty. It was unlikely, however, that they would be anywhere nearby, as the province is 341 miles from Bangkok.

Men in the dog business must be selective. If the dogs haven't eaten well, the meat may be stringy and possibly unhealthy, and many of the strays have rabies or mangy skins. In some Asian countries today the movement is not only to regulate the slaughter and promote cleanliness, but also to identify establishments where dog meat is served, because sometimes it is substituted for something else. For example, I was served "wild boar" in Saigon that I'm sure wasn't boar—the day after seeing a flatbed truck loaded with caged dogs on the highway leading into the city. A coincidence? Perhaps.

I have also eaten dog in China and Vietnam. As a photographer friend took pictures of a skinned dog just delivered to a restaurant in China's Yunnan province, a woman beckoned to us to come in. On the stove, she had some bite-sized, stir-fried haunch in a wok, left over from lunch, with a taste like cooked beef, slightly greasy, as dog, I'm told, often is. Two weeks later, in the mountainous region of northwestern Vietnam, near the Chinese border, I was served thin slices of dog tongue stir-fried with garlic and vegetables and while

visiting a weekend marketplace in the same province I saw more than a dozen well-fed dogs of various breeds for sale (for about $10 apiece), and later I observed members of the hill tribe prominent in that area leading dinner home on a leash. The same year, 1998, the Ministry of Agriculture and Rural Development said there were at least fourteen million dogs in Vietnam, their numbers swelling as more and more farmers turned to raising dogs instead of pigs.

In Thailand, I found dog in the open markets as well, butchered and ready to go, but also cooked into a rich stew that sold for about eighty cents a portion, and deep-fried into a sort of jerky that was very hard to chew. This was in the province that more or less declared a moratorium on dog during the British queen's visit, where on the average day, I was told, approximately a thousand dogs were killed for markets in the region. This region is also known for a kind of Oriental dog tartare, where raw dog meat is chopped almost to a mince, mixed with a few spices and finely chopped vegetables and served with the dog's blood and bile. Unlike Vietnam, where most of the dogs that are cooked are tender puppies, the adults wind up on the plate in Thailand, so tough that minced is the easiest to chew and most digestible.

In Korea, hundreds, perhaps thousands of restaurants serve rich soups (costing about $10 for a medium sized bowl), casseroles ($16 per serving), and steamed meat served with rice ($25). It is, as in other places, technically illegal to sell cooked dog meat, and restauranteurs do so under threat of having their licenses revoked. However, an appeals court in Seoul in 1997 acquitted a dog-meat wholesaler, ruling that dogs were socially accepted as food. Continuing government concern about the nation's image has led to periodic crackdowns, causing some restaurants to remove their outside signs or move from main streets to small lanes, away from the usual tourist haunts. And many now identify the special dishes not as dog, but instead use names like "Soup of Invigoration."

As a protein source for human consumption, cats

have a briefer history than dogs. At least, there are fewer historical references and while felines continue to find their way to the supper table from South America to Asia, the consumption level is comparatively quite low. This may be explained by the fact that through the ages, human regard for the cat has swung so widely—from worship to blasphemy and back—and at neither extreme did the small creature with the heart-warming purr and sharp claws ever seem as right for a stew or grill as their larger relatives, the cougar, the panther, the leopard, the lion, and the tiger.

There are, of course, numerous cases of the domestic cat being eaten for survival, just as Amundsen ate his sled dogs in the last century. In 1975, for example, the British correspondent Jon Swain was held captive in the French embassy in Phnom Penh following the invasion of the Cambodian capital by the Khmer Rouge. "With no end to our internment in sight, the shortage of food was becoming serious," he wrote in *River of Time* (1996). "Reluctantly, Jean Menta, a Corsican adventurer, and Dominique Borella, the mercenary who had been keeping a low profile in case he was recognized, strangled and skinned the embassy cat. The poor creature put up a spirited fight and both men were badly scratched. A few of us ate it, curried. The meat was tender like chicken."

So, too, in 1996, cats were skinned and grilled in Argentina under the media's harsh glare, causing an uproar in homes throughout the country and in the legislature. The press and politicians asked, were people so poor they had to eat pets? The answer, of course, was yes.

The same year, in Australia, Richard Evans, a member of Parliament, recommended the country do everything possible to eradicate the country's eighteen million feral and domestic cats by 2020 to prevent them killing and estimated three million birds and animals every year. John Wamsley, the managing director of Earth Sanctuaries, went a step further, urging people to catch and eat feral cats, recommending what he called "pussy-tail stew." Another uproar shook the media.

It isn't always need that puts the cat in the pot. At Guang's Dog and Cat restaurant in Jiangmen, a city in southern China, the owner, Wu Lianguang, told reporters in 1996, "Business couldn't be better. The wealthier the Chinese become, the more concerned they are about their health and there's nothing better for you than cat meat."

In northern Vietnam in the 1990s, cat joined dog on many restaurant menus in the belief that asthma could be cured by eating cat meat and that a man's sexual prowess could be aroused or enhanced with the help of four raw cat galls pickled in rice wine. As a food, it was enjoyed raw, marinated, grilled over charcoal, or cut into bite-sized chunks and dunked into a Mongolian hotpot with vegetables. According to a report from Agence France Presse, a dozen restaurants specializing in cat meat opened in just one district of Hanoi and about 1,800 cats were butchered every year in each of them, with the cost to the consumer rising from US$3.50 to $11 in just two years.

Cat meat—generally not so greasy as dog—was a favorite of Hanoi gourmets until 1997, when the government forbade all further slaughter. Why? Official figures showed that as the country's cat population dropped, the number of rats multiplied at an alarming rate, ravaging up to thirty per cent of grain produced in some districts around the capital city. The restaurants were held to blame.

The same year on the other side of the world, in Lima, Peru, a last-minute appeal from Peruvian animal-lovers persuaded authorities to halt a festival of cat cookery intended to celebrate a local saint's day. Organizers of the event announced with regret that the annual festival honoring St. Efigenica, scheduled in the southern coastal town of Canete, had been canceled at the insistence of animal rights activists. However, cat continues to be considered a delicacy and it remains on local menus, without any public display.

A Swiss chef who worked in a five-star hotel in Asia smiled when I mentioned cat cuisine. He said he ate cat in northern Italy and enjoyed it, and if anyone wanted to do the same and lacked a recipe, it tasted so much like squirrel or rabbit, all they had to do was find a recipe for one of those and substitute.

For now, the eating of dog—and to a lesser degree, cat—seems to have a healthy future, especially in Asia, where there is no social stigma attached. And in most cases, where laws forbid their consumption, those bans likely will go unenforced. This may change in time, of course. Chang Moon Joon, a managing director of the Korea Animal Rescue Association, and a strong opponent of dog eating, said in a press release issued in 1998 that "since young people these days don't eat dog meat, the market itself will dwindle and in twenty years' time it will disappear."

That may be so. Still, there is no accounting for, or predicting, the world's eating habits, nor the changes occurring rapidly in the harvest of unusual crops. A few years ago, ostrich was only a big, funny-looking bird. Today it's being farmed in large numbers in South Africa, Australia, China, and North America, where it is being praised as an answer to the need for low-cost, high-value protein. Canines and felines could fill the same role.

In April 1871, *Le Monde Illustré* depicted scenes of the Franco-Prussian War and the Siege of Paris, when market stalls selling cat and dog meat drew lines of people.

horse

Horse Tartare

5–8 oz. lean horse flank or
    rump (per person)
1 egg yolk
Worcestershire sauce or
    hot pepper sauce to
    taste
Salt and pepper to taste
1 garlic clove, minced
1 tbs. red onion, chopped
1 tbs. parsley, chopped
1 tsp. capers
Catsup, olive oil, soy sauce

Grind meat and form into a
ball, working in egg yolk,
garlic, Worcestershire
sauce or hot pepper sauce,
salt and pepper. Flatten
one side so the ball will
hold its position on a plate.
Place the onion, parsley,
and capers on the plate
around the meat; these
are then added to the fork
while eating. Serve with
catsup, olive oil, more
Worcestershire sauce,
and soy sauce as desired
for additional flavoring.

My friend Richard Lair, an elephant expert living in Thailand—where he says he has eaten just about everything except elephant—was attending San Francisco State University in the early 1960s when he was introduced to horse meat. A pal of his was a chef who often shopped for his dinner at a pet store, the only place where horse meat could be purchased (in America) easily—this, because it was regarded (in America) as food fit only for dogs.

This gentleman knew the various cuts of horse, my friend told me, and he knew fresh meat when he saw it, so when the "pet food" met his approval, he purchased some of the rump and took it home and prepared the horse meat in the same way he prepared beef bourguignon, coating the cubes of lean meat with flour and frying them in a heavy saucepan with onions and shallots, and perhaps a tot of brandy, set aflame just before serving with potatoes and vegetables.

Horse meat? Some Euro-Americans bristle at the thought. This was, after all, the mammal most closely identified with human activity. From approximately 2,500 B.C., the animal has been an indispensable part of society, primarily as a beast of burden and a means of transportation. As early as 900 B.C., the Assyrian horse was drafted into the forerunner of what became called the "cavalry." At the same time, in Greece, horse racing was included in the earliest Olympic games. They also pulled chariots into battle and plows across fields.

The horse was introduced to the "New World" by Spanish conquistadors in the seventeenth century, where it proliferated on the vast, grassy plains, and became a cowboy's (and in Argentina, a gaucho's) best friend and essential partner. Before trains traversed the United States, mail was delivered by Pony Express, people in stagecoaches were drawn cross-country by teams of four and six. Later, horses pulled trolley cars and fire engines. Teamsters and tradesmen transported their goods in horse-drawn wagons, much as the Budweiser Clydesdales pull beer carts for TV commercials today. In time, of course, the horse was replaced: by the train (initially called the "iron horse"), the tractor, the car, and truck.

The horse performs both essential and romantic tasks. Today, there are horses that pull carriages through New York's Central Park, others that perform tricks in circuses. There are horses that still help cowboys herd cattle and horses that race around tracks and horses that jump over fences. Polo is an international sport, dating back to ancient India, when a goat's head frequently was used as a ball. There are police horses and horses on dude ranches and there are ponies for little girls to ride on their birthdays. There also are horses on merry-go-rounds and, over the past century, dozens of horses that were stars in movies and in the international racing circuit. Equestrian clubs, riding competitions, and breed shows are everywhere.

With this background, it is no surprise that there are organizations, mainly in the United States, determined to halt the killing of wild horses in the American West and Canada for export to Europe as food. A 1996 equine survey counted seven million horses in America, about twenty percent more than a decade earlier. Of those sold at auction, most were "going to Paris," the local euphemism for the European horse-meat market.

We know that prehistoric man hunted the horse as a source of meat from cave paintings dating back to the Ice Age showing hunters and their equine prey. In fact, some historians believe the horse was domesticated as a source of food before it was used as a beast of burden. Although the flesh was forbidden by Mosaic law, Joseph raised horses for food during a famine and the Greek historian Herodotus told how horse was boiled and then cooked with ox.

In more modern times, Marco Polo told of the Mongols draining small but regular quantities of the blood from their mounts as they moved across central Asia, taking milk to make foods of the curd or yogurt type, and drinking mare's milk as well for sustenance. (See "Blood" section for further discussion.) "First they bring the milk [almost] to the boil," the early trader and explorer wrote. "At the appropriate moment they skim off the cream that floats on the surface and put it in another vessel to be made into butter, because so long as it remains the milk can not be dried. Then they stand the milk in the sun and leave it to dry. When they are going on an expedition they take about ten pounds of this milk; and every morning they take out about half a pound of it and put it in a small leather flask, shaped like a gourd, with as much water as they please. Then while they ride, the milk in the flask dissolves into a fluid, which they drink. And this is their breakfast."

Another early traveler in the east was William de Rubruquis, who published a record of his *Remarkable Travels into Tartary and China, 1253*, in which he told how the Mongols made *kumiss*, a fermented liquor. Just as the standing horse milk was about to ferment, it was poured into a large bladder and beaten with "a piece of wood made for that purpose, having a knot at the lower end like a man's head, which is hollow within; and so soon as they beat it, it begins to boil [froth] like new wine, and to be sour and of a sharp taste; and they beat it in that manner till butter comes. After a man hath taken a draught it leaves a taste behind it like that of almond milk, going down very pleasantly, and intoxicating weak brains, for it is very heady and powerful." The consumption of horse milk and its byproducts is not so common today, although a weak version of kumiss is drunk in parts of China. (Where the alcoholic strength is at a low two percent, no match even for the feeblest beers.)

The French, especially Parisians, have eaten horse meat commonly and openly since 1811, when it was decreed legal following a long ban. Today in France,

especially in the Camargue in the south where herds of wild horses dashing through water is a photographic cliché, some breeds are raised for meat and as is true of most meat sources, the young—the colts—are preferred for their tenderness. Easily digested, horse meat has fewer calories than beef—ninety-four per hundred milligrams, compared with one-hundred and fifty-six for lean beef.

To satisfy the market that now includes Japan, thousands of wild horses, donkeys, and mules are killed and butchered in the western United States each year. Oddly, it is an expensive government program that has created, or at least abetted, this industry. The program, managed by the U.S. Bureau of Land Management, is intended to protect wild horses on public lands, where they compete for water and forage with grazing cattle. What this means is that "excess horses" are rounded up and offered to the public for adoption. The government spends more than US$1,000 to collect, vaccinate, brand, and administer the paperwork for each horse and adopters pay US$125 for a healthy horse, as little as $25 for one that is old or lame. The new "parent" agrees to keep the animals for at least one year. Some do, many don't, most selling

Sources

In Europe and Japan, many butcher shops or meat departments in markets offer horse meat matter-of-factly. In other Euro-American regions, it is still stocked in some pet shops, but it is wise to have someone along who can recognize the cuts and freshness.

Zebra may be purchased on the hoof from rancher Audren Garrett, Rt. 7, Box 300o, Springfield, MO 65802, phone (417) 866-5113 or from Doug Smith, Bear Creek Ranch, phone (210) 367-2320, email <cdsmith@sat.net>. You'd better have a butcher standing by, along with a very large freezer or plans for a sizeable barbecue.

From The Plains to the Plate

BIG HORN, WYOMING—Last year, 85,000 horses met their end in the four horsemeat packing plants left in America. In 1996, these businesses shipped $64 million worth of horsemeat to Belgium, France, Switzerland, and Mexico. The prime candidate for slaughter, say buyers, is a 10–12-year-old well-muscled quarter horse. The hind quarters are chilled and flown to Europe; the front quarters are cooked and minced and sent by boat.

This is an all-but-invisible trade. Even the United States Department of Agriculture, the government agency responsible for inspecting horsemeat, is stingy with information. Studies and analysis of the industry are practically non-existent. Packing plants are about as open as a frozen oyster. The Central-Nebraska Packing Company of North Platte politely but firmly rejected this reporter's request to visit it. "With people burning down plants, we don't make a habit of giving tours," said the manager. He was referring to an incident in July 1997, when arsonists did $1 million of damage to the Cavel West packing house in Redmond, Oregon, which specialized in horsemeat. A torch-happy group, the Animal Liberation Front, claimed responsibility.

The Economist, May 23, 1998

This page, above: Of the fourteen retail horsemeat butchers still open in Paris, this establishment in the fashionable rue St. Antoine, owned by Jean-Pierre Houssin, has the most traditional façade, including glass paintings and three of the distinctive gilded heads above the shop.
This page, below: A mobile horsemeat butcher's shop does brisk business in a French Provincial town, selling freshly slaughtered steaks and mince.
Opposite: Saucisson d'ane– donkey meat dried sausage– is one of the specialties of the town of Arles in the south of France, seen on sale at the Saturday market and served with olive bread and a glass of *Côte du Rhone.*

them for slaughter eventually, usually receiving $700 apiece. More than 165,000 animals have been rounded up since the program was started in 1982, costing the government over $250 million. A tenth of that sum is considered a good year in the sale of the meat by export to Europe and Japan.

So it is not a big business, but it is a medium-sized one that likely will not go away. Some conservationists say it is a billion-dollar industry, a figure that makes people at U.S. slaughterhouses laugh and say, "I wish."

"Killed on Friday, processed on Monday, Thursday we load the truck and then it's flown to Europe," says Pascal Derde, proprietor of the Cavel West, a packing house in Redmond, Oregon. "Tuesday eaten."

However popular that horse may be today, it is unlikely there ever will be an event to top one held during the mid-nineteenth century, not long after Napoleon's pharmacist, Cadet de Gassicourt, and others publicly testified that horse meat had sustained a number of lives during the general's military campaigns. *Larousse Gastronomique*, the famed cookery encyclopedia, reported that on February 6, 1856, a number of butchers and chefs organized a banquet at one of Paris's grand hotels, offering horse-broth vermicelli, horse sausage, boiled horse, horse stew, fillet of horse with mushrooms, potatoes sautéed in horse fat, salad in horse oil, and a rum pastry with horse marrow. Guests at the feast included the novelists Alexandre Dumas, who not only wrote *The Three Musketeers*, but also the 1,152-page *Grand Dictionaire de Cuisine*, and Gustave Flaubert, author of *Madame Bovary*.

Horse may be substituted for beef in many recipes– the animals are related, after all–and it is particularly suited for raw dishes, the lean flank sliced thinly and presented with a hot sauce (horseradish is not inappropriate) or as "horse tartare," mixed with chopped onions and herbs and spices and served with Worcestershire sauce. In Japan, *umasashi*, horsemeat *sashimi*, is widely prized; in the south of France, the local sausage is based on ground horse meat, and is grilled, baked, or fried.

Other members of the horse family also are eaten, notably the zebra in Africa, where their extraordinary number have made them an inexpensive and readily available protein source for centuries. Laurens van der Post, a South African writer whose book *First Catch Your Eland* (1977) recalled his gastronomic adventures as a child and maturing adult, said zebra fillets and steaks provided "the tenderest and tastiest meat of all."

Today, zebra meat finds its way to open markets scattered across eastern and southern Africa, where the herds are most numerous. It is also, more or less, a staple in specialty restaurants and is usually spit-roasted, delivered for carving at the table.

rat & mouse

The first time I heard about the rodent as a comestible was when I was told about a restaurant in London where a French couple reportedly served a savory rat stew. The way the story went, the couple immigrated to England following the Second World War, bringing with them a recipe developed during the German occupation of Paris, a time of severe shortages. Meat was particularly scarce and of necessity, the couple caught rats in traps in the alleys and cooked them with whatever vegetables and herbs they could find, creating a distinctive and delicious dish. "Unfortunately," my friend told me, "the rats were as stringy and tough as the Parisians, so it was pretty chewy. Not to worry about that today, my lovely. The day of the alley rat is done. Today, they raise their own rats, feed them grain until they're plump and juicy."

My friend said the dish was listed on the menu in French for "rat stew," and next to it were the words "when available." That permitted the waiter to make sure it was understood just what kind of meat the customer was ordering. The only surprise the owners wanted to offer their patrons was how good it tasted. They did not want to hear anyone cry, "I ate WHAT!?!"

Sadly, the elderly owners of the restaurant had died and the establishment had closed, so it was many years before I actually got to eat a rodent. It finally happened the first time I stayed with my friend Samniang Changsena's parents, who are rice farmers in northeastern Thailand. There, field mice are not only savored as a gastronomical treat, but also are considered a superb way of disposing of agricultural pests, hated for their damage to the rice crop. Samniang told me that the rats and mice they eat are healthy, because they live in burrows in the mud dikes between the paddy ponds. Because they lived mainly on a diet of rice, they are fattest at harvest time, from November to January, which was when I took my trip.

My friend said she and her sister would pour water into a hole and when the small, furry residents ran out, they hit them on the head with a stick, and if they didn't come out, they dug for them. They then took them home and placed them directly on the coals of the outdoor wood fire that served as the family stove, turning them over with a stick until crisp. She said the babies were the tenderest, popped into the mouth and eaten bones and all, with or without a spicy dipping sauce.

And so it was when I visited my friend's family. On one of her visits home, she had brought an electric wok, but they still cooked nearly everything they ate over a wood fire outside their home. It was there that I watched several mice turned over coals until they were crispy, then ate them, bones and all, with a chili pepper and fish sauce dip.

When I returned to my home in Hawaii and told my friends, they said, "You ate WHAT!?!"

Rodents, after all, have an unfortunate reputation worldwide. For all the good Mickey and Minnie Mouse and other cartoon characters may have offered the rodent population's reputation, the rat and mouse are still creepy creatures that not many people seem to love and few might welcome to the dinner table.

In fact, in recent years the rat has been a detestable epithet, usually applied to someone who betrayed ("ratted on") his or her friends. Who can forget James Cagney calling some movie enemy, "You dirty rat!" (Or was it Edward G. Robinson?) When you joined the nine-to-five work routine, you were in the "rat race," from which escape was deemed desirable. With their twitchy pointed noses and whiskers, ominous yellow buck teeth, and hairless tails, rats aren't considered pretty to look at, either.

Worse, rats bit children in their cribs and spread a host of awful diseases, and newspaper stories appear all the time explaining how health departments in modern cities from Bombay to Berlin to Beverly Hills, struggle to stay a step ahead of rat infestation. A report in 1997 said one in twenty homes in Britain is infested—and that there are about sixty million rats in that country compared to a human population of fifty eight million.

Having said this, rats, mice, and other members of the rodent family have a long, palatable history, based in part on their vast numbers and variety. This is an order, after all, whose members constitute nearly forty percent of all mammals on earth, all of which are edible, among them the rabbit, squirrel, marmot, beaver, chinchilla, guinea pig, porcupine, gerbil, hamster, and in Latin America the agouti, coypu, and capybara—a large, tailless creature cooked in the same way as a suckling pig. In some areas, some of these rodents are considered common dinnertime fare. Between one and a half and two million squirrels are killed by hunters each year in the American state of Illinois alone. But most are eaten less frequently. And some are anathema to the prevailing Euro-American taste, most remarkably the mouse and rat.

The common black rat, sometimes brown in color, most likely came from Asia, reaching Europe on trading ships by the thirteenth century. Not long after, fleas on the rats were blamed for spreading bubonic plague and killing twenty-five million people, a quarter of the population at the time. Around the world today, rats and their parasites spread at least twenty kinds of disease, from typhus to trichinosis to Lassa fever. It is no surprise that *The Guinness Book of Records* calls this species "the most dangerous rodent in the world."

Yet, there are rats and mice that are easy to catch and not only safe to eat, but commonly eaten, both in times of hardship and as a staple or delicacy. And so it has been for millennia. In ancient Rome, caged dormice were fed nuts until they were plump enough for an emperor's demanding appetite. These animals, which reached a length of eight inches (not counting the tail), were so popular, they also were farmed in large pens and exported to satisfy the appetites of Roman soldiers then occupying Britain.

In imperial China, the rat was called a "household deer" and considered a special treat, and Marco Polo wrote that the Tartars ate rat in the summer months, when they were plentiful. In Columbus' time, when a ship's food store ran low during oceanic crossing, the ship's rat catcher became a man whose low station was elevated, and whose pay was raised when rodents—usually thought to be pests—became a valued protein source. In nineteenth-century France, many in Bordeaux traditionally feasted on grilled or broiled rat with shallots. Thomas Genin, a noted cook and organizer of that country's first culinary competitions in the 1880s, considered rat meat to be of excellent quality. Henry David Thoreau is reported to have said he enjoyed fried rats, served with relish, although some insist he was talking about muskrats, which probably lived around Walden Pond. During Vietnam's war with America, the Viet Cong considered rats an important food group. More recently, G. Gordon Liddy, one of the engineers of U.S. President Richard Nixon's Watergate scandal, boasted that he ate rat in the all-American way, fried, although it's generally believed that he did so to prove his courage, and not to expand his culinary experience.

In much of Latin America, Asia, and in parts of Africa and Oceania, rat remains a common hors d'oeuvre or entrée today. In parts of China, it still is prepared in more than a dozen ways in popular restaurants. Even in America, there are commercial sources for rats and mice. One outfit, called the Gourmet Rodent, will deliver the critters dressed and frozen by UPS, Express Mail, or alive, C.O.D., via Delta Air Freight. (In 1998, mice cost between US$0.47–0.67 apiece, rats from $0.62–$2.17 for the 10–14 ounce "jumbos." Discounts were offered on orders of more than five hundred units.) It should be noted that such companies advertised in magazines for people who kept snakes and that, according to the editors, it was known that some of the buyers were recent immigrants to the United States who did not keep snakes.

Deep Fried Field Rat

4 mature rats or
   8 small rats
10–15 garlic cloves,
   crushed
2 tbs. salt
$\frac{1}{2}$ tsp. pepper

Skin and gut the rats, removing the head and toes. Mix garlic, salt, and pepper into a paste, spread on the meat, then place in direct sunlight for 6 to 8 hours, until dry. Fry in deep vegetable oil for about 6-7 minutes, until crispy and yellow in color. Serve with sticky rice, sweet-sour sauce, fish sauce, or a hot chili paste, and raw vegetables.

Traditional Isan recipe, courtesy Samniang Changsena

Sources
Frozen or live rats and mice by mail from Bill and Marcia Brant, The Gourmet Rodent, 6115 SW 137th Ave., Archer, FL 32618, phone (352) 495-9024, fax (352) 495-9781, email <GrmtRodent@aol.com>; SAS Corporation, 273 Hover Ave., Germantown, NY 12526, phone (518) 537-2000; Kevin Bryant Reptiles & Feeder Rodents Inc., P.O. Box 4424, Evansville, IN 47724, phone (812) 867-7598, fax (812) 867-6058.

Also (frozen) from J&J Enterprise, P.O. Box 141, Grandfalls, TX 79742, phone (915) 5531; Kelly Haller, 4236 SE 25th, Topeka, KS 66605, phone (913) 234-3358; Ray Queen, The Mouse Factory, P.O. Box 85, Alpine, TX 79831, phone (915) 837-7100.

This page, above: Grilled whole baby mice, served with a Vietnamese dipping sauce of finely chopped ginger, garlic, chillies, and coriander in fish sauce and rice vinegar.

This page, below: At the end of a day's work hunting under rice fields near Madras, a group of rat catchers grill a small part of the day's bounty around an open fire.

The Rat Catchers of India

The greatest consumption of rats may be in India, where every year, swarms of mole rats, rice rats and field mice steal enough grain to feed the country's nine hundred million people for three months. Many are killed by chemicals that also poison the water and earth, at the same time rendering the animals hazardous to eat. Meet the nomadic Irula tribe, India's master rat catchers.

Not so long ago, the twenty-eight thousand Irulas, from the Chingleput District, earned a living as snake catchers, selling the serpents to the snake-skin industry. In the mid-1970s, when the government banned the trade, they offered their services as rat catchers and in the late 1980s, they proved their worth when a study conducted by the international aid organization Oxfam Trust showed that in fifty audited hunts, the Irula captured several thousand rats at a cost of about five cents (U.S.) per pest, where in parallel trials, the per-rat price using pesticides cost ten times as much.

The hunt is so simple it mocks modern eradication techniques. The men go into the fields and when they find a burrow they build fires in clay pots using grass and leaves to create a lot of smoke. The pots are then placed over all the exits of the underground tunnels and the smoke is blown into the burrows. After a while, the Irula dig into the earth to harvest the rats and mice, asphyxiated by the smoke. Some of the catch is sold to crocodile farms in Madras. The rest is taken to the market for human consumption, or taken home, where the small animals are prepared in a curry or grilled.

This page, above: One of the techniques used by the Irula is to smoke the rats out from their tunnels, having first identified all the numerous exits. A clay pot with a small hole drilled in the base and filled with smouldering rice stalks makes an effective smoke machine. Strategically placed, the smoke will drive the rats towards the exit where the rat catchers will be waiting.
This page, below: Working along the bund—the raised dike separating the rice fields—a group of Irula dig for a nest of rats that they have located by listening for movement close to the ground. Typically they will also recover a hoard of rice stolen by the rats, and this will be an additional bonus for dinner.

Opposite: Chockalingam, the most experienced of this group of Irula trappers, digs for a nest, helped by his wife and son.

This page, above: Two handfuls of rats that will either be eaten, or sold for one-and-a-half rupees each under a program set up by the Oxfam Trust and India's Department of Science and Technology.

This page, below: A hazy morning heralds a hot day at the end of the rice harvest, the preferred season for trapping rats, once the fields are clear of their crop.

bats

Stir-Fried Bat

6–8 bats
2 medium onions, sliced
2 turnips or similar
   vegetable, cut into
   small pieces
1 red chili pepper,
   de-seeded and finely
   chopped
2 garlic cloves, finely
   chopped
Salt and pepper to taste
Cooking oil

Singe hair over open
flame, remove wings and
heads, and cut bat meat
into bite-sized chunks. Fry
meat in a wok with a minimum amount of oil over
a medium flame until
tender. Vegetables and
other ingredients are
added only for the final
two or three minutes.

Collected personally in Thailand and
Indonesia, 1997

The Tri Ky Restaurant doesn't exist in Saigon any more, having been replaced by a high-rise office building not long after the city was renamed for the country's founder, Ho Chi Minh. A pity, too, because it had one of Southeast Asia's preeminent "strange food" menus, offering dog, bat, turtle, and a variety of wild game, as well as a selection of blood cocktails for the end of the difficult workday. The restaurant was in a fair-sized, ground-floor room in a building near the Saigon River. I discovered it in 1993, during its last days, when such drinks were supposed to gird your loins—so to speak—for what came later in the evening, probably in Cholon, the city's notorious Chinatown.

I entered, taking a seat by the large windows in the front near the door, looking out at a cluster of men in baseball caps napping in the seats of their three-wheeled cyclos, waiting for customers. I read the menu casually, as if I were used to encountering such dishes regularly. I recalled when I had decided not to drink snake blood in Taipei a few years before and figured this was the time to correct what I now hoped was a show of culinary cowardice.

"I'll have one of these," I said, pointing to a line in the menu. "The, uh, cobra."

"Bat very good, sir," the waiter said, pointing at the menu.

Obviously, I hadn't read far enough down the drinks list. "Bat blood?" I said. I tried to play it cool. "What sort of bat?" I asked, as if it really mattered and I would know what he was talking about, whatever he said.

"The fruit bat, sir. Also have bat stew. Very good."

I told the gentleman (actually about a third my age) that I'd try it. With a can of 333, the local beer. Two of them. First a bracer. Then a chaser.

What happened next surprised me. After the cold beer was delivered, the bat was brought to my table still alive, its legs and wings gripped in the waiter's hand as he cut the creature's throat with a small, sharp knife. The blood fell into a small glass.

"*Chuc suc khoe!*" the waiter said. It was the standard Vietnamese toast meaning good luck.

I raised the small glass and drank the warm liquid, tried to roll it around my tongue as if it were vintage wine, but then chased it rather quickly with a swallow of 333. The waiter smiled, still holding the limp bat in one hand, cupping the head with the other in a small bowl to prevent any blood from falling onto the floor.

"One more, sir?" he asked.

"Maybe after the meal." Still trying to be cool. As for the bat stew, think Dinty Moore with very stringy meat.

"How many foreigners order bat?" I asked as I paid the bill.

"You are the first this year," the waiter said.

In American cinema, Tom Cruise's presence in *Interview with the Vampire* (1994), and a number of actors playing Batman may have done something to soften the poor reputation held for so long by bats, but the fear of these creatures prevails in much of the world. The author Bram Stoker, who wrote the original *Dracula* (1897), must take some of the blame for this sorry state of affairs, but the American writer Anne Rice must share it for her series of best-selling vampire novels; it was the movie adaptation of her first that starred Cruise. With a hundred years of such inglorious history and images of neck-biting men who sleep during the day in coffins and who only can be killed by having stakes driven through the heart or shot with a silver bullet, is it any wonder that people turn away from the notion of deep-fried bat for dinner, or a glass of warm bat wine?

Nor is this all. Bats are grimly prominent in much folklore. The Bible calls it an unclean bird—although it is a mammal—and from India to Ireland to the United States it is regarded as a symbol of death. In many folk tales, the devil takes the form of a bat and there is a belief in much of the Euro-American world that bats will become so entangled in a woman's hair that nothing but scissors or a knife can get them free.

Bats may command such a prominent role because they've been around for so long—fifty million years, according to fossil evidence—and because they're so widely distributed and so numerous; it is estimated that one out of every four mammals on earth is a bat. There are more than nine hundred species, ranging in size from the bumblebee bat of Thailand that weighs less than a U.S. penny, right up to some flying "foxes" in South America and the Pacific, with bodies the size of small dogs and a wingspan of nearly six feet.

They're not very attractive, either. Their furry bodies look like those of rats or mice; their leathery wings stretch on a framework similar to an opening umbrella; their outsized, translucent ears are ribbed with cartilage and laced with blood vessels; their pig-like snouts are spoked with whiskery projections; and they sleep hanging upside down, clinging to a cave's ceiling with their feet...well, the picture is not appealing.

That said, bats are one of the most interesting of nature's creations, mainly because of their echo-location, or sonar, senses. Similar to radar, which uses radio waves to detect location of another object, sonar uses sound waves to accomplish the identical task: the sound goes out and bounces back, giving bats the precise location of obstacles—they don't want to be flying into buildings and trees, after all—and prey that may be moving at speed.

Most of the sounds humans perceive may be counted in hundreds of vibrations per second and humans can, with difficulty, hear sounds with a frequency of, maybe, twenty thousand vibrations per second. Bats hear sounds between fifty and two hundred thousand vibrations per second, and send out a series of clicks at the rate of thirty or so per second. This keen sense of hearing is unequalled in the natural and scientific worlds. Scientists say fishing bats have echo-location so sophisticated that they can detect movement of a

minnow's fin as fine as a human hair, protruding only eight hundredths of an inch above a pond's surface, while African heart-nosed bats can hear the footsteps of a beetle walking on sand from a distance of more than six feet. It also keeps them from banging into things. Most (but not all) bats are, as the old saying goes, quite blind and able to react to a "sonar" bounce with unerring and astounding speed.

So, how in the hell does anyone catch one? Easy. It doesn't take much effort to position several men with a fishing net outside one of the caves from which the bats emerge by the thousands at dusk to feed. A man with a shotgun at such times also can bring down twenty to thirty with a single blast, although when the cook prepares the meal, care must be taken to remove the pellets.

The easy catch is part of the bat's appeal, but there's more to it. Images of the devil and Count Dracula aside, there are millions in the world who believe that eating bats increases fertility and one's chances for long life and happiness. To the Chinese, a symbol of five bats indicates the five blessings: wealth, health, love of virtue, old age, and a natural death. Eating bats also is believed to improve eyesight and in India, bat oil—made from melted fat mixed with blood, coconut oil, and camphor—is sold as a cure for rheumatism and arthritis. In Cambodia, it is prescribed for a child's cough. And...it's low in fat.

The bat is regarded as food today mainly in Asia and the Pacific. One species of "flying fox" in Guam has been hunted to extinction, but elsewhere they are numerous and the bat is not considered threatened. Probably the most cherished is the fruit bat, found in much of the western South Pacific, including the Philippines, Indonesia, and most of Micronesia.

The preparation of bat always is simple. Bat has not yet breached the barrier that might one day make it more acceptable to a wider audience, much as emu and kangaroo have done in Australia and various wild game meats have in Africa, where "native" foods are now fashionable and for which chefs dream up

This page and opposite: Grilled bat is a local speciality of the foothills of the mountain range separating Burma and Thailand. Limestone provides abundant caves for the bats, and several small restaurants near Ratchaburi (about an hour and a half's drive west of Bangkok) serve them whole, grilled, or fried.

fancy recipes. Some day, there may be recipes for Bat Lasagna and Bat Casserole, but for now, it's mostly soup, with maybe a little ginger, soy sauce, or coconut cream.

Eating bat may also be difficult for those put off by its appearance on the plate. Rabbits don't look like rabbits when they are served, after the flesh has been hygienically distanced from any resemblance to living creatures, but bats often do still look like bats. Because most bats available for eating are small, and they are generally grilled or deep-fried, the entire creature may be cooked and consumed, including the wings, head, and brittle bones, bringing a crunchy sound to the table along with the undeniable reminder of what you are eating. Alternatively, the bat may be skinned, the head and wings removed—they contain only a little meat, after all—and the body cut into cubes for soup or stew.

A word of caution: most species exude a somewhat pungent odor as they cook. This can be alleviated by the addition of chili peppers, onion, or garlic, or any

combination. (An American friend living in Indonesia says that the cook's consumption of several bottles of the local beer also helps.)

There's a bat that lives on my street in Bangkok. I don't know where he or she hangs out during the day, but I see the solitary creature, swooping unevenly in the purpling dusk—sucking up mosquitoes, I guess. I don't know why I see only one. I do know that every time I see this small animal I remember cocktail time in Saigon.

More Reasons to Love a Bat

The larger species additionally are hunted for their skins and bat guano, the droppings deposited inside caves, valued for more than a century as an excellent fertilizer. In the wild, important agricultural plants, from bananas, breadfruit, and mangos to cashews, dates, and figs rely on bats for pollination and seed dispersal. A single brown bat can catch and eat six hundred mosquitoes in one hour and the twenty million Mexican free-tails that live in a large cave near Austin, Texas—the largest urban colony in the world, a tourist attraction—eat two hundred fifty tons of insects nightly.

Grilled or Barbecued Bat

6–8 bats
Salt and pepper
4 garlic cloves, finely chopped
4 chili peppers, de-seeded and finely chopped

Remove hair by singeing the bat over fire, then remove its skin. Remove head and wings if desired. Grind salt, pepper, and garlic together and work it into the meat, leaving it for at least an hour before cooking. Grill on medium heat, or over an open fire or barbecue until crispy. Sprinkle peppers on the meat and leave for about ten minutes before serving, until the strong odor dissipates. Serve with rice.

Opposite: Bats have inhabited the great twelfth-century temple of Angkor Wat for hundreds of years, roosting in the dark hollow interior of the famous towers. The two decades of turmoil and civil war in Cambodia left the temple in disrepair. The bat population has since increased.

This page: This local farmer found a way to supplement his family's diet by climbing the towers. He uses a hooked rod set in a bamboo handle to pull the animals out from the crevices, and then throws them down to his waiting nephew. His preferred way of cooking these small bats is to coat them in rice flour and deep-fry them.

primates & other bush meat

Sources

Antelope, bison, New Zealand elk, kangaroo, wild boar, and occasionally such rarities as lion (also ostrich and rattle-snake) from L.F.C., 3246 Garfield St., Hollywood, FL 33021, phone (954) 964-5861, email <eatgame@msn.com>.

Kangaroo and wallaby, ostrich and emu, crocodile, possum, and buffalo from Milligan's Gourmet Gallery, 5 Kirkwood Rd., Swanbourne, Australia, phone (61) (8) 9385-3455, fax (61) (8) 9385-3559, mobile (61) (4) 1990-7339.

Karl Amman discovered his burning "cause" in 1988 while traveling on the Zaire (now Congo) River in central Africa. Here, in what was the inspiration for Joseph Conrad's long short story *Heart of Darkness* (1902), on one of the legendary river boats he counted two thousand smoked primate carcasses and about a thousand fresh ones. Monkey. Chimpanzee. To Mr. Amman, it looked like a miniature human morgue.

Since then, Mr. Amman, a Swiss photographer, has spent a lot of time investigating the bush meat trade in Africa, where the gorilla is endangered (an estimated eight hundred are killed and eaten each year) and in Indonesia, where the orangutan is on the same long list of animals either at the edge of extinction or approaching it. Mr. Amman is a fanatic. He points out that chimpanzees share 98.6 percent of the human genetic code, and asks whether shooting them is not 98.6 percent murder and eating them 98.6 percent cannibalism.

Not everyone is so emotional, but the conservationist has a point. Yet it is undisputed fact that monkeys and other jungle rainforest animals have been the primary source of protein for tens, perhaps hundreds of thousands of years for the peoples of many parts of Central and South America, Asia, Africa, and Oceania. Even today, in west and central Africa, what is commonly called bush meat represents over half the animal protein consumed by millions of people and it is, in some areas, the only source of protein available. (Keeping livestock in the tropics is often impossible due to the lack of pasture, the cattle-preying tsetse fly, and a variety of animal epidemics.) The World Wildlife Fund (WWF) says:

- Bush meat comprises fifty percent of the protein consumed in parts of Equatorial Africa, seventy-five percent in Liberia.
- The half-million residents of the state of Amazonas in Brazil hunt and consume three million mammals every year (also half a million birds and several hundred thousand reptiles).
- Of the 214 species found in one forest in West Bengal, India, 155 are used by the local population for food, fuel, fiber, fodder, medicine, and religious rites.

Mr. Amman's question is: how long can this go on? The Biosynergy Institute, an American conservation outfit that runs The Bush Meat Project and is one of Mr. Amman's allies, is no less vehement, saying a "ragged army of fifteen-hundred bush meat hunters" in 1998 alone would shoot and butcher more than two thousand gorillas and four thousand chimpanzees in the forest region of west and central Africa, consuming

---

How to Make Real South African Biltong

Game meat
Rock salt
Black pepper, coarsely ground
Dried coriander, ground
Vinegar, preferably apple-cider vinegar

Start with half-inch thick strips of meat, cut with the grain, about six inches long. Liberally sprinkle rock salt on each side of the meat and let them stand for an hour. The longer you let it stand, the saltier it will become.

After the hour, scrape off all the excess salt with a knife (don't soak it in water!). Then get some vinegar — preferably apple-cider, but any vinegar will do. Put some vinegar in a bowl and dip the strips of meat in the vinegar for a second or so — just so that the meat is covered with the vinegar. Hold the biltong up so that the excess vinegar drains off. Then sprinkle ground pepper and ground coriander over the meat on all sides. Once you have done this, the meat is ready to dry. There are several methods of drying. One is to hang it up on a line in a cool place and have a fan blow on it. This method is a bit difficult because if the air is humid the meat can spoil. The method I use is a home-made "biltong box." This is basically a sealed wooden box (you can use cardboard if you like) with holes in it and a 60-watt light bulb inside. Just hang the meat at the top of the box, and leave the light bulb on, in the bottom. The heat from the light bulb helps dry the meat (even in humid weather) in about three to four days. Remember, the box must be closed on all six sides except for a few holes. The theory behind this method is that hot, dry air rises, thus drying the biltong. The holes are quite important as they promote good air circulation in the box.

more great apes each year than are kept in zoos and laboratories in North America.

That isn't all. It isn't just a centuries-old eating habit that's causing what CNN called "the biggest conservation issue facing Africa since the ivory crisis." Logging companies owned by Germans, British, Japanese, and Americans operating deep in the rain forest have caused a dramatic increase in the demand to serve the needs of their workers. Hunters in remote villages once killed only enough game to feed their families — a sustainable number of animals, thus no species were jeopardized — but now they are setting up camps in logging townships and hunting on a commercial basis. The construction of the new roads through the forests also eases transport of bush meat to the region's large cities, to Doula and Yaounde in Cameroon, Brazzaville and Pointe Noire in the Congo, and Kinshasa in Zaire, where it is not unusual to see a truck pull into the marketplace with dozens of animals tied to its sides. Bush meat also is commonly sold smoked or by the part (arm, leg, etc.) or cut to steak and stew-meat size.

Legal bans do not inhibit the sale of bush meat. "Bush meat from a wide variety of species was available for sale in all the major markets, irrespective of it being closed or open hunting season," Mr. Amman wrote in 1998 in one of his regular broadsides, published in various newsletters and on the Internet. "While the meat of protected species was disguised in some markets, it was openly on display in others. On our first evening in Ouesso, the gateway to the renowned Nouabale Ndoki National Park, we filmed a lorry carrying hundreds of kilos of bush meat, including the carcass of a silverback gorilla."

Mr. Amman said the bush meat trade had "been commercialized to the point where it has become an integral part of the economy, the problem well beyond the scope of conservation organizations." Even the loggers had to throw in the towel, he said: one executive of a major French firm told CNN that his company was now afraid of the poachers, who had automatic weapons; some German loggers, weary of the bad publicity, in 1997 asked the transporters of their timber to tell their drivers to stop carrying bush meat. The drivers went on strike, and the loggers and transporters gave in.

Mr. Amman did some shopping to compare the price difference between bush meat and that of domesticated species, such as pork and beef. "We went to the Yaounde bush meat market and bought two gorilla arms," he wrote. "We then acquired the equivalent amount of beef. Next, we bought the frozen head of a chimpanzee and matched it with a much bigger pig's head. We took all this back to the hotel and stuck on price tags to illustrate that beef and pork were less than half the price of gorilla and chimp."

For many outside third-world countries, mainly in Europe and the United States, eating primates is not within the range of acceptable behavior.

"Understandably, many of us who study and con-

In Trouble Again

Redmond O'Hanlon is an anthropologist–cum–travel writer of massive talent and eccentricity. His books which chronical treks into the jungles of Borneo, south America, and Africa, have won best-seller and cult status. In his second, *In Trouble Again: A Journey Between the Orinoco and the Amazon* (1990), he tells a story about shooting a howler monkey "about the size of a cocker spaniel."

"Chimo and Pablo spread palm fronds on the ground and began to prepare the Howler monkey, scalding it with boiling water and scraping off the fur. Its skin turned white, like a baby's.

"That night, when Pablo had jointed the body and Galvis boiled it, Chimo handed me a suspiciously full mess-tin. As I spooned out the soup, the monkey's skull came into view, thinly covered with its red meat, the eyes still in their sockets.

'We gave it to you specially,' said Chimo with great seriousness, sitting on a log beside me, taking another fistful of manioc from the tin and adding it to his own bowl. 'It's an honor in our country. If you eat the eyes, we will have good luck.'

"The skull bared its broken teeth at me. I picked it up, put my lips to the rim of each socket in turn, and sucked. The eyes came away from their soft stalks and slid down my throat.

"Chimo put his bowl down, folded his hands on his paunch, and roared with laughter.

'You savage!' he shouted. 'You horrible naked savage! Don't you think it looks like a man? Eh? How could you do a disgusting thing like that?'"

Redmond O'Hanlon, *In Trouble Again*

Above: A Bushman cave painting at Giant's Castle in South Africa's Drakensberg Mountains shows early spear-wielding hunters and their prey. Mankind's hunter-gatherer origins are responsible for a lingering fascination with "bush meat."

Opposite: A roadside restaurant sign in the town of Kulai, near Johor Bahru in Malaysia, advertises some of the "jungle food" popular in the region.

serve primates are uncomfortable seeing them on the menu," Dr. Anthony Rose of the Biosynergy Institute wrote in 1998 in *Pan Africa News*. "This discomfort may be ego-centric, born of our own personal eating taboos or our concern that animals at our field sites may be killed before we've finished our research. It may be anthropocentric—a manifestation of our reluctance to eat anything so human-like as a gorilla or baboon. Or it may come from a bio-centric concern for individuals and species that are on the verge of extinction, high on the food chain, or demonstrably sentient and subject to suffering."

Whatever the reasoning, there is now an alliance of more than thirty international organizations trying to change a diet that has existed for millennia, not only in Africa, but also in South America and in South and Southeast Asia. Together, they argue urgency, because hunting methods have changed. Not so long ago, the animals were hunted with bows and arrows, spears, and nets, the only goal being to put food on the family table, with occasional surplus carcasses being sold

in the village market or shared without charge with other villagers. Today, automatic rifles and shotguns are used and the same trucks that took the hunters into the forest also take the fresh meat out. Even some traditional riverboats now have freezers.

Thus, more bush meat is reaching the marketplace faster and more efficiently, as the market itself continues to expand. A study conducted in 1997 in Ouesso, a small town in Congo (pop. 11,000), reported more than six tons of bush meat was sold each week in a market that offered eight different kinds of monkey and gorillas.

Nor is the market limited to African dinner tables. The World Wildlife Fund for Nature reported in 1998 that chimpanzee and gorilla were on menus as far away as Paris and Brussels, where the meat was served dried, smoked, cut into steaks and cooked in a rich, gamey stew. Monkey is also a popular dish in rural areas of southern China and Southeast Asia.

However threatening all this may sound, many if not most of the jungle animals found on Equatorial restaurant menus or in diets in tropical countries around the world are not on any endangered list. While it can be said safely that so many primates are on such lists—the gorilla, the chimp, the orangutan, one species of baboon and more than a dozen species of monkey—probably they should not be eaten, even when their populations are sizeable. However, there are other kinds of bush meat, or what is called "bush tucker" in Australia.

Three countries in Africa—Namibia, Zimbabwe, and South Africa—export game meat to Europe, and a number of private game ranches now invite hunters to go on an old-fashioned safari reminiscent of the time when Ernest Hemingway championed big game hunting fifty years ago. Here, today, if the hunter can pay the price, he can shoot eland, impala, kudu, duuiker, springbok, bush pig, zebra, and hartebeest.

It's easy to guess what Hemingway would think of the number of "jungle restaurants" that opened in many cities worldwide. These included two African restaurants called Carnivore, one in his beloved Kenya and the other in South Africa. The first opened in 1980 just outside Nairobi and is now one of Kenya's most popular tourist attractions. Here, two different game meats are offered each day depending on what's available, cooked over a massive charcoal pit that dominates the entrance and is carried around the restaurant on traditional Masai machetes and carved right onto the diners' sizzling cast-iron plates. During the peak months of December and January in 1997, the Nairobi restaurant served thirteen thousand customers a month, seventy percent of them tourists. The restaurant's standard dinner included crocodile raised on a farm near the coast, along with zebra, eland, Cape buffalo, hartebeest, gazelle, giraffe, impala, camel, oryx, wildebeest, and ostrich. They call it "gnu-velle cuisine." (Their joke, not mine.)

Similar restaurants exist around the globe. In Australia, there are dozens of places where what is called bush tucker is served, "tucker" being slang for food, the menu offering what once was considered fit only for the aboriginal population. Today, kangaroo fillets and ostrich steaks and crocodile satay are not only acceptable, but desirable. Here and elsewhere, the "exotic" or "jungle" restaurants resemble the Hard Rock Cafe and Planet Hollywood, where the theme seems more important than the food.

For example, African Heartbeat in Singapore runs Discovery Channel documentaries on its closed-circuit television system as it dishes up Ostrich Potjiekos (stew) with Polenta and Fresh Vegetables, African Caesar Salad with Venison Biltong Shavings, and Pan Fried Crocodile with Papadums and Spring Onion Relish. Prices at such places are in the luxury class. It is as if the proprietors decided that the best way to make food that once was considered fit only for the "natives" was to ask an exorbitant price for it.

Most game meats tend to be drier and less tender than meats of domestic animals, and more pungent in smell and taste. Because wild birds and mammals forage for food, their muscles may develop more connec-

tive tissue than the muscles of domestic animals, thus exercise can be given as a reason for less tender meat, although the younger the animal, the less tough, of course—just as veal is preferred by some over meat from an older animal. In addition, it is generally agreed that strong flavors associated with game animals are more pronounced in the fat of the species, so trimming fat from a carcass can be important.

To assure tenderness, Carnivore chefs also marinate the meat for eight to twenty-four hours in a mixture of oil, water, soy sauce, lemon, tarragon, red wine, salt, white pepper, and cardamom seeds, and during cooking, baste it with a barbecue sauce made of honey, lime juice, oil, soy sauce, and cornstarch.

Almost all game animals lend themselves agreeably to stews and stroganoffs, or may be cooked on a grill, roasted in an oven, or baked. In South Africa, bush pig and several members of the gazelle family are routinely turned into biltong, or jerky, an age-old way of preserving meat for another day.

Elephant Stew

1 elephant
Brown gravy
Salt and pepper to taste
2 rabbits (optional)

First, find your elephant. Cut elephant into bite-sized pieces. Be sure to allow adequate time. In a large pot, cover pieces with brown gravy and simmer. Cook over an open fire for four weeks at 465ºF. This will serve about 3,800 people. If more guests are expected, 2 rabbits may be added, but do this only if necessary as most people dislike finding a hare in their stew.

Elephant conservationists may not think this is funny, because both species of elephant—the Asian and the African—are listed by every environmental group worldwide as endangered species. Where once large numbers of elephants roamed Africa from the Sahara to the Cape of Good Hope and occupied Asian forests nearly everywhere, now the numbers are small and the prospects are grim. Poachers continue to kill them for their ivory, a trade that is blamed for the slaughter of seven hundred thousand elephants in the decade before it was banned in 1989. Deforestation has removed much of their natural habitat, especially in Asia. Except for small numbers required in the tourism trade, few are needed now for transportation. At the same time, logging restrictions in many countries have taken away other traditional work.

That said, the African elephant is still being killed for food. Legally. And it is possible, if you visit one of the countries where elephant finds it way to a restaurant menu, to enjoy elephant stew—without hare—as well as elephant trunk steak, which is believed to be the tastiest part. You may even be able to find elephant meat in a tin to take home as a souvenir, to impress or offend your friends.

Elephant meat has been eaten for tens of thousands of years, going back to when primitive man hunted the modern pachyderm's ancestors, the mammoths and mastodons, with spears, or by driving them off cliffs with fire. Even in recent times, many African peoples included the animal in their diet. The Pygmies of Africa were known for their prowess in bringing down the giants with poisoned arrows.

Such activity did not affect the population; those killed numbered fewer than those born. The harvest was sustainable.

Today in most African and all Asian countries, the elephant population is threatened. Most, but not all. In Zimbabwe, protection efforts were so successful that the government initiated a program to cull the elephant population. In 1995, George Pangeti, deputy director of the Department of National Parks and Wildlife, said there were between seventy and eighty thousand elephants in an environment that could support only half that number. An adult elephant ate up to four hundred and fifty pounds of vegetation a day, he said, and large areas of the national parks were being ravaged by overpopulation, upsetting the ecological balance needed to sustain other wildlife.

The same argument was voiced in South Africa, where in Krugor National Park—a game reserve the size of Israel—the elephant population grew to eight thousand from the few hundred the ivory hunters left in the early 1990s. With park officials warning that the reserve could provide for only seven thousand and that larger numbers would endanger other species, pushing *them* to the brink of extinction, or at least to hunger. The government proposed a culling program that included selling the hides (for expensive luggage and so on) and the meat, which in turn would bring up to US$500,000 a year, to be assigned to conservation programs.

Animal welfare groups in Europe and the U.S. argued that the culling would weaken the ivory trade ban as well as encourage more poaching by creating new markets for the meat and skins. Why not send the unwanted beasts elsewhere? South Africa did that, relocating hundreds to smaller reserves, as did Kenya, moving elephants from crowded areas to parks where the herds had been decimated. But the overpopulation problem remained in some areas and it was prohibitively expensive to transport the animals over longer distances, say, from one country to another.

With politicians nervous about endorsing any law that sanctioned the killing of elephants, the beasts were put up for sale and "adoption." Understandably, there were few takers and finally the herds were thinned by government hunters in helicopters using drugged darts, at last sending the meat and hides to the marketplace.

Such government programs were not cheap. Skinning an elephant required a team of people several hours and five hundred pounds of salt to treat a single animal, while hauling a thousand or more pounds of meat a long distance was no easy matter. In fact, the scale of the economics brought one effort at culling to its knees in 1965. This was funded by the United Nations, creating an abattoir in Zambia that was designed to cut five per cent of the local populations of elephant, hippopotamus, and buffalo. By 1970, the program was scrapped, due largely to the cost of transporting the carcasses over long distances and poor marketing. Today in South Africa, most elephant meat feeds the poor living in densely populated areas surrounding the game reserves.

Historically, elephant meat usually has been consumed on the spot, or smoked and dried for later use. The trunks and feet are considered the choicest cuts; elephant fat has been made into cooking oil.

Even after twelve or more hours of cooking (or long aging in the open air), the meat is regarded as somewhat chewy. The flesh, which is muscular and gelatinous, compares with beef tongue, which it also resembles in taste, only gamier.

If you wish to try this delicacy in Africa, book a flight soon. In Johannesburg, politicians are talking about putting the elephants on birth-control pills.

Opposite above: A waiter at the Carnivore restaurant in Nairobi serves up the bush meat *du jour,* carved right at the diners' table.
Opposite, below: Kangaroo has found recent favor in modern cuisine. In London's Sugar Club, renowned chef Peter Gordon, a New Zealander, serves a Thai-style spicy kangaroo salad, and likes the meat for its taste and tenderness.

Opposite left: A chimp, such as this one, occasionally may serve as a family pet, but only for a short time, and then it's into the pot or is sold at a central African market.

This page, above: Monkeys are smoked over open wood fires in the wild, then packaged for shipping to the city or put aside for later consumption. In the Congo Republic in 1997, the prime minister officially announced that all school children should spend their holidays hunting and fishing, an announcement made during the closed season.

This page, below: Gorilla meat is easily smoked and passed off as buffalo, which makes it easier to sell openly in some areas. The nine-ball Chevrotine cartridge designed to bring down a gorilla is sold over the counter.

Photos this page by Karl Ammann.

This page: This chimpanzee baby was frozen and transported by riverboat to Kinshasa where it is found on many restaurant menus.
Near right: Antelopes make up a large share of commercial bushmeat, whether rare species or not.
Opposite, left: A young boy carries a trophy gorilla head.
Far right, above: A village woman holds a cooked monkey.
Far right, middle: Fresh and cooked meat is moved from the jungle by dug-out canoes, then by larger river boats or on logging trains like this one, offloaded within walking distance of the open market.
Far right, below: A central African market.

All photos on this page and the next are by Karl Ammann.

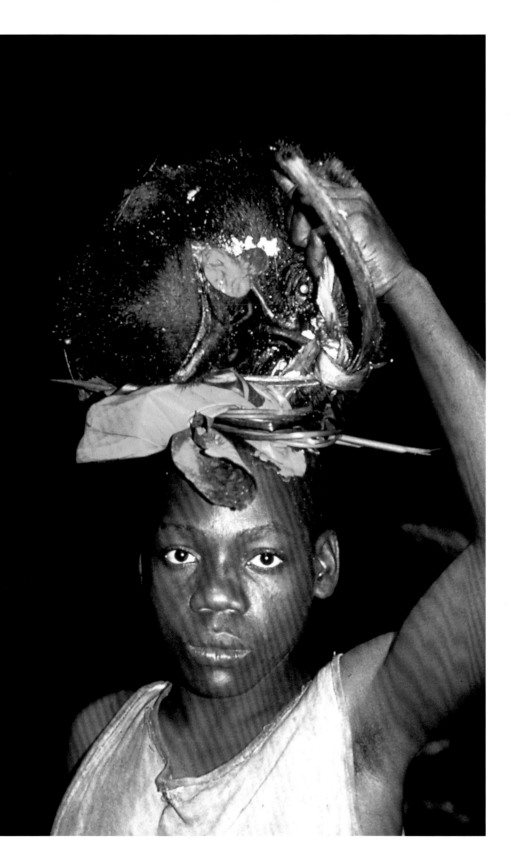

bison, water buffalo, & yak

Sliced Water Buffalo Meat Stew

2 pieces of water buffalo meat, each the size of a hand
salt
4 straight-bulbed spring onions
2 (small) heads of garlic
5 slices galingal
1 large onion, sliced vertically
fish sauce
2 fresh red chili peppers, chopped crossways
2 Kaffir lime leaves, finely chopped
2 limes
chopped coriander leaves
ground black pepper
young cucumbers

To prepare the meat, remove the tendons. Then wash the pieces, rub salt into them, and toast over a fire until the outside is golden. Take the spring onions and chop the bulbs and adjacent green parts only (not the leaves). Place the garlic in the embers of a charcoal fire until they are partly cooked but not well done, then remove them, take off the charred outer skin, and chop them vertically.

Put the meat, galingal, sliced large onion, and a sprinkling of salt into a pot with enough water to cover the meat. Put the pot on the fire. When the water boils, sprinkle in some fish sauce and continue boiling until the water is reduced and the meat tender.

(Continued opposite)

Roasted American buffalo, also called bison, was the main dish served to me at a Boy Scout ranch in New Mexico in the 1950s after a month spent hiking and riding horses across the rough, dry mountains and plains. At the time, one of the coins in American pockets had a picture of an Indian chief on one side, a bison on the other; thus, it was called a "buffalo nickel," and as a Boy Scout, Indian lore was something I knew well. At home, my mother hated to cook and my father's bland dietary demands made dinner time quite mundane, so eating the same food that nourished countless American Indians was quite exotic, permitting me to ignore the fact that it tasted like a slightly pungent version of my mother's overdone roast beef. (Sorry, Mom.)

The bison was once so numerous, its shaggy, humped-back herds roamed the Western U.S. plains like zebra and gazelle still inhabit parts of the African veldt. Before the white man arrived, an estimated forty to sixty million bison ranged from central Canada south into Mexico, where it was a primary source of food for the nomadic Indian tribes, including the Cheyenne, Cree, Kiowa, Sioux, Osage, Blackfoot, and many more. Like other grazing animals, bison relied more on a keen sense of smell than sight and hearing to detect approaching harm; native hunters frequently approached the herds on their hands and knees, with wolf skins hiding their human forms, their bodies smeared with buffalo fat to hide their human odor, bow-and-arrow at the ready. The hunters also constructed high walls of brush along either side of known buffalo migration routes, forming a sort of funnel leading to a rough corral, where they easily killed the targets of their choice. When the geography permitted, they stampeded the buffalo over cliffs. After acquiring horses and rifles from early European hunters and explorers, the tribal hunt became more efficient.

One kill, averaging between a thousand and fifteen hundred pounds, could provide for a tribe for days. Usually the first parts consumed were the offal, although the favorite parts—generally either roasted or dried for future use—were the tongue and meat from the hump, which was considered the tenderest and sweetest. Eaten soon after slaughter, the meat was roasted on a spit or boiled in a skin bag with water and stones heated in an open fire, a process that produced a nutritious stew or soup.

The Indians wasted nothing, using every part of the shaggy beast. Clothing and moccasins were made from the tanned hide, along with river rafts and boats; the cured hide also covered the Indians' tall, conical tents, or tipi. With the hair left on, the hides became blankets for the bitter winter cold. Tanning agents were produced from the brains, fat, and liver, soap from the leftover fat, glue from the rendered hooves. War shields were crafted from the tough neck hide, arrowheads and knives from the bones, powder flasks, spoons, and drinking cups from the horns. Sinew was used as thread. Hoes were fashioned from the shoulder blade, and stomachs were sewn into water bags. The long hair was plaited into halters. Even the dried dung was used, as it is today when no wood is available, for campfires, producing little smoke.

The Indians killed an estimated three hundred thousand buffalo a year, well below the natural replacement rate. That changed tragically in the early nineteenth century, when a vogue for big game hunting swept much of the world and white settlers with rifles began populating the American plains, followed by entrepreneurs and adventurers. The bison were killed by white hunters first for their meat at a rate of about two million a year, but frequently only the tongues were taken for the menus of fashionable restaurants in Chicago and New York and the huge carcasses were left to rot. The slaughter accelerated to about three million a year in the 1870s, when bison hides were first made into commercial leather.

William F. Cody, an early plainsman, acquired his nickname "Buffalo Bill" for shooting bison as food for railroad construction crews and is reported to have killed 4,280 animals within one seventeen-month period. Once the railroads were in place, the white man shot millions more each year, blasting away from trains passing through the diminishing herds. Some contend that this was a plot to beat back the native Americans; slaughter the primary source of their survival and you wipe out the Indians, too. More likely, the hunters got some sort of thrill from banging away at the beasts.

Whatever the motivation, now the entire animal was left to waste and with the introduction of fences erected by sheep herders and other homesteaders, the surviving animals' freedom to range was restricted, their natural lifestyle inhibited. By the end of the century, the American buffalo was driven to the point of extinction; unbelievably, from tens of millions, only about a thousand still grazed the plains.

Happily, the tide has turned. Small wild herds survived in parts of the U.S. (notably in what became Yellowstone Park) and Canada and in the twentieth century, efforts were introduced to protect the animal and reconstitute the once-great herds. Today, the buffalo's future seems secure as more than a hundred thousand of them range parklands and private ranches from New York to California, from Canada to Oklahoma. Some of the herds, including the largest in existence—numbering twelve thousand—are on ranches owned by American media mogul Ted Turner and his wife, actress Jane Fonda, and the corporate emblem of the company that administers their ranches is a charging bison.

Many of today's herds, including Mr. Turner's, are being managed at least partly for the production of food, so today it is becoming more common to see charbroiled bison steak and stew on menus in the U.S. and Canada. Because of its resemblance to beef, in

appearance as well as in taste, it has found ready acceptance wherever it is available; limited quantity and distribution, however, has kept the meat unknown in most places. The bison also is being cross-bred with cattle, producing what is called "beefalo," and sometimes "cattelo." (However, the male of the mixed breed so far is infertile.) The North American Bison Cooperative, backed by scientific studies, boasts that the meat is lower in cholesterol and saturated fat than beef, non-allergenic, and free of chemicals.

Bud Flocchini of Gillette, Wyoming, president of the American Bison Association, says the membership has doubled to twenty-three hundred since 1993. "We've never seen such interest," he says. "Heifer calves are selling now for about US$1,600 each, and two-year-olds for up to $3,500. Last year, a champion blue-ribbon bull sold for $15,000. But most buyers are small operators. We advise them to study the animal very carefully before getting started, and pay a lot of attention to fences. These animals are much tougher to work with than beef cattle. To produce income, you need between fifty to one hundred head and around fifty acres of good pasture, with supplementary feed in the off-season."

Much of the bison consumed by the Indian nations was in the form of pemmican, a word that comes from the Cree, meaning "journey meat." To make pemmican, or jerky, the Cree dried strips of buffalo meat in the sun, a process that took a few days. They then pounded it into a pulp, mixing it with the fat from a bear or goose, or the bison itself, and, if available, pulverized dry fruit. More colorful was the description by C. Levi Strauss in *The Origin of Table Manners* (1978): "They placed thin slices of hard meat carefully on a bed of charcoal, first on one side then on the other. They beat them to break them into small pieces, which they mixed with melted bison fat and marrow. Then they pressed it into leather bags, taking care that no air was left inside. When the bags were sewn up, the women flattened them by jumping on them to blend the ingredients. They put them to dry in the sun."

Take out the meat and slice it thinly. Spoon out and throw away the galingal. Return the sliced meat to the pot. The amount of water should be just sufficient to keep the meat moist. Taste, and check the saltiness. Stir in the chopped ingredients and the juice of the two limes.

Put the soup in a large bowl, garnish it with ground black pepper and the chopped coriander leaves, and serve it with young cucumbers.

Sources

Jerky made from bison is available from the Tasty Jerky Company, (800) 537-5988. Check the company's web site at <www.info2000.net/~tastymilk/hnybuff.html>.

Yak breeders in the U.S.: Harlan Leer, Ranchos Dos Osos, P.O. Box 1103, Steamboat Springs, CO 80477, phone (970) 879-1789, email <dososos@cmn.net>; Cynthia and Dave Huber, Duckett Creek Ranch, Hillside, CO 81232, phone (719) 942-4181, email <dhuber@mariner-energy.com>; and Nancy Allen, Allen's Ark, P.O. Box 133, Dixon, MO 59831, phone (406) 745-2838, email <sti4472@montana.com>.

The bison has numerous cousins around the world, many of them also cherished as a renewable, non-threatened protein source. These include the Cape buffalo in Africa, and in Asia, the water buffalo and yak.

Of these, surely the water buffalo is the most commonly consumed. With an estimated 140 million in existence, this largely domesticated, cud-chewing, plant-eating animal is now spread over much of the world, but it is in Indonesia, Thailand, Malaysia, the Philippines, Myanmar, China, Laos, Cambodia, and Vietnam where the majority live. Here, they labor as the developing world's tractor, while serving as family friend, object of competitive sport (battling head-to-head during festivals or in long, bouncy dashes in a race against the clock, riders clinging precariously to their asphalt hides), and household symbol of status, wealth, and tranquility. Sacrifice a buffalo at a funeral or in a religious rite or offer one as part of a dowry for a bride and your local status goes up, or put them to work in the paddy fields and, between shifts in front of primitive plows, let them and children mind each other in muddy peace. Surely no other Asian beast of burden is so revered.

Given this status in Asian society, it may seem surprising that the water buffalo so easily becomes dinner. In fact, until most Southeast Asian countries first imported real beef from Australia and elsewhere about twenty years ago, most of the "beef" consumed in Asia was water buffalo—sadly much of it rather chewy, due to the animals' advanced age; after all, there was no advantage in butchering a key member of the family work force.

Related distantly to domestic cattle, the water buffalo—so called because they like to wallow in mud and water—labored in fields in Iraq and the Indus Valley as long as four thousand years ago, and domesticated populations existed in southern China a thousand years later. Wide hooves, flexible joints, and tremendous strength allow them to pull a plow knee-deep in mud. They also have a docile nature and thrive on low-quality forage, surviving happily on wild grass and the stubble left behind following a rice harvest. Despite such a humble diet, adults often reach nine feet in length, can be nearly six feet high at the shoulders, and weigh more than a ton, as much as a small automobile.

Today, water buffalo are a major source of milk, contributing about half of the milk consumed in India. This liquid, which has much more fat, more nonfat solids, and less water than cow's milk, also is important in China and the Philippines. In India, the milk is also used for making a kind of liquid butter, and herds created for commercial purposes, as far apart as Italy and Australia, provide the milk that is turned into mozzarella cheese. Similarly, the Cape buffalo contributes much milk to the diet in Africa. Still, mainly the beast is valued for its flesh.

In 1993, for example, when the United Nations was in Cambodia helping organize and supervise the country's first election, one of the UN vehicles slammed into a water buffalo as it ambled across a rural road.

The water buffalo plays an important role in the cultures of rice-growing Asia, here celebrated in the Philippines at the annual *carabao* (Tagalog for "buffalo") festival in Pulilan, north of Manila. Farmers parade their animals dressed and decorated for the occasion.

The driver panicked and hurried back to the capital, Phnom Penh, where he was told by his superiors that he must return to the scene of the accident and pay the villagers for their loss. When he arrived next day, the buffalo already had been butchered and partially consumed. The UN representative was invited to stay for supper.

Water buffalo may be consumed raw (usually ground, as in steak tartare), dried, or cooked as beef would be prepared. Some of the earliest written recipes survive from the nineteenth century, when, in Laos, the king's chef included instructions for making "hot boiled water buffalo sauce" to be served with slices of raw eggplant or cucumber, "slow-cooked water buffalo tripe," and the meat in a kind of stew seasoned with lemon grass and chili peppers. Even today in Laos, there is a restaurant in the capital, Vientiane, known for its buffalo specialties, including placenta, fetus, udder, and brains. As is true for other animals, the older the beast, the tougher the meat, so tenderizers may be warranted.

Today, the water buffalo population is shrinking, worldwide. The average population growth rate in Asia has, over the past three decades, declined by more than half. As farmers replaced these four-legged tractors with three-wheeled ones (the earliest were called "iron buffalo"), interest in breeding dropped. At the same time, more and more farmers sought work in the cities, leaving much of the rice farming to large conglomerates. In the past, four hundred families in one village might have owned as many as a thousand buffaloes. Nowadays, the same number may have only twenty-five.

In the high plateaus and mountains of Central Asia, in eastern Kashmir, Nepal, and Tibet, ranging from the lower valleys to twenty-thousand-foot elevations where the climate is cold and dry, there lives another cousin of the bison and water buffalo, the yak. Known for an unusually luxuriant coat almost reaching to the ground and its long, curving horns, it looks like a large brown or reddish shag rug thrown over a long-horn steer with a hump. Despite their relative immensity—yaks also weigh as much as a small car—they are nimble climbers and sure swimmers, roaming icy mountainsides and valleys, grazing on native grass.

Like other members of the same family, they are favored for the variety of their uses and services. They carry heavy loads. The hair is spun into rope and woven into cloth. The hide is used for leather, shoes, coats, bags for storing grain, and for the construction of simple boats, as well as for tent-like, temporary housing. (More permanent homes may include some of the bones for structural support.) Its horns serve as a bugle, emitting a distinct sound when properly shaped and blown, used by monks or yak-herders to signal the time of day, to call for help, signal danger, or simply to communicate. And, as is true for its American relative, the dried dung is used for fuel.

During the funeral rites of the Akha hill-tribe in Burma, Thailand, Laos, and Yunnan, a sacrificial buffalo is committed to the deceased. The dead animal is laid out for a day and covered with paddy, while the spirit priest prays over it. Later, it will provide a feast for the entire village.

Yet, it is its use as a food that gives the yak its reputation. The milk yields excellent butter and curd, and the flesh is of high quality, eaten roasted or dried, fried, boiled, baked, broiled, or made into a stew or soup, with or without noodles. Its meat is available everywhere in Lhasa, Tibet's capital, where it is found on most restaurant menus, stuffed into dumplings, sliced into steaks, air-dried, and minced into "yak burgers." (When China invaded the country and the Dalai Lama and some eighty thousand Tibetans fled to neighboring Nepal and India, they took this cuisine with them. In Nepal's capital, Kathmandu, several Tibetan restaurants offer a full range of yak dishes.) Because the yak, like other animals, tends to get tough and stringy with age, most of the meat will have been ground to ease the chewing process. The taste is like cheap hamburger meat.

However popular the flesh, it is the butter that likely will give this mammal its culinary immortality. Read any book about Nepal or Tibet, or check the staggering number of Internet web sites about these countries—hundreds and perhaps thousands of them posted by foreigners who recall their visit as if in a state of religious transcendence—and it is inevitable that the subject of yak butter is mentioned.

Yak milk is rich, valued for its seven percent fat content, compared to half that for cattle. The butter is used as a thickener for soups and mixed with ground barley in a tea called *tsampa*, a drink consumed in vast quantity at all hours of the day and night. The whitish-yellow fat may also be burned in lamps to illuminate tents, homes, and temples, and is applied as a body lotion or hair pomade. In Buddhist monasteries, monks boil up huge cauldrons of the stuff to offer visitors in tea. The natives' clothing is redolent, committing to the air a sort of greasy, smoky smell. The odor is strong—some say rancid—yet it is so pervasive that because you cannot avoid it, after a while you stop noticing it. It becomes a part of you.

And you hold out your cup for more.

This page: When CNN founder Ted Turner bought this Montana ranch west of Yellowstone National Park, he replaced the cattle with bison, which now number 12,000.

Opposite, above left: An Akha spirit priest in northern Thailand sacrifices a tethered buffalo with a single stab from a spear. Immediately, water will be poured down its throat so that it will make no noise in dying.

Opposite, above right: At the ritual slaughter of another buffalo, in a Pathan village on the Northwest Frontier of Pakistan, the butcher washes his hands after cutting the animal's throat.

Opposite bottom left: Pathan tribesmen from the village of Kado, near Peshawar, enjoy a buffalo biriani feast from the animal pictured above right.

Opposite bottom right: The sleek braided hair of a Tibetan pilgrim praying outside the Jokhang in Lhasa owes its lustre to a yak butter pomade.

whale

All hell broke loose in 1998 when the school district of the seaside city of Shimonoseki in Japan announced an addition to the upcoming year's school lunch menu: whale meat.

Greenpeace went ballistic and thousands of save-the-whale crusaders worldwide—along with fans of the *Free Willy* movies—went to bed angry. When the Japanese defended their move, saying it was designed to teach some 25,000 elementary and primary school students pride in their town's historical role as a major port for their country's whaling fleet, it only made people madder.

No food harvest in the present time stirs more controversy than the killing of whales. Not the tiger, panda, elephant, dolphin, monk seal, manatee, bald eagle, gorilla, orangutan, gibbon, chimpanzee, or any other endangered or threatened species. People who killed whales were crazy, the "save the whales" contingent argue: "Didn't you read *Moby Dick*?" Of course, it's not that simple.

Surveys show that most people believe Japan is the only country defending this age-old harvest and that only the Japanese continue to regard the meat, blubber, and other by-products as a part of daily life. While it's true that Japan leads all other countries in its whaling activity—sending the meat into markets and onto dinner plates, as well as including it in school lunches—Japan is not alone. There are other countries that approve whaling, Iceland, Denmark and Norway among them, as well as Canada, Russia and a handful of South Pacific nations, which have refused to agree to international bans. In addition, aboriginal subsistence whaling is permitted by native peoples in Alaska, the far-eastern part of Russia, in Greenland, and in Saint Vincent and the Grenadines. What's more, there is a strengthening international voice to cancel the commercial whaling ban altogether.

In fact, as long ago as 1972 and 1973 the Scientific Committee of the International Whaling Commission (IWC), the committee responsible for counting the world's whales, by consensus at its meetings said that "there is no scientific justification or need for a whaling moratorium." This opinion did not match that of the anti-whaling member nations who controlled the IWC, however, and the judgment was ignored. This same opinion was put forth by the committee once more in 1993, but again brought no change.

Then, in 1997 at the bi-annual meeting of the highly esteemed Convention on International Trade in Endangered Species (CITES), the organization generally regarded as having the last word on the subject of any creature thought to be in jeopardy, member nations stunned environmental advocates everywhere by supporting the sustainable use of abundant whale stocks, voting to allow trade in whale products fifty-seven to fifty-one. Thus, the majority endorsed the notion that whales could be killed and eaten, but since a two-thirds majority was

Moby Who?

To understand how whale meat found its way into school lunches in Japan and onto grills in faraway Iceland, Norway, Denmark and elsewhere—and why it is not eaten in most places today—suggests a fast look at whaling history.

Many whales are threatened with extinction today because unregulated whaling activity—led by the United States, England, and Norway—annihilated the oceanic population in much the same way many other large mammals were hunted to near-extinction in the North American and African continents. Whaling by these countries was conducted to collect whale oil, the market for which died with the discovery of petroleum. The market for whale bone,

used in the construction of corsets and other female foundation garments, also died when those garments became obsolete. It wasn't concern for the survival of the great beasts that ended whaling. It was commerce.

With the market for the oil gone and no apparent interest in the meat, commercial whaling became unprofitable and the United States quit whaling in 1940, the United Kingdom in 1963. A resolution calling for a ten-year moratorium on commercial whaling was adopted at the United Nations Conference on Human Environment in 1972 and the IWC followed with an open-ended moratorium effective from 1986. Iceland withdrew from the IWC six years later and Norway resumed whaling in 1993.

needed to overturn a ban, the prohibition remained in place.

The operative phrase in the frustrated proposal was "abundant whale stocks." What, after all, is "abundant"? There are nearly two million sperm whales; is that "abundant"? Certainly that number would make the defenders of any other endangered species ecstatic. Yet, the sperm whale, found in all the earth's oceans, is still one of the eight whale species on the CITES list. (The others are not so fortunate: the blue, bowhead, finback, gray, humpback, the right, and sei have populations far smaller, many in the tens of thousands and one, the right, is estimated to be down to 3,000.)

It is important to note that Japan reportedly claims to hunt the minke whale almost exclusively, a species whose estimated numbers, while smaller than those of the sperm whale, are regarded as sufficiently large to justify limited hunting and are, therefore, not on anyone's endangered lists. (Smaller numbers of the Pacific Brydes whale are also taken—another whale not on any threatened list.) According to the Scientific Committee of the IWC, charged with maintaining population figures, there are approximately 760,000 minke whales in the Antarctic, another 118,000 in the North Atlantic, a further 25,000 in the Okhotsk Sea and Western Pacific.

Initially, Japan objected noisily to any controls, but then it discovered it could continue limited whaling with IWC approval under the cloak of "scientific research"—where it was believed that safe management of marine resources was not then possible because knowledge of the number of whales, age composition, sex ratio, and natural mortality rate was unknown or ambiguous. The research catch by Japan was thus introduced, with the IWC limiting the capture to 2,000 whales a year, to answer such questions and eliminate uncertainties.

While it is true that the Japanese are completing their task, contributing to the world's knowledge of the Antarctic and its *cetacean* population, it may be noted that they also get to keep the whales. After scientific examination and removal of necessary tissue and organ samples, the remains of the whales are frozen and marketed in compliance with further provisions of the IWC, which forbid any part of the carcass to be wasted. Voilà! Whale blubber and steak.

Environmentalists contend that Japan is hiding behind "research" to keep whaling fleets intact, and whether or not this is true, there is ample evidence that eating whale meat in that country has a long history. Discoveries at archeological digs in Japan show that whale meat has been eaten at least to the second century B.C. (Whaling began in Norway, France and Spain in the ninth century A.D.) Furthermore, after the acceptance of Buddhism in Japan, which in its early years prohibited the consumption of flesh from four-legged animals, whale meat became an important source of protein. It has been found recorded on menus from a thousand years ago and by the Muromachi Period (1333–1568) it had come to be regarded as so important as to merit inclusion on a menu contained in official literature.

Japan's whale meat consumption was about 10,000 thousand tons in the early 1920s, jumping to 40,000 tons by 1939. Its popularity accelerated again following World War Two, when other protein sources were severely limited, reaching a high of two hundred thousand tons in 1962. Since then, the market has fallen, to just under fifteen thousand tons in 1985. Today, it appears to be less than that, although figures are not revealed because of the controversy.

The Japanese people know that the whale is a mammal, but it is commonly treated as a "fish." (As is the dolphin or porpoise.) For instance, a quarterly journal published by the Japan Whaling Association is called *Isana*, a word from the ancient Japanese language composed of two Chinese characters, for "brave" and "fish," denoting a whale. The whale to the Japanese in earlier times was, therefore, a kind of courageous fish, thus it was served at joyous occasions such as weddings and other communal celebrations.

Japan has long been, and still is, a nation of fish-

Whale Steak with Vegetables

4$\frac{1}{2}$ lb. whale meat
2 cup red wine
1 cup water
15 juniper berries
2 dessert spoons black currant cordial
cream
cornflour

Brown the meat on all sides in a stew pot, add the red wine, water, and mashed juniper berries. Simmer under lid for about 30 minutes. Remove the meat and wrap it in aluminum foil while finishing making the gravy.

For the gravy, add the black currant cordial to the juices in the pan. Add cream to taste and thicken with cornflour. Cut the meat into thin slices and serve with potatoes, green peas, sprouts and mountain cranberries.

High North Alliance, 1994

This page, and opposite: So-called "whale bacon" is a popular snack in Japan—thin slices that include the blubber, seen below for sale in a Kyushu fish market. The Japanese katakana letters spell the English word, pronounced "bacon-o."

eaters and the whale was regarded as just another part of the harvest from the sea; just as it has been judged by indigenous peoples from the northwestern United States, where the Maah Indian tribe won the right from the IWC to resume a 1,500-year-old whaling tradition, pointing to a treaty with the U.S. government that dated back to 1855. On the southern tip of South America, the Yahgen people used smoke signals to summon neighbors whenever a whale was caught or found beached; families would come for miles around and camp out and feast for as long as a month.

For a tribe of native North Americans, the Kwakuitl, such a find was highly ritualized. Preparing food was women's work and the honors, in this case, went to the daughter of the hunter who found the whale. The choicest piece was given to the village chief and others received a share, according to their status, starting with the neck and working from the top down and from head to tail.

The harvest was then loaded into the canoes and taken home, where the blubber was cut into half-inch strips and boiled in water. When the oil separated, it was ladled into watertight storage containers and the remaining strings of blubber were threaded onto long thin pieces of cedar bark and hung to dry in the rafters of the house for at least a month. It could then be taken down and reboiled as needed.

It was back in 1931 when the International Convention for Regulation of Whaling (ICRW), one of the earliest monitoring groups, set rigid standards for "aboriginal/subsistence whaling." The concept was to aid "local, aboriginal, indigenous, or native" communities in meeting their nutritional, subsistence, and cultural requirements, but the regulations soon proved unworkable. Aborigines, who themselves were never very clearly defined, were to use only canoes or other exclusively native craft propelled by oars or sails and were forbidden to carry firearms. In effect, IRCW was saying that if an exception was going to be made for the hungry natives, they would have to stick to ancient means of pursuit and capture, a inefficient hindrance that resulted in much wasted time, effort and meat. Over time, the rules were relaxed and today, modern whaling boats usually assist in providing the limited catch.

Some of these ships are from the former Soviet Union, one of several countries—Japan is another—accused of illegal whaling. According to figures released in a report commissioned by the Australian

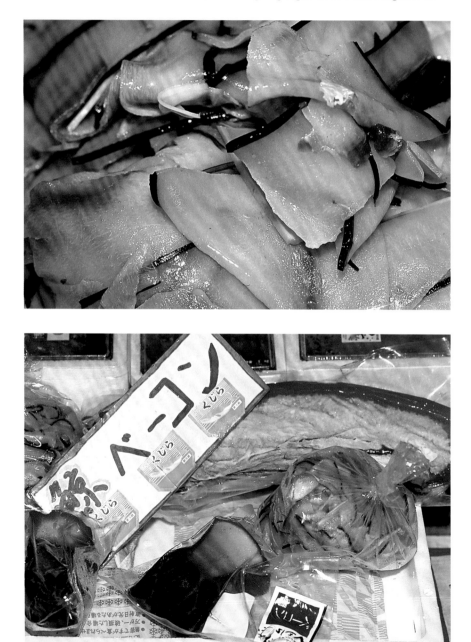

government, one of the loudest anti-whaling voices, Soviet fleets between 1947 and 1972 killed 48,000 humpback whales, one of the most endangered species, yet reported a catch of fewer than 3,000. The Soviets also were charged with killing 8,000 pygmy blue whales, while admitting to a catch of only ten. Anti-whaling critics also said that in Japan, as recently as 1998, DNA testing of whale meat on sale in local fish markets showed some of the meat was not from Japan's "scientific" catch, but from protected species caught thousands of miles away from the authorized hunt areas.

Whatever its legal—or ethical—status, there is no doubt about the healthy nature of whale meat. Though richer in protein, whale meat has fewer calories than beef or pork, and it is substantially lower in cholesterol. To many Arctic peoples, salted whale meat has long been an indispensable part of the diet during the winter months, as it keeps longer than salted fish and tastes good as well.

Whales are classified into two groups, baleen whales and toothed whales. Unlike toothed whales, which actively hunt their food, baleen whales "graze" on zooplankton called krill, comprised of extremely small shrimps and fish. It's believed that this is what makes the meat so tender and juicy. The Japanese consume nearly every part of a whale, including the internal organs, the blubber, even the tail and flukes. The tastiest part is thought to be the *onomi*, the marbled flesh found at the base of the tail.

Surely, the controversy over killing whales will continue. Many whale species are now increasing in numbers and the political climate is changing. When CITES voted fifty-seven to fifty-one, supporting the trade of whale products in 1997, Ginette Hemley of the World Wildlife Fund told the Associated Press, "This indicates a significant decrease in opposition to whaling. The whole tone of the whaling debate has changed."

Peter Bridgewater, chairman of the ICW, added, "The numbers [favoring an end to the ban] were much stronger than they have ever been. The interpretation being put on this by a number of countries is that the way is open for trading and people are interested."

Greenpeace and other conservationists continue to say "No way! Feed the school children something else!"

guts

"Guts" is an interesting word. Literally, it is a reference to the alimentary canal, a tubular passage functioning in the digestion of food and extending from the mouth to the anus, a path that includes a lot of anatomy, and provides a great deal of food itself.

It's also now thought of—colloquially, at least in English—as a synonym for courage and fortitude. So, a robust and daring individual may be described as being "gutsy" or "having guts," and to be without such character is to be "gutless." Sometimes, this attribute is called "intestinal fortitude." The famous World War Two army general George Patton was known as "Blood and Guts."

In addition, many people talking about their instincts say, "I feel it in my gut."

This is one of those rare instances when positive endorsement—using the word to mean courage and intuition—don't do anything to make the namesake appealing as food. However many people in the world today savor the deliciously prepared parts of the alimentary canal, as many more would never even consider putting "guts" on their dinner plate. And it is interesting how many of those who *will* eat guts often give the meat an innocent-sounding euphemism, as if that would distance the food from its anatomical origins. Just as feet are called "trotters," the pancreas and thymus glands are called "sweetbreads," lungs are called "lights," the spleen is called "melt" and testicles have a variety of more socially acceptable names, the stomach of ruminants, especially the ox, calf, or sheep, is called "tripe," as, sometimes, are the intestines, while the intestines of young pigs are called "chitterlings." (Or in the southern United States, "chitlins," usually consumed with grits and collard greens.) Such foods, along with other internal organs, are called offal, meaning, literally, the "off-fall" or off-cuts from the carcass; many call these items "variety meats." Even in

Chinese households, you will never hear anyone say, "Pass the stomach" or "Could I have some more intestine, please?"

Eating entrails has a history as long and twisting as the gut itself—proving that no matter what something may have once contained, with the proper preparation, a tasty meal can be made of it. Many European countries are known for their sausages; Germany alone boasts nearly 1,500 varieties. What is used to hold all that beef, pork, mutton, chicken, game meat, fat, egg, cream, beer, wine, blood, breadcrumbs, oatmeal, potato and soybean flour, dried milk solids, onion, garlic, herbs and spices, salt and pepper and assorted additives and preservatives together? Although some of the casings are now made from digestible plastic—the horror, the horror!—the tube-like sleeve tied off at the ends usually is a length of pig's intestine. For large sausages, the large intestine is used, and for the smaller ones and chitterlings, meat packagers employ the small intestine or the cecum, an abdominal appendage that is also used, from sheep, to make condoms that are sometimes called "skins." (Falling into disfavor nowadays because they are porous and while it will keep back spermatozoa, the HIV virus may slip through.)

The intestines themselves also may be minced and added to the sausage's other ingredients. Chitterlings, for instance are not only encased in short sleeves of pig intestine (or cecum), the insides are pork intestine, too. They are enjoyed in France, as well as in the United States, and usually are fried or grilled. Calf's mesentery, part of the peritoneum, the membrane lining the abdominal cavity, is a sausage ingredient that may also be fried or prepared in the same way as tripe, about which more in a minute.

Ox intestines also are a common ingredient in blood sausage (black pudding), a dish most often associated with the north of England, but found in many other European countries as well. In Asia, the carefully cleaned bowels of pigs are chopped and simmered along with other innards, such as the stomach, in anise-flavored broth and poured over noodles and the large intestine, similarly thinly sliced is simmered and deep-fried, then served as a snack that goes down well with beer. In Singapore, I've eaten entrails cut into quarter-inch wide rings and cooked in a rich soup with blood used as a thickening. A disadvantage: improperly cooked, such foods have the chewability of thick rubber bands.

The somewhat snooty *Larousse Gastronomique* calls offal, "particularly intestines and tripe," inferior, saying that only kidneys, liver, calves' sweetbreads, lambs' brains, and animelles have any "real gastronomic importance." Having said that, *Larousse* then devotes two pages to stomach—tripe if you and *Larousse* insist—to praise and recipes.

Tripe comes from the first and second stomachs of oxen, the former providing "plain" tripe, and the latter looking much like a honeycomb, and regarded as the tastiest. As is true for intestines, preparation of tripe is lengthy, requiring ninety minutes of simmering before becoming tender. The good news is that most tripe is sold in stores cleaned and prepared for cooking, so the repeated lengthy washings and soakings are unnecessary, although it still must be simmered at home. Tripe also is available ready-cooked or pickled. *Tripes a la mode de Caen*, the most famous of French tripe dishes—cooked with calves' feet, garlic, thyme, bay leaf, beef fat, cider, and Calvados—is available tinned. Pickled tripe is usually sold thoroughly cooked, but should be parboiled before using. Canned tripe is ready to heat and serve.

Tripe is eaten throughout most of Europe. In France, tripe may be cooked with pig's trotters, goose fat, or white wine, and the pig's caul, the lace-like, fatty membrane around the paunch, is the binding used for *crepinettes*, small forcemeat sausages made from lamb or pork. The French also use it to wrap patés. Although occasionally found fresh, usually caul is sold frozen; thaw it until you can peel off as much as needed, then refreeze.) Another French sausage, the *andouillette*, is made almost entirely of tripe and mesentery. The Spanish garnish tripe with chorizo, chili peppers, garlic, and thin strips of sweet red pepper. In Bulgaria, there is a popular tripe soup. In Arabian countries, it is boiled with cumin, pepper, and the rind of citrus (oranges and lemons most commonly). In Mexico, it is a part of *menudo*. It also may be cut into one-inch squares and batter-fried or dipped into egg and breaded and fried until crisp, another beer snack. Almost everywhere, the classic dish is a white stew with onions.

In China, honeycomb tripe is simmered for an hour and a half with soy sauce and star anise, then sliced and eaten. Bruce Cost in his book *Asian Ingredients* (1988) suggests simmering in water or a light stock with wine and ginger, then sliced and stir-fried or tossed in a Beijing-style salad with a mustard-sesame sauce. Asian cooks also use caul fat to wrap pork liver. In Sri Lanka, it is cut into one-inch cubes and cooked in a rich curry. It may also be marinated, then fried or grilled; stewed with tomatoes and other vegetables; and cooked in broth, wine, or cider.

Americans may be surprised to learn that it is often one of the ingredients in hot dogs.

Pass the mustard.

Call it Grass Soup

"I don't know why," my friend Richard Lair told me, "but the people in the north of Thailand like their food to taste bitter."

Richard is an American expatriate who's lived in Thailand since the late 1960s, working much of that time with elephants. He told me he had eaten just about everything while traveling in northern Thailand (where most of the remaining elephants are) and living in the jungle for up to two years at a time with the mahouts, the native elephant trainers.

"One of the bitterest foods is called *phia*," he said. "This is fluid from the second ruminant sac of a water buffalo or cattle. Grass that's been fairly well digested and one step away from the intestines. Some say it's from the intestines, but that's not true. It's dark green and carefully collected when an animal is slaughtered, then sold in buckets in the street markets."

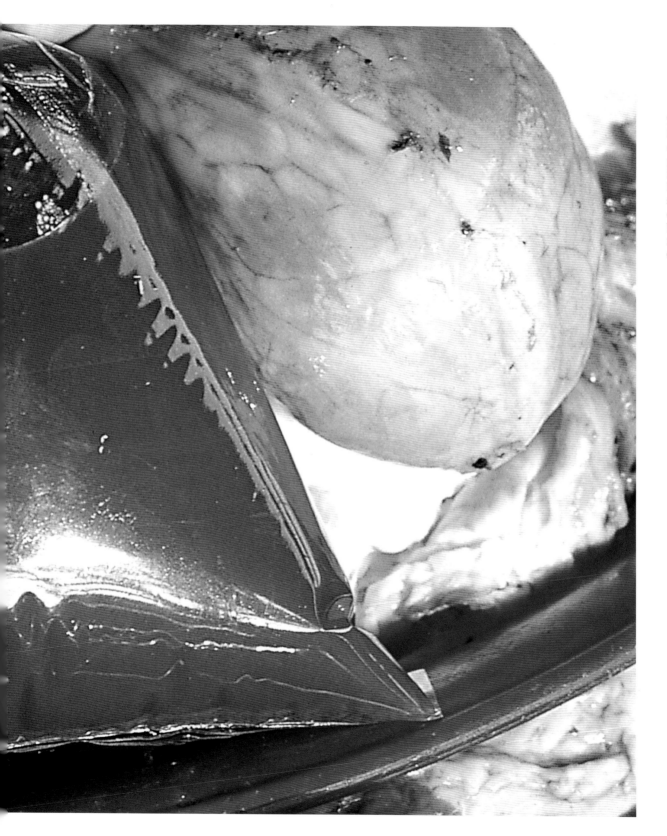

The northern Thai town of Phayao is known for its culinary use of all possible parts of cattle and buffalo, including the cloudy green liquid called *phia*, from the second ruminant sac. Locals call it *khi phia*, the prefix being the word for excrement, and use it to flavour dishes such as spicy salads.

ears, eyes, noses, lungs, tongues, lips, gums, glands, & feet

Mannish Water (Sheep's Head Stew)

4 quarts water (or enough to cover head)
2 lbs. sheep head, feet, or both
2 lbs. lamb stew meat
2 small onions, chopped
2 garlic cloves, minced
10 pimento (allspice) berries
10 whole black pepper corns
3 bay leaves
Salt
½ cup vegetable oil
4 carrots, diced
2 dasheen, peeled and cubed
2 lbs. potatoes, peeled and cubed
¼ pumpkin, peeled and cubed
6 green bananas, peeled
5 scallions, finely chopped
3 whole Scotch bonnet peppers
2 cups white rum

In a large, heavy pot, combine the water, head, meat, onions, garlic, pimento, peppercorns, bay leaves, and salt. Bring the mixture to a rolling boil, and skim off any scum. Cover the pot, and over medium heat, cook for 30 minutes, or until the meat falls off the bone.

(Continued opposite)

I was 14 or 15, a Boy Scout going cross-country by train from the U.S. East Coast, where I lived, to New Mexico, where I would spend a month on a Boy Scout ranch (and eat my first bison meat). On the way, we stopped in Chicago, where the two places selected for our group to visit were the Lincoln Park Zoo and the Hormel slaughterhouse. I don't remember a thing about the zoo, but the visit to the abattoir remains as vivid today as it was then.

Our guide led us past hundreds of cattle, sheep, and pigs, crammed together in rough plank pens between the rail lines and the slaughterhouse, waiting, unknowing, placidly, for their imminent demise, and then into a huge building where the butchering of pigs was done. As we entered, a large hog was released into a room about the size of my small bedroom back home, except this one was wall-to-wall cement and there was no furniture, only a large handcuff-like device hanging from the ceiling at the end of a chain.

A man in a blood-stained butcher's jacket that went to his knees grabbed the disoriented pig by one of its hind legs and attached the handcuff. Instantly the hog was lifted up so that it was suspended at a height that made it easy for the man to open its throat with a knife. Gravity quickly emptied the beast of its blood supply, which splashed onto the cement floor and disappeared down a nearby drain, destined for I didn't know what. The hog was then transported along an overhead rail, still hung by its hind foot, to the next station in the slaughterhouse, to be steam-cleaned and have its bristly hair removed.

We were told that we would follow that hog through the building, to watch it being butchered and packaged for sale nationwide, and that it would provide the nourishment that kept our nation great, building fine young bodies like ours. Maybe when we got home again, we were told, we'd have some of the bacon from that pig for breakfast. Our guide then said something that I remember to this day: "Every part of the pig is used, everything except the oink."

And so it is with many animals. Little or nothing is wasted. Other sections of this book consider blood, guts, and genitalia. In this one, I consider the other bits: the feet, the ears, the bones and marrow, the tails and snouts and tongues, the heads, some of the glands, the eyes, the gums, the lips, even the noses.

A friend of mine tells a story about why he won't eat sausage. He says he once took the time to read the list of contents on the package and while he found it (barely) acceptable to consider consuming most of the ingredients that went into the pulpy mix, when he got to the ingredient identified only as "parts," he blanched. No way, he says, would he eat "parts." That's too bad, because probably those parts are not only edible, but most of them tasty and nourishing.

The head of the animal offers such nutritious variety, I wonder why it is discarded or ignored by so many when the eyes, ears, the tongue, the brain, and the flesh on the skull itself, especially the fleshy cheeks, give up such valuable protein, minerals and vitamins, as well as a succulent taste. Many cultures, now and in the past, have savored the head of the ox, pig, and calf as a delicacy, most notably nowadays in Asia and Asian groceries, where you will find heads of animals staring at you, usually between the pigs' feet and the gigantic slabs of tongue.

Many nice things can be done with the heads—which have a surprising amount of meat attached to all that bone—although usually they are roasted whole in much the same way any other large piece of meat or poultry is cooked, for three to four hours on a rack in a baking pan, basted every thirty minutes or so, served when the skin is crisp, or as the centerpiece for a hearty stew.

The heads of pigs and calves, and sometimes sheep, are the most common in Oriental and specialty meat markets, usually bought whole and skinned, although it is sometimes sold split in half with the tongue intact and the eyes removed. The flesh is tender and gelatinous, perfect when corned for making head-cheese (called brawn) and other jellied meat dishes. In Britain, smoked pig's cheeks, called bath chaps, are usually boiled and eaten cold like ham, while the meat of the calf's head is eaten cold as a luncheon dish with a light vinaigrette sauce.

Laurens van der Post wrote in *First Catch Your Eland* (1977), "I have in my youth seen even the head of a slaughtered ox, not discarded, but grilled until it was tender and the distinguished historical gathering for whom it was done in the bush fall on the meat as if it were the best caviar from the Caspian Sea."

Among the Eskimos, the head of the moose—or at least a prominent part of it—is turned into Moose Nose Jelly. In recipes from both Canada's Ministry of Indian Affairs and the Cooperative Extension Service of the University of Alaska, the upper jawbone of the moose is cut just below the eyes and boiled, then chilled. After the hairs have been removed, it's washed and boiled again, this time with garlic, spices, and vinegar. The large, fleshy nose is next simmered until the meat is tender. When cool, the meat is removed and the bones and cartilage are discarded. The meat—white from the bulb of the nose, dark from along the bones and jowls—is sliced thinly, the original broth is brought to another boil and poured over the meat in a loaf pan. It is then cooled until the jelly sets, sliced and served cold.

Some internal organs—lung, spleen, pancreas and others—may comprise some of the "parts" that my friend the former sausage eater is worried about. In most parts of the west, notably in the United States and some European countries, these meats are sold to pet food canneries, a waste, because the spleen is a fine sausage ingredient and, along with the heart and lungs, may be used in stews; the pancreas and thymus glands from the neck and heart of young animals can be braised, fried, or sautéed. In some areas, however, lung is a major taboo; in the United States, Japan, and several other developed countries, the import of haggis, a Scottish dish, has been banned because sheep's lung is an integral ingredient.

Holding the head and body upright are the feet, or trotters, of slaughtered animals. The hooves of pigs, sheep, and calves and a number of other animals, as well as the scrawny legs and feet of chickens and ducks, are eaten today in Asia matter-of-factly, and are sold with other offal in groceries wherever Asian populations have taken up residence.

Lambs' and pigs' trotters generally are sold already blanched, but must be boned, singed (to remove the little hairs between the hooves) and generally are cooked in a bouillon, then braised, broiled, grilled, or fried and eaten hot with or without a sauce, added to stews for extra richness, or jellied for eating cold.

Shoppers for pigs' feet might keep in mind that the front ones are meatier than the hind ones, and may also wish to ask the butcher to cut them into eight pieces each. (They are hellaciously hard to chop into sections with a cleaver at home, unless you have a huge chopping block and a wicked overhand swing with the cleaver, or perhaps will use a chainsaw.) The Chinese use the feet to make a somewhat bony but delicious stew, with sweetened black vinegar and fresh ginger. In Sri Lanka it is more common to boil the trotters, adding cinnamon, coconut milk, and curry leaves, serving the meat with boiled potato or cucumber.

Calves' feet usually are used as a source of gelatin in stock, but also may be dipped in beaten egg and breadcrumbs and served with a piquant or tartar sauce. There is even a sausage called Zampone, a pork sausage that is stuffed into a hollowed-out pig's trotter instead of a casing. Serving this whole and letting the luncheon guests slice their own portion is guaranteed to make the afternoon memorable.

Sauté the carrots, dasheen, potatoes, pumpkin, green bananas, scallions, and peppers in the oil for 3–5 minutes, then add to the stew. Cook the stew at least an hour (2–3 hours is better) and then add the rum. Cook one hour more before serving. This should serve 10–12 people. Adding finely chopped banana peel makes the soup extra mannish.

Courtesy of Maple Leaf Farms

Marrow Bones

2 thigh or femur bones of
    beef cattle
Flour and water paste
Bread for toasting

Have the bones sawn into 3-inch lengths and seal the cut ends with a stiff paste of flour and water. Wrap the bones tightly in a floured cloth and put them to simmer in plenty of salted water for an hour. Or bake them at 300°F in the oven for an hour. Serve the bones as they are, with a knife or a long thin spoon to scoop out the delicious marrow onto fresh, hot toast.

Elisabeth Luard,
European Peasant Cookery (1986)

Pickled Lamb Tongues

6–8 lamb tongues
3 peppercorns
6 whole cloves
2 bay leaves
2 tbs. salt
1/2 cup vinegar (5% acid)

Place tongues in saucepan and cover with hot water. Simmer for an hour. Add peppercorns, cloves, bay leaves, salt, and vinegar. Cover and simmer until fork tender. Cool in broth. Peel and clean. Put peeled tongues in sterile canning jars. Skim fat off broth in the pan and bring to a boil again. Pour broth through a strainer over the tongues. Seal and refrigerate or freeze.

Maine Whole Lamb Cookbook
courtesy of Maple Lawn Farms

Opposite, left: Roasted bone marrow is a starter dish on its own at the fashionable London restaurant St. John. Chef Fergus Henderson has a passion for more unusual parts of animals, and the restaurant's motto is "head to tail eating."
Opposite, right: On a sidewalk in the Burmese town of Maymyo, a Shan trader offers a variety of dried animal parts for sale, including the dorsal scales of pangolins. All are considered to have medical value when consumed.

Bones and marrow play a larger role in what we eat than most of us realize. How many times did I watch my mother put leftover chicken or turkey bones into a pot of boiling water to produce a healthy soup stock? Some bones may also be crushed and browned in an oven, then cooked with vegetables and herbs to make stock for sauces. Lamb chops, chicken legs and wings, turkey drumsticks, and most other bones are also fun to gnaw on, and nourishing, although it is considered by some to be coarse or impolite. (Except in yuppie bars where Buffalo Wings—which have nothing to do with buffalo—are dipped into bleu cheese dressing by hand between cell phone calls.) Put a little paper collar on the bone at the dinner table and everything will be alright.

Marrow, the soft, fatty goop in the centers of long bones (shoulder bones, fore and hind legs), is one of the richest protein sources available. Just breaking the bones and sucking the marrow is a wonderful experience, even when it's the little dollop of glop found in the middle of a slice of baked ham. Marrow is used in sauces, soups, stews, and in the Italian rice dish (cooked in fat and stock) called risotto. Elisabeth Luard in her book *European Peasant Cookery* (1986) recommends marrow bone as "a treat for high tea or a savory after the meal instead of a pudding."

Now, imagine a tongue that is more than a foot long and weighs four or five pounds. While thinking about such a thing, it almost makes talking impossible. But that is about average for an adult ox and even the smaller tongues of calves, young pigs, and lambs have impressive heft and size. The most commonly served tongues, those of the larger mammals—and these may include wild game and horse—may be prepared in a variety of ways: in stews or ragouts, boiled or grilled, pickled and smoked, *au gratin*, and often cold, sliced thinly and delivered to the table with a vinaigrette sauce. Pork tongue may be marinated and roasted, simmered, and fried. Tongue sliced thinly and served with mustard and fresh, sliced onions makes a delicious sandwich, as any habitue of a Jewish deli will

affirm. And dog tongue—I tried it once near the Chinese border in Vietnam—sliced and stir-fried in oil with Chinese cabbage makes for a tasty, if somewhat chewy dish. In fact, the tongue has been cherished all the way back to Roman times, when flamingo tongue was on more than one emperor's dinner plate.

Tongue often is sold ready-to-serve, but it is more usual to buy it fresh, smoked, corned or seasoned in brine, for cooking and eating hot or cold, with or without a sauce. Beef and veal tongues are the commonest, lamb tongues thought to be the most tender, although all tongue is tough and requires long, slow cooking. (Stop for a minute and pinch your own tongue between your thumb and forefinger; that is not a piece of meat that is quickly tenderized.) If purchased fresh, it is necessary to soak the tongue for some time—up to twelve hours—in water that is changed several times. Fat is then removed and the tongue is placed in boiling water and skinned. (After making an incision at the root and along the top, pulling the rough outer layer toward the lip.) Sprinkle with salt and let sit in the refrigerator for a day. Now you're ready to go.

Pigs' and calves' ears offer another protein treat that may be boiled, fried, sautéed, braised, grilled, stuffed, made into a gratin, or added to a stew or soup. In parts of China, they are cooked for up to two hours until the cartilage is crunchy, then cut into narrow strips and mixed with sprouts and garlic, and served with soy sauce and chili oil. They may also be cooked until tender and combined with thinly sliced carrots, cucumbers and onions and tossed lightly with plum sauce, then served on lettuce, chilled. (This is a salad that could also incorporate sliced duck web or jellyfish.) Brushed with crushed garlic and deep-fried until crispy, they also make a delicious alternative to potato crisps. Before cooking, they must be cleaned thoroughly, blanched, scraped, and dried.

Now we get to the funny bits, the "parts" that some may consider the most difficult to eat: the eyes, the snouts, the gums, the lips. Even *Larousse Gastronomique*, known for its patrician but generally open mind, doesn't mention eyes, lips, or gums, although calves' and pigs' ears get a full page of mouth-watering recipes. Yet, all are eminently edible.

Eyes may be plucked from virtually anything cooked—from chicken to cow to fish—and chewed or chased with a shot of liquor.

In many cultures, they are considered a delicacy, although making a meal of them is logistically challenging. In the Middle East, sheep's eyeballs are considered a great delicacy, removed with the point of a dagger and eaten straight from the skull or with a sauce or extra seasoning.

Lips and gums comprise an even rarer treat. I've seen them on a menu only once, at a Laotian restaurant in Bangkok where *nguak wua thot* (fried beef gums) is one of the dishes that attracts a crowd that oohs and ahhs over the choice, but usually orders something else. (The same restaurant also serves a piquant salad with ant eggs, but that isn't one of the favorites, either.)

Perhaps my friend, who rejected sausage that contained "parts" might welcome them if they were identified and served as good parts should be served, rather than hidden in mystery.

This page, and opposite: A Pathan village butcher skins and trims the head of a water buffalo that has been slaughtered for a feast in Pakistan's Northwest Frontier Province. The head will be cooked whole.

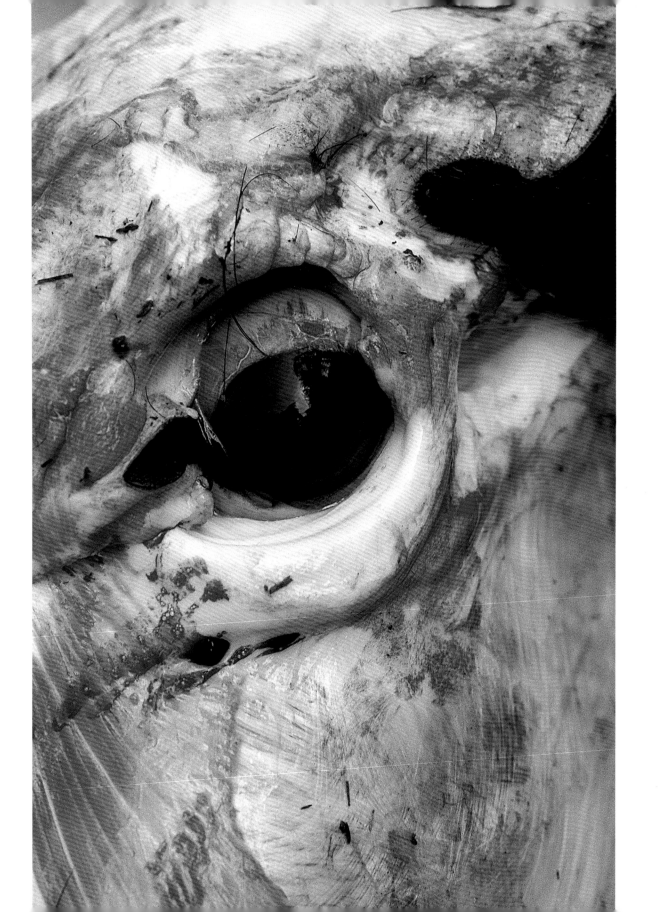

genitalia

Lamb Fries

1 quart lamb testicles
1 onion, chopped
4 green peppers, chopped,
   or 1 small can of chili
   peppers
1 to 3 cloves garlic,
   chopped
3 tbs. parsley
7 oz. can Mexican salsa
¼ cup white wine
Salt and pepper to taste

Cook testicles in salted water for about 20 minutes or until done. Skim foam from water as it appears. When done, drain and rinse in cold water. Fry onion and peppers in small amount of oil. When onion and peppers are limp, add garlic and parsley. Add meat and fry a few minutes. Add salsa, salt, pepper, and white wine and simmer, covered, for about 15 to 20 minutes.

Courtesy of Maple Leaf Farm

It is not difficult to understand why most modern diners might turn their noses up and roll their eyes in despair at the idea of eating an animal's genitals. Offer a soup made from deer or cow penis, or sheep testicles that have been deep-fried, and he or she likely will flee.

There is, however, one compelling reason that has made the genitals of four-legged creatures attractive to two-legged diners. In a word, it's "testosterone," the sex hormone secreted by the testes. A feminist friend of mine calls the whole macho syndrome, of which slurping penis soup and masticating sheep testicles is a small part, "testosterone poisoning," defined as man's desire to be manly, and more manly, and even more manly than that. I confess I may be one of the men she's talking about.

It first happened in Mexico City, when in 1969 I found myself traveling with an American rock and roll band, the Doors, a group not known for its sissiness, whose lead singer wore leather trousers made from cowhide and unborn horse and who called himself the Lizard King. So when we all were taken to one of the Mexican capital's finest restaurants and one of the dishes served was a platter of deep-fried bull's testicles, most of us nervously tucked in. Some joked about how they'd always wondered what happened to the bull's balls following its humiliation in the *corrida*. Some

pushed the gristly meat around the plate, as they had done with so many other uninvited dishes as small children, hoping it would appear that they were eating, when in truth they were trying to hide the evidence under a taco shell or beneath a pile of refried beans.

Still, most of us did consume at least a portion. Why? Because we were men, that's why. And that is why in parts of the world today there is something on many menus that has been euphemized for more than a century. They were called "lamb stones" in nineteenth-century England, and today they are called "lamb fries." *Larouse Gastronomique*, the French encyclopedia of cookery that has a fancy French word for everything, calls them animelles, the culinary term for testicles, and in the United States they are called mountain or prairie oysters. Sometimes, they're found under the vague linguistic umbrella called "variety meat."

This macho attitude—testosterone poisoning, if my friend is correct, and I suspect she is—may have its variety meat cloaked in euphemism to suit contemporary conservatism, but it has historical roots that sink deep. Animal genitalia have been devoured to improve one's bedtime prowess and cure a number of ills as well as one's status among male friends for thousands of years in many parts of the world. What is termed "organotherapy" dates back at least to Roman times, when it was believed that eating a healthy animal's organ might correct some nagging ailment in the corresponding human organ, a belief and practice that continues to the present day.

In a pharmacologia published in 1696, deer testicles were hailed as an aphrodisiac and in 1739 and 1750 in medical texts sold in Sweden the deer's penis was also prescribed against poisoning, bladder stones, and blood in the urine. The better-known *Kama Sutra*, the first-century Hindu guidebook to relationships and sexual dexterity that found a following in the newly liberated 1960s, recommended ram's testi-

Will Viagra Save the Tiger?

The scientists who invented Viagra were awarded a Nobel Prize in 1998 for giving millions of men an solution to impotence. Because the prescription drug also is finding widespread acceptance as a sex-enhancer, even when erectile dysfunction may be a minor factor, those scientists may soon be given an award by organizations struggling to protect endangered species.

According to a report from Tokyo by Agence France Presse in early 1999, "ancient cures, most based on Chinese medicine, are being swept aside" by Viagra sales. "Viagra, already a hot black-market item in Japan before its official release, is threatening sales in Tokyo of tiger and seal testicles" the news agency said.

cles boiled in milk and sugar.

More recently, in the nineteenth century, a Victorian explorer and amateur anthropologist named Richard Burton (not to be confused with the actor, although he probably suffered from testosterone poisoning, too) translated a fifteenth-century Middle Eastern treatise titled *The Perfumed Garden* for the *Soul's Delectation*, originally written in Arabic and now regarded as an erotic classic. (Burton is better known for his translation of a book of Near Eastern tales, *Thousand and One Nights*, born in what is now Iraq, which may explain Saddam Hussein's testosterone level.) The author of the *Perfumed Garden* was Shaykh Nefzawi, who wrote, "Pleasure is only given and felt by those who are well developed. He then who, having a little penis, wishes to improve and strengthen it for its task, should bathe it in warm water until it becomes red and swollen by the blood which will be drawn to it; let him now anoint it with honey mixed with ginger, and he will then be fully primed for his part. So great a pleasure will he now bestow upon the woman that she will be loathe to let him go. Another method is to make use of a donkey's pizzle. The organ is boiled with onions and wheat, and the resulting mess is fed to fowls with care, afterwards killed and eaten. Or the pizzle may be soaked in oil and the oil then drunk." What kind of oil was not specified, although likely it didn't matter.

Such genital imagination runs rampant in cookery even today, especially in Asia, where the belief that tiger penis soup will improve one's sex life has been blamed for helping drive the tiger to the window of extinction. The Wildlife Conservation Society in 1996 used this notion as the basis of an international advertising campaign, showing a bowl of soup with the headline, "SOME MEN BELIEVE THAT TIGER PENIS SOUP IS A POWERFUL APHRODISIAC. ACTUALLY, IT'S A LOAD OF OLD BULL." The advertisement went on to say that a single bowl of "tiger" soup cost as much as US$300, warning buyers that they should expect to be disappointed: "Firstly, because tiger penis

soup usually is a load of old bull. Or ox. Or deer. Or any number of more commonplace substitutes. The counterfeiting of tiger penises (and tiger bones or other potions) is something of an art in Hong Kong and China. (At US$300 a bowl, it's something of a temptation.) And for those drinking the real thing? More depressing news. Testosterone simply cannot, we repeat, *cannot* be ingested through eating animal genitalia. Cooking steroids only inactivates them."

What the conservation society didn't mention, and might consider in any future campaigns, is that it isn't such a wondrous thing to gain the sexual prowess of a tiger, a beast that normally makes love for only fifteen seconds and then goes into the jungle to take a nap. Sound like someone you know?

The society also failed to warn that what is sold as a tiger's penis may not even be a penis. "Many people, including staff at non-governmental organizations and members of the media, slam the trade in wildlife and their body parts, which seems to continue in Thailand," said Dr. Schwann Tunhikorn, head of the wildlife research of that country's Royal Forestry Department, in an interview in the Bangkok Post in 1998. "What they don't realize is that most of the merchandise is fake. I have never seen a real tiger's sexual organ in the market." The doctor went on to say that the phony penises usually were carved from cattle tendons. I have seen several for sale in northern Thailand. Even if I never saw a real tiger's penis to compare them to, the ridiculously low price of US$20 to $30 should have made it clear; the price for what is claimed to be the real thing is far pricier.

The illegal slaughter of tigers and sale of the great cat's genitals goes on, of course. Despite widespread efforts to control poachers, another conservationist group, the Wildlife Protection Society of India, estimates there are still one hundred million potential users of tiger-based potions in the world. Most of these consumers are in Asia; with the increasing cost and illegality attached to eating an endangered species, other genitals are being used widely as substitutes. In

Rocky Mountain Oysters

40 lamb testicles
1 or 2 cloves garlic, chopped
1/2 onion, chopped
2 tbs. corn starch
1 cup white wine
Salt and pepper to taste
hot pepper sauce to taste
1 cup water

Wash and clean testicles thoroughly. Boil until tender, about 30–45 minutes. Drain thoroughly. Fry testicles, onion, and garlic until brown. Dissolve corn starch in water; add to the oysters. Add wine and let simmer until sauce thickens. Add seasonings and serve steaming hot. Serves four.

Bull's Ball Pie

Boil four bulls' testicles together with salt. Cut into slices and sprinkle with salt, pepper, nutmeg, and cinnamon. Then, in a pie crust, place layers of sliced testicles alternated with mince of lamb kidneys, ham, marjoram, cloves, and thyme.

Bartomolo Scappi
Sixteenth century chef
to Pope Pius V

Double-Boiled Penis Soup

4 oz. penis (deer, beef,
   etc.)
1 cups rice wine
10–12 cups water
Herbs and spices,
   packaged at Chinese
   pharmacy

Soak meat in rice wine for
a few minutes to remove
the strong smell. Scrub
with salt, rinse with hot
water, and boil for 1–2
minutes. Take out and
scrub again, then chop
into small pieces.

Put meat and herbs
together in the double-boil-
er with water and cook
over a high heat for 1½–2
hours. Usually there are
several herb packages
available, the mixtures created according to the
customer's needs. Some
are for the blood (circulation), others for stamina,
etc. When purchasing,
merely tell the pharmacist
what you are doing and
ask his advice.

When ready to serve,
remove the meat and
drink only the broth.

1994, for example, a Canadian company delivered fifty thousand seal carcasses to China. And while the pelt meat and oil of one seal sold for US$20, the genitals each went for more than US$100.

All that said, it is not difficult to include genitalia in your diet without endangering any threatened animals. As mentioned, many restaurants in the United States serve Rocky Mountain Oysters, which generally are made from lamb's or sheep's testicles, and in Mexico, deep-fried bull's testicles are still a savored delicacy, thirty years after I passed a plate of them to Jim Morrison. And throughout much of Asia, especially where there is a large Chinese population, a restaurant or food stall serving some kind of penis soup is seldom far away.

In Singapore, there's a pricey place called the Imperial Herbal Restaurant, only a few steps from the famous Raffles Hotel. It may be the only restaurant with a resident Chinese herbalist, Dr Li Lian Xing, who emigrated from Tianjin, China, and now diagnoses

offers a choice of wines where the ingredients include deer penis, starting at $12 a glass, with a two-liter bottle costing as much as $450!

At smaller sidewalk establishments in Singapore, penis soup is less expensive, but not always available. When I visited one, shortly after the Chinese New Year, the sign on the wall advertised bull penis soup for about $6 a bowl, and turtle penis soup was double that, but I was told that the restaurant's compete supply of penises had been consumed. (In Asia, that's expensive compared to, say, a bowl of noodle soup with pork or chicken, selling for less than a dollar.) The taste? Nothing special, sad to say, as it's rather like any red meat broth. It's the anticipation of pleasures to come that gives the dish its kick.

No less interesting is the Five Penis Wine available at the Snake King Completely & Restaurant in Guangzhou in China. Although this is a place that focuses on the reptile in its odd name, this wine reportedly is a drink that blends with the snake penis the genitals of ox, sheep, deer, and dog. When I tried it during a visit in 1997, it went down quite smoothly, although the dark sediment floating in it was a bit worrying. I also had to wonder how effective it might be in delivering its sexual promises after consuming several glasses. I was the only foreigner in the restaurant that night and was asked to join several tables for after-dinner drinks of it.

"*Ganbei*!" my new friends cried again and again. "Empty glass!" And perhaps empty of subsequent performance, too.

Like other organ meats, testicles may be cooked in a variety of ways—deep-fried whole as I experienced in Mexico; cut into broad, thin slices and marinated in oil, lemon juice, chopped parsley, salt and pepper, then fried in batter; and sliced and cooked in butter and a cream sauce with blanched and sautéed sliced mushrooms. Like the heart, kidney, and some other organ meat, it tends to be a bit chewy.

Opposite: Dr. Li, herbalist at the Imperial Herbal Restaurant in Singapore, displays one of his prize deer penises infusing a jar of wine. The wine is sold by the glass, but dried penises are also sold, for home use. *This page:* At a restaurant in the northern Thai city of Chiang Mai, a member of the kitchen staff prepares the primary ingredient of buffalo penis stew. The long flaccid organs sell by the piece in local markets, and are known euphemistically in Thai as *tua dio an dio*, which translates approximately as "one body, one thing."

customer ills or imbalances, recommending certain dishes or drinks on the menu as being helpful. On entering the restaurant, the first thing you see are large glass display cases containing deer antler and dried penises from assorted unthreatened species, and behind that a full-scale herbal pharmacy where, if one's luck holds, Dr. Li will suggest one of the house specialties—Bull Pizzles with Chinese Yam, perhaps. Prices start at about US$20 and go up, depending on the number of pizzles, to $40. The restaurant also

urine

Some years ago, when my former wife and I were unsuccessful in our efforts to have a child, we sought means by which we might better our odds and fertility. One of our friends at the time was Dave Guard, a musician and singer who was one of the founding members of the Kingston Trio, American recording artists popular during the early 1960s folk music boom. Twenty years later, he was spending much of his time in Tibet and when we told him about our predicament, he said that when Tibetans wanted to get pregnant, the husband and wife drank each other's urine. We were aghast. We told him that we'd think about it.

As it turns out—and neither my wife nor I knew this at the time—there were many besides Dave Guard and the childless Tibetans who believed in "urine therapy," a field of study that says human urine—usually your own, not someone else's—may be a cure for a number of illnesses, good for the skin tone, and a way to cleanse the physical body of impurities as well as promote spiritual growth, while offering something nutritious. So widespread was this belief that in 1996 some six hundred delegates from seventeen nations traveled to India, meeting in Goa in what may be one of the most unusual "scientific" gatherings in modern times, the first World Conference on Auto-Urine Therapy.

The three-day meeting was organized by the Indian chapter of the Water of Life Foundation, bringing together leading proponents of what was declared to be a 5,000-year-old therapy that fell into disuse in this century and was considered taboo in most of the world. Conference delegates didn't care, thumbing their nose at the world's majority by hanging posters that showed a young boy urinating into a glass. They also paid loud and approving tribute to Morarji Desai, who, shortly after succeeding Indira Gandhi as India's prime minister in 1977, shocked the international community by announcing that his excellent state of health could be explained by his longtime practice of drinking his own urine, a glass each morning, taken in much the same way others have a cup of coffee or tea.

Are these people quacks, or what? Drinking urine certainly seems radical. As it turns out, consuming the yellow liquid excreted by the kidneys has a long history, much of it in India, where it has been associated with the yoga and tantra tradition for perhaps as long as five millennia. A document said to be that old, called *Shivambu Kalpa Vidhi* ("the method of drinking urine in order to rejuvenate"), calls urine "a divine nectar capable of abolishing old age and various types of diseases and ailments. The follower should first ingest his urine and then start his meditation." *Shivambu* literally means "the water of Shiva," the highest god in the Indian pantheon, whose name

---

The Cure for Everything?

For three days at the 1996 conference, men with "Dr." in front of their names presented scientific papers regarding the therapeutic benefits of drinking urine, appearing on stage with the regularity of steady beer-drinkers visiting a tavern loo.

Dr. Shigeyuri Arai, manager of the Fujisaki Institute and a researcher in the Hayashibara Biochemical Laboratories in Okayama, Japan, said gargling with small amounts of urine could cure many diseases including cancer, hepatitis B, and influenza.

Dr. Ryoichi Nakan, chairman of Japan's Miracle Cup of Life Institute and one of Dr Arai's colleagues, said he gargled with urine for thirty seconds every morning, and affirmed that about 200,000 other Japanese joined him in the daily exercise.

Dr. N. N. Dalwadi of Bombay said

urine therapy had arrested the symptoms of eleven of twenty-seven terminally ill cancer patients he had treated since 1992. "They have at least lengthened their life span," he told delegates.

G. K. Thakkar, head of India's Water of Life Foundation, said urine cured him of amoebic dysentery and eczema and made him a "bold orator overnight." He also said animals with mad cow disease could be cured if they were made to drink their urine.

Claude Jacot of Switzerland said he suffered from sinusitis for fifty years, then started pouring urine into his nose every day and the ailment hasn't recurred since.

Coen van der Kroon of the Netherlands, who has written what is regarded as a definitive book, *Golden Fountain: The Complete Guide to Urine Therapy*, added, "I splash it on my face as an after-shave."

means "auspiciousness." In India, at least among urine enthusiasts, one often hears the phrase "drinking Shiambu," which simply means drinking the water of auspiciousness. Urine also is described as harmless in the Buddhist text *Phra Traipidok* (or *Triptaka*).

Definite rules for ingesting urine were established early. Only "midstream" liquid was recommended, meaning that the first and last ten milliliters were to be discarded, because the first flow was too pungent and the last was lacking in strength. Before drinking, the mouth was to be cleansed and the urine sipped like tea one to four times a day, usually upon awakening and following meals. The rule-makers also suggested a urine fast, where it was consumed only with water and no other food or liquid. It is clear that believers take this urine-drinking seriously.

In 1747, German author Johann Heinrich Zedler wrote, "One can best heal injuries to eyes with honey dissolved in the lightly-boiled urine from a young man." He also said that mixing it with sulfur and potato helped prevent hair loss and "in the beginning stages of dropsy, one should drink one's own morning urine on an empty stomach for a prolonged period of time." In the same century, French and German physicians used it to treat jaundice, rheumatic disorder, gout, sciatica, and asthma, and in wartime, soldiers who manned the cannons, which tended to overheat, kept a bucket of urine nearby, plunging their hands into it when burned.

In more modern times, Dr. John W. Armstrong, a British convert to urine therapy and author of a book called *The Water of Life* (1994), claimed to have treated more than forty thousand patients starting in 1925 for ailments ranging from cancer to tuberculosis. In the 1940s, many German doctors routinely gave urine enemas to children exposed to measles or smallpox and today, according to Dr. Johann Abele, a delegate at the conference, an estimated five million Germans are regular consumers. "It has spread over Germany like a huge wave," he said.

Mainstream physicians scoff at the claims made by those who advocate drinking urine. There is general agreement that small amounts probably won't hurt anyone—but it is difficult to find anyone in the Western medical establishment willing to endorse it. They say there hasn't been sufficient study and insist that the literature of urine therapy is not scientifically based, and some insist that becoming exposed to any body fluids—from blood to saliva to urine—is to risk becoming HIV positive.

Supporting literature is substantial, nonetheless. Books on the subject have been published, and remain in print (although sometimes difficult to find) in the U.S., England, and India, the latter nation appearing to be where most of urine therapy's proponents reside. Adherents contend that it is not a toxic waste. They agree that urea, making up 2.5 percent of urine, can be poisonous when present in large amounts in the blood, yet it also is urea that is used worldwide as a key ingredient in many skin products. They also warn that urine therapy is based on the principle of "natural cycles." So long as we do not interfere chemically with the body's natural cycle, they say, the body produces urine that is suitable for recycling. However, if you ingest chemical substances—and processed foods contain chemicals—some of them will end up in the urine, in which case the composition of the urine changes. Literature suggests a variety of other ways of utilizing this pungent yellow liquid: using it as a gargle (good for toothaches, colds, and sore throats), as an enema, ear- and eye-drops, or as vaginal douche (for yeast problems). When you step on a sea urchin or get a bee sting, and you don't have any meat tenderizer handy (this being the most widely accepted first aid), urinating on the wound is the next best thing to do. I've done that. But, drink it?

Who knows? In one of the most expensive Hollywood movies ever made, *Waterworld*, in the opening scene, a web-toed Kevin Costner urinates into a cup and drinks its contents. It could start a small trend. Even if it doesn't, the movie is certain to find an audience in India.

Mango Urine Lassi

1 cup unflavored yogurt
2 tbs. sugar
$\frac{1}{2}$ cup urine
$\frac{1}{2}$ cup mango pulp
Ice cubes

Put all the above into a blender. Blend well and serve immediately. Other fruit may be used when mangoes are out of season.

Vanda Balbir, owner-chef, Mrs. Balbir's, traditional Indian restaurant, Bangkok

human flesh

When I tell people that I took the placenta home following the birth of my son and the next day served it as a paté, they generally (1) don't believe me or (2) recoil in horror, calling me a cannibal. My dictionary defines the word as "a person who eats human flesh" or "an animal that eats its own kind." I guess that makes me, technically, a cannibal, but I feel a long distance from all the images of cannibalism in history, where a missionary or white hunter is being cooked in a large iron pot by natives with bones in their noses.

This is how it happened. I was married, I had a daughter about two years old, and I was living in London. My wife and I decided we wanted to have our second child born at home, but when the doctor, who agreed in principle, learned we lived in a fifth-floor walk-up apartment, he said no; what if there were problems and we had to get my wife down four flights of stairs? So we accepted his offer of a private room in a small clinic a block away from our flat and decorated it with cloth we had purchased on a trip to Africa, fired up some sandalwood incense, and with a British doctor, a German nurse, and a South African midwife in attendance, Nicholas Sky Hopkins was born. I think it was then that I told the doctor that I wanted to take the placenta home with me.

The placenta is the organ attached to the lining of the uterus that provides for the nourishment of the fetus. It is expelled by the woman's body following the child's delivery and as a rule it is discarded, at least in developed nations. In some other places—including our London flat—it was considered food, and trashing it along with bloody bandages and used rubber gloves and other medical debris seemed to us a waste. After all, this was the organ that had nourished our unborn child and although the baby no longer had a need of it, it remained rich in protein, vitamins and minerals.

My wife was to return home the day following and my plan was to cook the placenta and make it into a paté to serve visitors who had been invited to meet the baby. When I asked, the doctor agreed in wonderment, but then didn't know what to put it in for transport to the flat. Unlike restaurants, medical clinics don't have Styrofoam "take-away" containers for leftover food. We settled on a large, plastic "garbage" bag. As I was walking home, at four in the morning, the bag slung over my shoulder, I wondered what I'd say if a British bobby stopped me and asked what I had in the bag.

Fortunately, I encountered no policemen and the next day I sautéed the placenta in butter and garlic, then chopped it into small pieces, and turned it into a dark brown paste in the blender. Oops. I had forgotten to de-vein the organ, so there were small bits of gristle throughout. This was a major faux pas in cooking, I guess, but I served it anyway, chilled, with whole wheat crackers and slices of raw onion for garnish. Much to my amazement, a couple of our guests actually tried it.

Our serving placenta paté may seem a deliberate oddity, designed to shock our friends, or may be written off by some as something only hippies would do. (My wife and I then would have admitted we belonged to that group, happily. It was 1972, after all.) The truth is, from a historical perspective, what we were doing was not unusual. The consumption of human flesh had a long and sometimes approving history.

Archeologist Tim White of the University of California Berkeley in 1981 found a six-hundred-thousand-year-old skull from an early human ancestor in Ethiopia, noticing that the skull had a series of fine, deep cut marks on the cheekbone and eye socket where the flesh appeared to have been stripped away with a knife. The marks were judged to show the "signature of cannibalism," which differed from damage done by war, normal injury, burial practices, and scavenging animals. Dr. White compared that skull to the bones of twenty-nine individuals from the Anasazi pueblos in Colorado in the United States, the spectacular, apartment-like cliff dwellings that are now a major tourist attraction. Carbon dating the bones, tools and pottery found back to the twelfth century, and using an electronic microscope to examine 2,106 bone fragments to identify cut marks, burn traces, and so on, he proposed a new category of bone damage called "pot polish." These were the shiny abrasions left on bone tips that came from being stirred in pots. He concluded that the Anasazi people processed their colleagues by skinning them, cutting the muscle tissue into chunks and roasting it, baking their long bones, crushing their skinny bones, putting all of the pieces into pots over open fires, stirring vigorously.

"People were being systematically captured, killed and eaten," he said. "Thigh and arm bones were broken open for their marrow, and smaller fragments were boiled in pots to extract the last fatty residues. It is quite incredible. You suddenly catch your breath and think, my God, this must have been ghastly. These people—the ancestors of modern Hopi and Pueblo Indians—used cannibalism to instigate a reign of terror that lasted four hundred years."

Well, maybe. There have been reasons other than terror for anthropophagy, the scientific name for consuming human flesh. In caves and digs in France and Germany dating back to Neanderthal days, archeologists have uncovered piles of hollowed-out human leg and arm bones—thought to be the leavings of a sort of marrow buffet—as well as bone fragments that showed "clear cut marks, undoubtedly resulting from a flint tool." According to Dr. Yolanda Fernamdex-Jalvo of Madrid's Natural History Museum, in an eight-hundred-thousand-year-old settlement at Atapuerca in Spain, "the evidence is strong. Human bones found at Atapuerca have cut marks and had clearly been stripped of their flesh. They also were mixed up with the bones of animals that had been eaten." Precisely why human flesh was eaten at that time is not known. Most believe the defining force behind most early

consumption of human flesh by other humans was hunger.

Later, there were other reasons. Beginning in the Tang, and especially during the Ming and Ch'ing dynasties in China (seventh through eighteenth centuries), for example, it was common when all normal medical resources failed to cure a dying parent, the daughter or daughter-in-law (or, less often, a son) would cut a piece of flesh from her or his thigh and cook it in a broth to offer it to the patient to drink. Evidence to the contrary, it was believed that miraculous recovery would be made.

The consumption of human flesh as medicine, called *ko ku*, or *gegu* in Chinese literature, may be rooted in a story about Princess Miao Shan, the human incarnation of Kuan Yin, the goddess of mercy, who offered her eyes and hands to save her dying father. This theme is also prominent in the stories of the previous lives of Buddha, representing the Buddhist tenet of compassion. (Although Buddha urged no one to kill anyone or anything, nothing is said in the teachings about eating from the living without destroying it.)

Most of the incidence of modern cannibalism has been reported by explorers, missionaries, and other Euro-Americans who discovered it in primitive societies and always cited it as evidence of native savagery. In literature, this attitude goes back to the Greek myths of Saturn devouring his children and the Cyclops eating Odysseus's sailors. Homovores also are a staple ingredient, so to speak, of early tales as diverse as the *Thousand and One Nights*, in which Sinbad the Sailor was shipwrecked and rescued by a king who then fed him human flesh, and Marco Polo's highly imaginative narrative in which he said the soldiers of Kublah Khan ate the flesh of men who died on the battlefield. "I assure you," Polo wrote, "that they go about every day killing men and drink the blood and then devour the whole body."

The eighteenth century satirist Jonathan Swift, best known for writing *Gulliver's Travels*, used the same subject when he penned an essay in 1729, "A Modest

Placenta Paté

1 placenta
Salt and pepper to taste
6 oz. red wine
3 garlic cloves, minced
2 shallots, chopped finely
Paté pastry
6 strips bacon
1 egg
Green onion

Use a thin, pointed knife to remove all the veins in the placenta by opening the larger end where the main vein can be spotted easily. It should come out with a tug. Remove other, smaller veins.

Cut placenta into thin strips, sprinkle with salt and pepper, and marinate in wine for at least 6 hours. Mince about half of the meat and the garlic and shallots. Blend the minced meat with the minced vegetables.

Line a mold with paté pastry, covering the bottom and sides with the bacon, then add the minced forcemeat and remaining slivers of meat mixed together.

Cover the top with pastry and glaze with egg. Bake in a preheated oven at 375ºF for about one hour. Let cool.

Serve with unsalted crackers and garnish with green onion.

Proposal," suggesting that the solution to the food shortages in England and Ireland might be to eat some of the children. Even novelist Robert Louis Stevenson, who lived his final years in the nineteenth century in the Marquesas in the South Pacific, reported seeing "the last eater of long-pig in Nuka-Hiva" striding along a beach with a dead man's arm across his shoulder. "So does Kooamua to his enemies!" Stevenson said the man roared to passers-by, taking a bite from the raw flesh.

Missionaries returning from Latin America told similar stories and one writer described a tribe of man-eaters in Africa as having pointed teeth that fit together like those of a fox; that he had never been to Africa, nor had any hard evidence to support his claim was unimportant. The invading Spanish in the Caribbean similarly said that the Caribs salted and dried their victims' flesh at a time when salting was unknown to them. While some of the tales appeared to ring true—the Aztecs are thought to have eaten thousands of prisoners of war—much of what was reported at the time is now known to be poppycock. What emerged from such overwhelming attack is, as one contemporary writer put it, "greater evidence of a prurient curiosity within developed cultures about cannibalism than of its widespread practice outside them."

In fact, many cannibalistic practices had strong cultural roots, in the belief that existed in many parts of the world that eating one's ancestors would incorporate their benevolent spirits, or that making a meal of one's enemies would give the diner the deceased's strengths; eat the brains and you gain his wisdom, eat his heart and you ingest his courage, and so on. When Captain James Cook was killed by Hawaiian natives in 1779, his remains were returned the following day to his surviving officers in the form of bones, the flesh having been boiled and eaten so that the natives might absorb the great explorer's numerous powers. Even the tyrant who ruled Uganda in the early 1970s, Idi Amin, was known to boast at mealtime that he had consumed human flesh, justifying his act by saying, "In warfare, if you do not have food and your fellow soldier is wounded, you may as well kill him and eat him to survive. It can give you his strength inside. His flesh can make you better, it can make you full in the battlefield." Perhaps it was for a similar reason that at about the same time Michael Rockefeller, the young, adventurous son of American millionaire Nelson Rockefeller, disappeared into the jungles of Papua New Guinea and was presumed eaten by some of the last remaining cannibals on earth.

Not far away, in Fiji, cannibalism was practiced as early as 700 A.D., when Fijians sacrificed captured enemies to appease the warrior-gods. Afterwards, the flesh was consumed by the victors because to eat your enemy was the ultimate disgrace to the victim, having a lasting effect on the victim's family. Thus, religious ritual and revenge justified the practice. So common was this—lasting into the early twentieth century—that most Fijian households included among their belongings what came to be called "cannibal forks." These forks today are beautifully hand-carved and sold as souvenir items. They are, adhering to tradition, made from a local wood, buried in black mud for several weeks and then polished. They come in a variety of sizes, small forks for eating the eyes and brains, larger ones for consuming the fleshy parts. "Tender as a dead man" is an old Fijian phrase occasionally heard today to compliment a modern dish.

Accounts of humans being consumed outside Euro-American locales are well documented. Less frequently discussed is the flesh-eating that took place in Europe, including incidents of prehistoric cannibalism among the Anglo-Saxons and early Irish Celts, as well as in Scandinavia, Czechoslovakia, and France, and among the Germanic tribes of Gaul, where human flesh usually was eaten for medicinal reasons, in some areas as late as the eighteenth century.

It was Christianity and not the emergence of a "civilized" society that changed Europe's view of such behavior. Spanish missionaries in Latin America, for

example, set about to change the diet as well as the religion they found, both of which were declared barbaric. If they recognized the irony in espousing a faith where the blood and body of Christ are fed to believers during communion as wafers and wine, as a replacement for the real thing, it was never recorded. For the Christians, in the phrase of one scholar, Gian-Paolo Biasin, "cannibalism is [thus] metaphorized," as it was in the Bible itself, when Jesus said (John 6:51–57): "I am the living bread which came down from heaven. If anyone eats of this bread, he will live forever; and the bread that I shall give is My flesh, which I shall give for the life of the world. Most assuredly, I say to you, unless you eat the flesh of the Son of Man and drink His blood, you have no life in you. Whoever eats My flesh and drinks My blood has eternal life, and I will raise him up at the last day. For My flesh is food indeed, and My blood is drink indeed. He who eats My flesh and drinks My blood is in Me, and I in him."

As was true when the Neanderthal roamed the earth, much human flesh has been consumed in modern times not for eternal life, but for immediate survival. The story of American settlers snowbound in a blizzard while crossing the Donner Pass into California in 1846, eating their friends as they died, is well

Above: This archival print depicts cannibalism in what is now Brazil.
Opposite: Modern reproductions of nineteenth-century cannibal forks are a staple tourist item in Fiji. From the collection of Jonathan and Daphne Socher, Big Wind Kite Factory, Molokai, Hawaii.

known. In an almost identical situation, British explorers on a doomed nineteenth-century Arctic expedition to find the imagined Northwest Passage between the Atlantic and the Pacific Oceans in Canada's frozen wastes, resorted to cannibalism in what turned out to be a vain attempt to survive—a story substantiated by the recent discovery of their remains, which showed knife marks on over ninety bones. There is also the somewhat humorous account of a man named Alfred Packer, who, while prospecting for gold in Colorado in 1873, became trapped in a shack during a blizzard, surviving by eating his fellow prospectors. "You are a low-down, depraved son-of-a-bitch," the judge said when sentencing Packer to thirty years. "There were only seven Democrats in Hinsdale County, and you ate five of them."

In a more contemporary tragedy, the members of an Uruguayan rugby team whose plane crashed in 1972 in the Andes Mountains in South America survived by eating their dead teammates, their story later told in a best-selling book and movie, *Alive*. Some Vietnamese boat people reportedly avoided death the same way. In a story not acknowledged until recently, in Guangxi, China, during the Proletarian Cultural Revolution of 1966–76, there was widespread cannibalism practiced against "class enemies"; a book published in 1996, *Scarlet Memorial: Tales of Cannibalism in Modern China*, by Zheng Yi, quoted an official saying that some ten to twenty thousand people from that county alone ate their fellow citizens. More recent reports have come from North Korea, where widespread famine in 1997 and 1998 drove the hungry to eat family members and neighbors who had already starved to death.

Other contemporary reports about cannibalism focus on its grisly aspects. This, in fact, seems to be all the media care about. In England some years ago, there was a well-credited story of the infamous Kray brothers, who controlled much of London's organized crime, cutting out the liver of an enemy and frying it on a sizzling shovel held over an open fire. Similarly,

the American serial killer Jeffrey Dahmer, called the "Milwaukee Cannibal" by the press, slaughtered and ate his victims. Except for the contents of his freezer—which included lungs, intestines, a kidney, and a liver—police found no food in his apartment, only condiments. Dahmer asked prison physicians after his arrest in 1994 if there was anyone else in the world like him, or was he the only one? He was not.

I have dozens of stories from 1994–1998 in my files telling, for example, how eight people in Brazil unwittingly ate the liver of a murder victim served up fried with onions and garlic in a bar in Rio de Janeiro; how a 76-year-old woman in Moscow was arrested for killing her husband, then eating and canning his remains; how two men in northeastern India murdered a neighbor they thought was trying to kill them with black magic, cutting his heart in half and eating it raw; and how a Portuguese historian studying World War Two atrocities uncovered documents showing that a hotel in Macau bought babies, who were fattened, then cooked and served to the hotel customers. From a small village in Russia's Ural Mountains in 1995 came a story that police had arrested four men who were selling human flesh, telling restaurants it was veal. Another the same year tells of two Cambodian men who were helping a friend bury a stillborn child and, with the father's permission, made a soup instead. In Hong Kong in 1997, a police officer's head was chopped off by a doctor who said his wife was having an affair with the man; when police, tipped off by the policeman's wife, arrested the physician, they found the head in a pressure cooker. More shock—or, at best, black humor—informs a literal film noir genre in Hollywood, with low-budget exploitation films such as *Cannibal Attack* (1954), *Blood Feast* (1963), *The Undertaker and His Pals* (1967), *Night of the Living Dead* (1968, followed by two sequels and one remake), *The Folks at Red Wolf Inn* (retitled *Terror on the Menu*, 1972), *Cannibal Girls* (1973), and *Return of the Living Dead* (1985, with two sequels), to name, believe it or not, just a few, all of them eminently forgettable, some

This historical print is entitled "Polynesians Bring Home Supper."

of them unintentionally hilarious to watch. Still, they had an effect on how the public felt about eating human flesh, all negative.

Slightly more palatable were productions made with larger budgets and by more talented film makers. When Harry Harrison's science fiction classic *Make Room! Make Room!* was turned into a movie called *Soylent Green* (1973), the futuristic food that gave the film its title was discovered to be made from human flesh. In Jean Luc-Godard's satirical *Weekend* (1968), terrorist wannabes who claimed "the horror of the state can only be answered by horror" demonstrated their return to a "natural," anti-industrial way of life by dining on captured bourgeois picnickers. Similarly, in *The Cook, the Thief, His Wife and Her Lover* (1989), an iconoclastic assault on sacred cows set in a smart restaurant, the meal served in the final scene is a whole, naked, roasted human. While Thomas Harris's character Hannibal (rhymes with cannibal) Lecter in *The Silence of the Lambs* (1991) and its lesser-known predecessor *Manhunter* (1986), is an human ghoul jailed for, among other things, his taste for human liver washed down with "a nice Chianti."

None of these movies or contemporary events presents cannibalism in a favorable light, and it is difficult to imagine when, or how, attitudes about the consumption of human flesh might change, even if what I served my guests as a paté in 1972 became a sort of yuppie fad in England in 1998. At that time, *Esquire* magazine interviewed several people who had eaten it, as well as a number of professional chefs. One cook suggested braising it slowly and serving with herb dumplings. Another advised cooking with olive oil, onion, vin santo capers, and anchovies, blending in a food processor, spreading it on a toasted crostini—"the perfect canapé for a Christening party," he said.

The same year, William Arens, professor of anthropology at the State University of New York at Stony Brook, surveyed the academic literature in his field, reporting that various cultures had varying methods for cooking humans. He said pots of water were favored in Africa, clay ovens in the South Pacific, charcoal pits in America, and the New Guineans had a penchant for steam.

"Boiled, broiled, baked, and steamed—but no recipes," he said, glumly.

I'll be happy to send him mine.

reptiles &
water creatures

reptiles & water creatures

After Hollywood discovered the dinosaurs, many people probably thought reptiles ate us, even if most, in fact, were then and are now vegetarians. Whatever the reason, in today's world, there are many who consider eating reptiles unattractive. However, there are others who think a lizard on a spit quite ordinary, really nothing to talk about.

In Colombia, natives open the abdomens of pregnant female iguana and remove the eggs, then smear wood ash into the wound and release them into the wild, where the wound quickly heals, while in Mexico they grill the iguana, males as well as females. Crocodiles and alligators are on the menu wherever they are not on an endangered list and sometimes where they are. Armadillo is a treat in Texas, geckos are eaten matter-of-factly in parts of Asia, and snakes are consumed almost everywhere that they're found.

Yet, these descendants of ancient reptilian majesty are scorned and loathed at most Euro-American dinner tables. Probably only insects are more repellent. Perhaps it is the bony skeletons and the covering of dry scales and horny plates that is so off-putting. The word "reptilian" itself is an epithet when used as an adjective to describe someone regarded as cold-blooded and sneaky. In science fiction's long history, both in literature and film, many of the most terrifying villains were reptiles or had reptilian features, as epitomized by the *Godzilla*, *Jurassic Park*, and *Alien* movies.

I've always liked reptiles. When I was young, I had turtles as pets and while I don't think I ever thought of them as food, I don't believe I would have rebelled if someone suggested it. Nor do I find lizards and their limbless, scaly, elongate cousins, the snakes, very threatening today, however many movies I've seen that employed the image to scare (did you see *Anaconda*?).

Such widespread prejudice is now beginning to fall in the developed world, where "jungle" restaurants and gourmet dining are coming together in a way that may make such creatures acceptable as food, even if the notion is wrapped in a sense of adventure and fashion. Never mind. However a reptile finds its way to the dinner plate, it can only enhance one's protein choice.

Some of the other creatures in this section come from the sea or freshwater lakes and rivers, among the greatest sources for nourishment since the first humans started grabbing fish from the tide pools with their hands. However much a staple most fish are today, there are several that are widely dismissed. Shark, for instance—like reptiles, rejected because of what it represents alive rather than cooked. And *fugu*, the highly publicized poisonous fish that continues to be regarded as a delicacy in Japan despite the lock put on wallets when the economy collapsed in the late 1990s.

This is an amorphous section of the book, with chapters on an assortment of unrelated creatures, including not only foods from both the land and sea, but also both vertebrate and invertebrate, the latter category represented by the jellyfish and worm, neither of which are related to each other.

Previous: A jellyfish drifts in the clear tropical waters of the Philippines. Plucked straight from the sea, the flesh is eaten by local fishermen simply dipped into the juice of a *kalamansi*—the small local lime.
This page: In a market on the Khorat Plateau of Northeast Thailand, a bucketload of the ground lizards known locally as *yae* await customers. Small lizards like this are usually gutted and barbecued.
Opposite: Popular medicine stalls in Hwa-Hsi Street in Taipei feature treatments commonly based on snake blood.

snake

When I was in secondary school in the United States back in the 1950s, a classmate of mine told me and his other pals a story he thought was hilarious. Over the weekend, his father, a respected local physician, had hosted a barbecue at his home, serving what appeared to be small fish steaks, with potato salad, coleslaw, and plenty of beer. Everyone assumed the meat was fish, although it tasted a bit like chicken and was a little on the chewy side. The consensus was that it was delicious. Many went back for more.

After the meal, my friend's father announced that what he had served, and everyone had consumed, was rattlesnake. My friend, practically falling on the floor as he told the story, said that several of the guests promptly rushed to a toilet and vomited.

Happily, the dietary tolerance of many Americans has changed, with rattlesnake appearing rather matter-of-factly in restaurants and on home barbecues, especially in the Southwest, where rattlesnake round-ups are now an established tourist attraction. However, snake still has not slithered very far onto the Euro-American plate, not as it has in Asia, anyway. In Asia, snake is king. And in much of Africa and Latin America, at least prince.

This was made clear when I visited one of the top destinations of culinary adventurers, Guangzhou, an easy commute from Hong Kong, where I went to one of the city's most famous eating places, the Snake King Completely and Restaurant, a nice-tablecloth joint that offered—and I swear this is true, I copied the entire menu; there was only one in English, well worn by years of use, and they wouldn't let me take it with me—seventy-five different snake dishes! The live serpents were stored in cages on the ground floor and on order were brought to the second level where the kitchen was, to be sliced, diced, minced, flaked, shredded, stuffed, cut into fillets, and rolled into balls, then baked, salted, steamed, boiled, double-boiled, stir-fried,

pan-fried, deep-fried, stewed, braised, baked in a casserole, cooked in paper, served raw (as in sashimi), and presented with rice, vermicelli, a staggering selection of vegetables, herbs and spices and sauces, as well as with other protein, including quail, abalone, silkworm, and cat.

The cat was not in stock, I was told—I noted that a live one wandered confidently around the restaurant, mouthing dropped morsels—but I was assured that they did have the seventeen different snake wines listed on the menu, along with steamed fish lips with sour bamboo shoots, baked fish intestines, pig's blood and marrow with Chinese chives, and something called "cattle oil and flower rolls." Overwhelmed by the choice, I forgot to ask what that was. I ordered a baked snake plate "with special sauce" that tasted like soy and sugar, a stir-fried snake with vegetables, and a glass of the five-snake wine. The snake tasted like—what else?—chicken and the wine looked like and burned like tequila going down; I also quickly learned to be careful of the tiny snake ribs, about the size of fish bones. I was the only *gwailo* (foreign devil) in the restaurant and so I was as much an attraction to the local residents as the menu was to me.

Snake eating has long been a valued part of the diet in southern China, especially in Guangdong province (Guangzhou is the capital), where it was praised by Liu An, a sage during the Han Dynasty (206 B.C.–25 A.D.), who said, "Whatever good southerners can do with a snake, it is useless in the rest of China." Snake meat later became a delicacy in the north as well, and figured as one of the dishes in a famous banquet of Qing Dynasty emperors (1644–1911), an indulgent, 196-course culinary marathon that reportedly lasted three days.

Usually snake is consumed in the cooler months, from late September, say, to March. The Chinese believe that during this period, when the snakes are entering winter dormancy, their flesh is more delicious. Snake also is categorized as a yang food, representing the positive, bright and masculine half of the Chinese yin/yang philosophy (yin being negative, dark and feminine). Eaten in winter, it is believed that its consumption will warm the blood. However, good quality snakes are available throughout the year and if there is a real snake-eating "season," it is determined by customer demand.

Such interest is year-round at the Snake King Completely and also in a village called Le Mat, three miles north of Hanoi, in Vietnam. For generations, people have come here to eat snake. Other exotic dishes are sold in the restaurants lined up along a rough street—including porcupine, lizard and raccoon—but it is the signs for *thit ran* (snake meat) that line the street where customers come seeking the serpent's medicinal properties.

Once entering one of the establishments, the snake of choice—cobra is always preferred by connoisseurs—is brought to the table and washed in a tub of water. The snake is then held by two men as one of them cuts a hole in the abdomen, allowing the heart to pop out, falling onto a dish where it continues to beat. The blood is drained into a glass and mixed with snake wine made from rice whisky and the fermenting corpses of several snakes. The heart is added last and the glass is offered to the customer before his or her order is taken. There is one dish on the menu called "South of the Five Ridges with Fresh Snake Balls." Who could resist?

Many could resist, of course. Snakes have been denigrated for as long as history has been written. Was it not a snake that was the evil symbol in the Garden of Eden? An asp that killed dear Cleopatra? How many movies have used snakes as threatening props? (*Raiders of the Lost Ark* used six thousand in one scene; many more films have featured boa constrictors, which if we are to believe Hollywood, can swallow a school bus.) There is also the inarguable evidence that of the some 2,400 species, about two-hundred are dan-

gerously poisonous to man. Venomous snakes are divided into several groups—the pit vipers, including rattlesnakes, copperheads and water moccasins; the cobras and their relatives; the mambas and coral snakes; the true vipers, including the various asps; and a group of snakes called sea snakes that are found in salt water.

Snakes also have a positive role in history and mythology. Invocation of the serpent's magical powers shows up in snake dances from Haiti to Bali to many American Indian tribes. In Mayan culture, the snake represented fertility and Quetzalcoatl, the mythical "plumed serpent," was worshipped as the "Master of Life" by Aztecs in Central America. Some African cultures worshipped rock pythons and considered the

Rattlesnake Round-Up!

In the United States, several rattlesnake "round-ups" are held each year—a scheme originally dreamed up by farmers and ranchers to cut back the swarming rattler population, but now a tourist attraction in a number of cities and country towns, from Kansas to Texas and through the American southwest.

The largest and oldest of these is administered as a charitable event by the Junior Chamber of Commerce in Sweetwater, Texas, drawing tens of thousands of visitors the second weekend every March. The round-up's promotional brochure—boasting that over one hundred tons of Western Diamondback rattlers have been captured and consumed since the event's introduction in 1958—says it all in the section called "Things to See & Do," offering a calendar that begins with a Rattlesnake Review Parade, includes a Miss Snake Charmer Queen contest and Friday and Saturday night "Rattlesnake Dances" (with country-and-western bands), snake-handling and milking shows, brisket and chili cook-offs, a rattlesnake-meat-eating contest, guided snake hunts and bus tours (for

those who want to either capture snakes or merely photograph the critters in the wild—an experienced guide is provided, and the awarding of prizes and trophies to individuals and groups who turn in the most pounds of rattlesnake and the largest one. An "OFFICIAL RATTLESNAKE ROUND-UP SOUVENIERS SALES BOOTH" offers tee-shirts, caps, pins, jackets, and keychains with a rattle attached.

An "official" Jaycee rattlesnake recipe may be unimaginative, but it is easy: "Kill it; remove head, suspend by tail for 1 hour. Skin; gut. Chop into chunks. Marinate in sweet milk for two hours. Dredge in corn meal or bread crumbs, or a combination of both. Deep-fat fry until brown. Serve with Louisiana Hot Sauce, Texas Pepper Sauce, or Tartar Sauce." Figuring the recipe would work with any kind of snake, I tried this with a snake bought at a market in Bangkok and made a terrible mess in my bathtub (hanging the carcass from my shower head as I drained the blood), but it was delicious, cut into one-inch chunks and fried in soybean oil, then served with a local chili sauce and the ubiquitous steamed jasmine rice.

This page: Live snakes lie coiled in the window in Snake Alley in Taipei.
Opposite, right: A cobra, artfully arranged so that its hood is spread, infuses a bottle of Chinese snake wine. The small red lozenges are wolfberries.
Opposite, left: A vendor offers fresh snake blood to passers-by in Taipei's Hwa-Hsi Street, known popularly as Snake Alley. The blood and bile are believed to strengthen eyesight and the lower backbone, to invigorate and to promote virility.
Overleaf: An assortment of tiny strange foods available at the Imperial Herbal Restaurant in Singapore, including baby snakes, crickets, bark, and a scorpion.

killing of one to be a serious crime. In Australia, the Aborigines associated a giant rainbow serpent with the creation of life.

Other cultures have associated snakes with medicinal powers or rebirth. In India, cobras were regarded as reincarnations of important people called Nagas. The snake appears on many flags and currencies, and in the United States, its motto and flag during the revolution against Britain in the 1700s carried a picture of a snake cut into thirteen parts (representing the thirteen colonies) and the message to Britain: "Don't Tread on Me." And so on. Our modern medical symbol of two snakes wrapped around a staff, or *caduceus*, comes from ancient Greek mythology; according to the Greeks, the mythical figure Aesculapius discovered medicine by watching as one snake used herbs to bring another snake back to life. Among Catholics, Saint Patrick is credited with ridding Ireland of snakes.

Practically all snakes, poisonous or not, are edible: the cobras of Asia, the boas of South America, the pythons of Africa, the garden snakes of Europe, the rattlesnakes of North America. The poison is restricted to a small area of those snakes, which is simply removed while cleaning. And all parts of the snake are used—the blood and bile for rejuvenative drinks, the flesh as a nourishing protein source, the skin for crispy snacks (deep-fried), as well as for shoes, purses, belts and other wearables.

It is as a food that the snake is most cherished. "People can now afford it," says Yip Kwok-leung,

Snake...with a Hart

Tim Hart, a resident of Thailand with an inquisitive palate, suggests a soup that calls for one snake, one tablespoon of chili peppers, one tablespoon of dehydrated rice, fresh coriander, finely chopped onions, two tablespoons of fish sauce, and five or six cups of water. The chilies are chopped, the rice is pounded into a fine powder, and the

snake is scorched over an open flame (or in a pan) to remove the scales. The scales are scraped off, the intestines are discarded, and the flesh cut into strips three to five inches long. The water is heated to boiling and the meat is simmered for one hour, or until tender, then is removed and boned. The snake is returned to the pot with the other ingredients, cooked until piping hot, and served with sticky rice.

owner of one of several snake shops in Hong Kong. "They don't see it so much as exclusively a tonic any more, but take it like ordinary food, like porridge." At Yip's, a bowl of soup costs under US$2 and at the Snake King Completely, the only dishes over $10 called for the addition of tortoise or cat. Some of the snake wine is expensive—a pint-sized bottle of cobra wine, complete with coiled cobra inside cost $40 at the airport in Saigon in 1998—and the gall bladder where the greenish bile held within is believed to improve libido and cure impotence, today costs as much as $1,000 in Hong Kong. But the meat itself almost everywhere is reasonably priced.

In Europe, the eating of snake has a long history, although its consumption has declined in the past hundred or so years. Before the eighteenth century, adder diets were fashionable in France for what was believed to be beneficial effects on beauty and health; recipes of the time suggested baking the snake with herbs, using it to stuff a capon, simmering it in a soup stock, and making it into an oil.

It is not only weekend adventurers (like me) and middle-income diners who relish snake. Restaurants in Hong Kong alone imported nearly fifty thousand snakes in a recent year to satisfy the local demand; in the western United States there are at least fifty restaurants serving rattlesnake chili and steak, and in some Asian cities with large Chinese populations there are an equal number.

It is another story in the jungles of equatorial Africa, Central and South America, and rural Southeast Asia, where snake may be considered quite ordinary, consumed not as a special treat but as a regular part of the diet along with monkey, rodents, grubs, and insects, whenever it is available. While in parts of Latin America, "rattlesnake salt" is sprinkled on other dishes at least once a day; to make it, a rattlesnake (rattles and all) is chopped up and salted, and after six months the dried meat is discarded and what is left is ready for use.

If the snake isn't roasted or grilled over an open fire—the most common preparation—the basic dish found in Asia, as well as in parts of Africa and the Americas, generally is a soup or stew, many of them hard to tell apart; the ingredients may be identical, only the amount of liquid varies. Some soups and stews in these regions—usually tropical—are thickened with arrowroot, rice, tapioca and other local starches, while in other areas the snake meat is merely cooked with vegetables and seasonings.

Last I heard, my high school friend, who went on to become a thoracic surgeon, was living in a section of southern California where snakes probably outnumber humans. I wonder how he would react to a snake dish today. Would he still fall down laughing, or tuck in?

lizards

In a Hollywood movie called *The Freshman* (1990), Marlon Brando, portraying a Mafia don named Carmine Sabbatini, hired Matthew Broderick, who played a college student in desperate need of cash, to pick up a "package" at the airport in Newark, New Jersey. The "package" turned out to be a live Komodo dragon on a leash—the Komodo being named for the remote Indonesian island where only a few thousand remain. Once upon a time, this largest of the world's lizards, growing to eleven feet and weighing up to four hundred pounds, was hunted for meat, but today it's an endangered species, protected by the Indonesian government.

Much of what followed in the movie detailed the silly adventures involved in transporting the lizard, when it got loose at a petrol station, ran wild inside a shopping mall, and so on. Finally, came the flimsy plot. Each year, Brando invited members of a private gourmet club to a banquet comprised entirely of endangered species. Cost per serving started at US$200,000 and went to US$1 million, depending on the animals' rarity. In the film, there were supposedly only eight Komodos left in the world—the actual figure is between 2,000 and 6,000—so the price tag for the meal was $350,000. Per person.

The movie, so far seeming politically incorrect, to say the least, became socially acceptable in the final scenes when it was revealed that no matter what endangered species Sabbatini promised the club members—after marching the poor beast on-stage during cocktail time, to prove the animal was real—year after year they always got smoked turkey; after all, didn't every unusual food taste more or less like chicken? And afterward, the animals were donated to the Carmine Sabbatini Wing of the Bronx Zoo.

The point that must be made is that every unusual food doesn't taste like chicken, and certainly that's true of lizard, whose flavor is more like, well, smoked turkey, but varies from species to species, the reptiles' diet, and locale.

Lizards live on all six continents, from the southern tips of South America and South Africa all the way to the snowy Arctic, but most of the 7,350 or so species make their homes in more temperate climes, and many of the largest and most unusual—and most popular at mealtime—are in the tropics. Especially in Asia and Latin America, the lizard is considered a delicacy.

One of the most popular is the iguana, standard mealtime fare in Mexico, Central America, South America, and parts of the Caribbean, at least since the days of Christopher Columbus, whose sailors reported it "white, soft, and tasty." (As recorded in *The Life of the Admiral Christopher Columbus* [1942], written by his son.) Today, it is sold in markets, restaurants, and such places as Iguana Park, a tourist attraction whose name surely was inspired by *Jurassic Park*, a book and brace of movies that have done nothing to improve the image of ancient lizards. In the park's first five years in Costa Rica, owners say more than 80,000 iguanas were released into the wild, claiming that the population is now of such size that the park managers have a permit to sell iguana meat and make other commercial use of the animals. (The skin may be turned into leather belts, purses, and shoes.)

In size, the iguana is no match for a Komodo, but males can reach six feet in length, over half of which is tail, and females usually grow to four feet. They also have a distinct, prehistoric appearance, characterized by large round scales beneath their ears that look sort of like high-fi speakers, prominent spines along the neck, back and tail, and a large dewlap hanging beneath their chins, which they display to defend their territory and attract mates. And, they are bright green. The effect is that of a miniature dinosaur crafted from pistachio ice cream.

Sold in the native markets, the iguana is far cheaper than when sold in a store as a pet. Usually they are sold live, although some of the smaller ones are grilled on skewers and in small cafes sold in a stew or soup with local vegetables, and seasoned with garlic, cumin, cloves, and nutmeg.

It is in Colombia where one of the most unusual egg-collecting practices is conducted. Iguana eggs are valued highly, so when the mama lizard is thought to be about ready to lay her eggs, hunters capture the slow-moving creature, slit open the abdomen with a sharp knife, gently remove the eggs, rub wood ash into the wound, sew her back up, and away she goes, waddling into the underbrush to resume life and, presumably, seek another mate, while the Colombians go off to cook the eggs or sell them in the marketplace. Of course, the eggs may be dug out of the ground once laid, but many aficionados and hunters know that it is easier to spot a pregnant iguana than follow one until she lays her eggs.

Iguanas are not difficult to catch, although they can sprint for short distances at considerable speed and are skilled at climbing trees. Usually, hunters creep up on them as they lounge on low tree limbs, snoozing in the sun.

Opinions differ about lizard as food. Some say most species are hard to catch and don't have enough meat on them to justify the energy spent capturing and butchering them. However, most of the beast is meat, as opposed to, say, small birds, which seem to be all bones and feathers. Lizard is also regarded as an exotic delicacy and restaurant diners must expect to pay a premium, just as exotic leather goods cost more than those made from cattle, pig, or other domestic species.

Another popular, large lizard is the chuckwalla, found in the mountains and deserts from Utah in the United States across the border into Mexico. Here, it is happiest in barren, rocky ground where there are small caves and crevasses in which to hide while pursued by hungry Indians. Once inside such a hole, it hyperventilates, filling its lungs to maximum capacity, causing its body to increase up to sixty percent in size. To get the chuckwalla out, hunters pierce its lungs with a sharp stick to deflate them.

This grisly routine is deemed worthwhile. (And, after all, is sending a pack of dogs after a wild boar, then gutting it in the wild, a pleasanter exercise? Or slaughtering a hog in an abattoir?) A large chuckwalla may be a foot to a foot and a half long and may measure about three and a half inches wide, its thick tail as long as the head and body and containing nearly one hundred percent meat. Usually it is roasted, grilled, broiled, or cooked on a spit over an open fire and consumed with vegetables, tequila and lime. Sometimes, as with other lizard species, the chuckwalla is cooked in its rough, leathery skin. After gutting it and removing the head, it is placed directly on hot coals and turned continually. When the skin splits apart, the meat can be removed. (This is, in fact, precisely how John Wiseman suggests preparing lizard in the *SAS Survival Handbook*, a handbook for British soldiers—boiling it after grilling if the meat is not yet tender enough.)

A number of monitor lizards, looking like small versions of the Komodo, also are hunted from the Nile to Southeast Asia to Australia, where the aborigines

Sources

Leopard geckos, retail and wholesale, by mail from Bill and Marcia Brant, The Gourmet Rodent, 6115 SW 137th Ave., Archer, FL 32618, phone (352) 495-9024, fax (352) 495-9781, email <GrmtRodent@aol.com>; leopard and fat-tail geckos from the Golden Gecko, P.O. Box 292304, Davie, FL 33329-2304, phone (954) 584-4590; thirty-nine species, Gecko Ranch, P.O. Box 318, Davis, CA 95617-0318, phone and fax (916) 759-8158.

Chuckwallas, desert iguanas, other species, Whyte Ark Reptile, P.O. Box 1430, Pahrump, NV 89041, USA, phone and fax (702) 751-8623 various species, Atomic Lizard Ranch, phone (520) 432-9161, fax (520) 432-2352, email <atomic@theriver.com>.

The Iguana as Jewelry!

Iguanas are nearly extinct in some areas today, due to rainforest destruction and over-collection for the tourist and pet trade. Most iguanas found in pet stores are raised on farms, but there also is an illegal market because the demand is high. In Thailand in 1996, for instance, the iguana became almost as popular among youthful trendies as the cellular telephone and one pet shop owner in Bangkok admitted he imported more than a thousand from El Salvador and Guatemala every month, this, despite the fact that the legal monthly import quota for the entire country was about five hundred. Costs ranged from US$12 for a juvenile less than a foot in length and worn on their owners' shoulders like costume jewelry, to $1,600 for a full-grown adult.

Sadly, many of the pet iguanas in Thailand died within a month of purchase because the young owners didn't know or weren't told how to care for them. Others escaped or were released into wooded areas. Over the years, such practices have established populations in the United States in southern Florida, the lower Rio Grande Valley in Texas, and sections of Hawaii. They also are being farmed not only in El Salvador and Guatemala, but in Surinam, Nicaragua, and Indonesia, the latter being another country that prizes lizard meat.

This page: To harvest iguana eggs, the gravid female
is not killed, but felled from
a tree with a slingshot. An
incision is them made with
the blade of a machete, and
the string of eggs pulled
out. The iguana's ability to
recuperate is remarkable—
once the wound has been
protected with a coating of
old ashes, the animal runs
off back into the forest.
Opposite: Iguana eggs, with
their rich and tasty spherical
yolks, are a favorite snack
to accompany the local
white rum on the Caribbean
coast of Colombia.

coat the animals with mud before roasting them on hot coals, realizing the same "baked" effect accomplished when fish or poultry are cooked in clay or *en papillote*. These and other smaller lizards are usually clubbed when caught basking in the sun, or snared by a noose at the end of a stick.

By comparison, even the largest geckos of Southeast Asia are smaller and it always takes more than one to make an entrée, especially if you're using the smallest (up to three inches long) variety found zigzagging along the walls and ceilings in a house. This is the variety I watched in my home when I lived in Hawaii and now watch chase mosquitoes and other insects in Bangkok, where the small creature is called a *jing cho* for the clicking sound it makes. There is really only one practical way to cook geckos and that's by deep-frying them in hot oil, although the larger species, maybe six inches in length and found in the jungle and infrequently in the home, may be gutted and grilled as any other large lizard.

In Vietnam, Hong Kong, and China, the gecko also is made into a strong alcoholic drink, by adding the reptiles to a bottle of strong rice wine or whisky, then left alone for about a year. In restaurants—usually where snake is sold—the wine sells for about US$1 a shot-sized glass, and is drawn from five- to ten-quart jars. Smaller bottles, most containing one large gecko, can be purchased for under $2 in Oriental groceries and some airport souvenir shops in Asia. Dried geckos are also sold in street markets in China and in herbal shops in most of the world's Chinatowns, to be ground up and mixed with hot water and drunk to cure a variety of ills.

Live lizards are available in many pet stores, as well as through the mail, but the cost almost gives Sabbatini competition. Some common species are priced as high as US$100 and more, while many of the larger monitors cost up to $500 apiece. The sources also sell them as pets.

This page: A young water monitor rests on a branch in southern India.

Opposite: The stages in the preparation of *yae,* a ground lizard found in Northeast Thailand:

(Above, left) The live lizards as bought from the local market.

(Above, right) Once the lizard has been killed with a blow to the head, an incision is made from neck to tail.

(Below, left) The intestines are removed and discarded and the two eggs reserved.

(Below, right) The lizards are grilled both sides over an open stove, together with their eggs.

alligator & crocodile

**See you later,
alligator.
After a while,
crocodile!**

When this refrain topped the pop music charts around the world in the 1950s, the alligator and the crocodile had a cheery, unthreatening image. An American television show of the time, *Kukla, Fran & Ollie*, featured a friendly, gregarious character named Oliver Dragon. A gator or croc, take your choice, who engaged in happy repartee with the other hand puppets and the program's hostess, an ageless ingenue named Fran Allison. In the popular comic strip *Pogo*, one of the regular characters was Albert Alligator, a cartoon figure that stood on its two hind feet and was always non-threatening and frequently funny. More recently, the world flocked to see Australia's Paul Hogan in somewhat screwy films about an adventurer named Crocodile Dundee.

On the other side were numerous adventure dramas of the Indiana Jones ilk depicting this large, scaly creature as some sort of junior-varsity Godzilla, where alligators and crocodiles became a cliché in cinema fright. For decades there has been a persistent "urban myth" that baby alligators that had been kept as pets were flushed down toilets when the owners tired of them, thriving in the city's sewers. When floods hit Thailand in 1996, several crocs escaped from commercial farms, leading the government to send armed teams in boats with orders to shoot to kill, and the media reported the "threat" worldwide.

At the same time, alligator "wrestling" has been a staple roadside attraction in the American South for generations, just as crocodile shows are a tourist draw in Australia and Southeast Asia; how many hundreds of thousands (millions?) have gasped when one of the trainers opened the reptile's mouth and stuck his or her head inside between those rows of pointy teeth?

Of course, people actually do get killed by gators and crocs in the wild occasionally, just as they're killed by sharks every now and then, and surely there is some hazard in sticking one's head inside a toothy mouth. The thing is, the media always report such things with more than appropriate drama. It makes for a good story, but the truth is, the crocodile and alligator are, like snakes and most "dangerous" carnivores, totally uninterested in humans, unless they themselves feel jeopardized.

Such clichèd reporting and the attitude attached to it—by both reporters and audience—clearly affects how we now feel about alligators and crocodiles. Most people in the developed parts of the world think of them as animals not only threatened (some species are, anyway), but also personally threatening. It's too bad, because, the unthreatened species offer a tasty, healthy meat that is now finding a growing market on several continents.

In Singapore, stir-fried crocodile is a staple on many restaurant menus, while in some parts of India the preferred dish is a crocodile curry, and in Australia, crocodile pie is a part of that country's traditional "bush tucker." In Japan, crocodile dishes are served as a delicacy at pricey Tokyo restaurants. In the United States, alligator gumbo is a recognized New Orleans dish, a part of Creole cuisine, and alligator ribs are barbecued in the same region. In black ghettos in the north, they're served with collard greens and black-eyed peas. The meat is also eaten matter-of-factly in parts of Latin America and Africa, usually grilled on an open fire or as part of rough stews and soups.

Crocodile and alligator lend themselves to wide culinary artistry and choice. They mix well with many herbs, spices, and vegetables. They are well-suited for numerous dishes, including not only soups and stews, but also casseroles, stir fries, omelettes, pies, pasta, and pastries. The meat beneath that armor-like skin is easily butchered and cut into chops and steaks, to be char-grilled like a chicken thigh or breast, whose flavor it resembles. (The preferred, or tenderest, meat is from the legs and tail of the young.) More exotic recipes abound, from crocodile tripe, a delicacy in Ethiopia, to omelettes made from the eggs and "Dragon's Palm," the roasted crocodile foot, offered in some restaurants in Southeast Asia.

It's also low in cholesterol.

Several species of crocodiles and alligators are endangered, but others are described as "controlled," meaning that the populations are closely monitored and carefully culled for commercial use only when the numbers warrant it. The American alligator, for example, went onto the endangered species list in 1967 when its number dropped to about one hundred thousand, and today the gator is thriving both in the wild and in captivity. There are an estimated million gators in the wild in Florida alone, another hundred thousand on commercial ranches. No longer on the endangered list, this species today provides hides for a variety of products, and meat for the table through much of the Southern United States, especially in Florida, Louisiana and Texas, the primary alligator-farming states.

Similarly in Australia, where the menacing saltwater croc once stood on the verge of extinction, after years of protection the population of "salties" living along the northern coast has rebounded to the point where they are now on the verge of being a dangerous nuisance. In the tropical Northern Territory, the population has grown from an estimated five thousand in 1971, when hunting was banned, to between sixty-five and seventy thousand in 1998. The prohibition remains in force, banning the meat from the Aboriginal diet, where it had been for thousands of years. This is a touchy issue today, as the Aborigines argue for revival of traditional ways. During a state visit by German Chancellor Helmut Kohl in 1997, however, croc stew was served along with kangaroo satè. Why? The meat came from a licensed farm.

If you want crocadillia on your plate anywhere nowadays, it must (legally) come from one of the commercial ranches and farms that stretch from Cuba to Cambodia, where even governments are in the business. Although some facilities are still small, as is one

in the Philippines, also government-run, large commercial operations exist in many parts of the world. Many in the Southern United States, where alligators are now hunted in the wild and trucked to slaughter-

World's Biggest Croc!

Fossil crocodiles appear in the rocks at about the same time as dinosaurs, varying little in size and appearance from the beasts today, preying on small, antelope-sized dinosaurs when they came to the rivers and streams to drink. Through recorded history, they have played a widely varied role. An ancient Egyptian god, Souchos, was a crocodile himself and at one period the creatures were believed to be oracles and were embalmed after death. The custom of "ordeal by crocodiles" was popular for a while in Arabia in criminal proceedings, in which the accused's guilt was determined by whether the crocodile ate or rejected him. In the Philippines, Borneo, and parts of West Africa, crocodiles were regularly fed prized livestock and other animals for religious reasons, although it isn't difficult to see that a well-fed croc is a better neighbor than a hungry one. Numerous popular tales from the South Pacific tell of women who had crocodiles for lovers.

Many people use the words "alligator" and "crocodile" interchangeably. Technically, both may be called "crocodilians," but they are two distinctly different, if related, species; the shapes of their heads providing the most obvious variance. The snout and jaws of the crocodile are broad, from the eyes to the tip forming a sort of rounded, lumpy rectangle, while the alligator's head tapers so that it appears almost triangular in shape. The alligator is also known to be far less aggressive than the croc when it comes to interaction with humans. I once watched a photographer get into a soupy Florida swamp almost nose-to-nose with a gator to take his picture; the gator looked totally bored.

Like most cold-blooded animals, they spend much of their time basking on sand banks, maintaining an even body temperature. They also open their massive jaws and gape, so that air plays over the soft skin inside the mouth, a natural posture for the animals — which may make it easier for those who work in alligator and crocodile tourist attractions to put their heads between those rows of awesome teeth. Of course, there are never any guarantees, so most of the head-in-mouth shows take place *after* the animals have been fed.

Some think that the alligator is exclusively North American, but there is a species, lesser-known, in China. The crocodile is found in many parts of the world, even in the United States (in southern Florida), but mainly in Latin America, Africa, and Asia, where different species are at home in either fresh or salt water. Records show that the estuarine or salt water croc, now extinct in many areas, is one of the largest reptiles on earth, ranging from India, Sri Lanka, southern China, and the Malay Archipelago to northern Australia, Papua New Guinea, and the Solomon Islands. One, killed in Bengal, India, about a hundred years ago, was thirty-three feet long; a twenty-nine-footer was killed about the same time in the Philippines. The largest alive today, according to *The Guinness Book of Records*, is believed to be nineteen feet, eight inches from snout to tail, and is in a wildlife sanctuary in India. Most mature males average about fourteen to sixteen feet in length and weigh from nine-hundred to 1,150 pounds, although old individuals may be half again as heavy.

Sources
Big Al's Gourmet Delights
(for gator tail fillets, bits, and
pieces), phone (800) 294-
0492 or (717) 992-4816,
email <bigal@noln.com>.

Louisiana Foods (for gator)
4410 West 12th St.,
Houston, TX 77055,
phone (800) 799-3134,
fax (713) 957-1659

houses and factories that process them into steaks and shoes. Not surprisingly, the U.S. dominates the world market and is the biggest exporter. The big buyers include France, Italy, Germany, and Japan for the leather. In Australia and Southeast Asia, where the beasts are raised in captivity, China and other Asian countries are the big markets for selling meat.

Oil derived from crocodile flesh also is in demand, widely used as a stabilizing agent in cosmetics and perfumes. In Brazil, Bolivia, and Madagascar, crocodile oil is praised as a cure for everything from asthma to baldness. The reptile's teeth, head, and bones are sold as souvenirs. And, because the commercial use of the beasts is almost everywhere rigidly regulated, limiting the numbers allowed to reach the market, the cost of anything made from alligator or crocodile is high.

In Southeast Asia, the most famous commercial operation is located only a half-hour's drive from Bangkok in Samut Prakarn. Called simply the Crocodile Farm, it is the source of the croc meat sold at restaurants throughout Asia. By its own boast, it is also the largest reptile ranch in the world, claiming a population of some forty thousand crocs of nine varieties. Whatever the census may be, it's clear that there is no shortage. When I visited in 1997, I saw thousands on open display behind metal mesh fencing or in shallow ponds, ranging in size from almost newborn (six to eight inches in length) to old enough to be gathering real moss and large enough to qualify for the scariest movie you've ever seen.

The crocodile is extinct in the wild in Thailand, but once past the turnstiles of the Crocodile Farm (admission: US$6 for foreigners, a twelfth that for Thais), it is threatened only by the farm's owners, who have a habit of turning the reptiles into profit-making leather and soup. One store near the entrance is full of luggage, briefcases, purses, shoes, belts, key chains, and other items made from the polished, brown skin. In another shop, stewed crocodile meat is sold in cans whose labels boast: "Product of our crocodile farm. It is selected by the first class breeding crocodile and pre-

pared under the Chinese medicine with the modern stew processing. Stewed croc-meat strengthens the libido. It is a nutritious and a tonic food for good health. It provides a pleasant taste. Stewed croc-meat stimulates the appetite, good for old people and growing children. It is an appreciated gift." The same shop also sells "essence of crocodile" in small bottles, reputed to be a healthy drink that can be served hot or cold, as well as a "crocodile oil," which is sold as a massage oil.

Near the two shops is a small, open-air restaurant, where those who have seen the crocodile show and have exhausted the rest of the farm's low-key amusement park-like entertainment may relax over a bottle of beer or soda and a zesty bowl of soup before getting back into Bangkok traffic. Only the tenderest (young) crocs are used, so visitors should be prepared to see little crocodile feet taking a final swim in the broth. Those little feet were on the bony side, but overall the taste was quite sweet. And a bargain at US$1.50.

Opposite: A bowl of crocodile soup served at the Crocodile Farm near Bangkok.

This page: Cans of prepared crocodile soup, priced at 200 baht—a little over US$3.00—are stacked for sale at the Crocodile Farm.

Overleaf: The Great Saltwater Crocodile, or "saltie," is not only one of the largest living reptiles, but one of the most aggressive. This specimen, one of the largest in captivity, is called "Jaws," and resides at the Croc Bank south of Madras, India.

Crocodile, 39 Ways

Crocodile Steak
Hot Spicy Spare Rib Crocodile Soup
Fried Spare Rib Crocodile with Peppers and Garlic
Fried Crocodile with Chili Paste
Fried Crocodile with Crispy Basil Leaves
Sweet and Sour Crocodile
Fried Crocodile with Ginger and Chili
Fried Crocodile with Cashew Nuts
Fried Crocodile with Pepper and Garlic
Fried Salted Crocodile
Crocodile Spicy Salad
Crocodile Tail Soup
Crocodile Satay
Crocodile with Chinese Bread
Baked Crocodile Egg
Dried Crocodile Meat
Crocodile Roll
Fried Crocodile with Vegetables
Crocodile Curry
Deep Fried Crocodile Meat
Crocodile French Bread
Fried Crocodile with Matsu-take Mushrooms
Fried Crocodile with Tiger Palm

Mushrooms
Fried Crocodile with Beef Liver Mushrooms
Fried Crocodile with Chinese Kong-chai Vegetables
Fried Crocodile with Asparagus
Fried Crocodile Liver
Baked Crocodile Egg
Fried Crocodile Egg with Ham
Crocodile Gastro
Dragon Palm [the foot]
Crocodile Palm in Red Sauces
Fried Crocodile Tongue with Garlic and Pepper
Dragon Soup with Ginseng
Tian-chi Crocodile Soup
Crocodile Liver Soup
Tian-ma Crocodile Soup
Bamboo Tissue Crocodile Soup
Steamed Crocodile Egg

— Menu, Sri Racha Tiger Farm Restaurant, Thailand, 1998, where the tigers are just for show, not to eat

frog & toad

How many cartoons have we all seen about frogs' legs? Remember the one showing a legless frog sitting on one of those wheeled platforms, begging with a tin cup? Or the ones with frogs on crutches? It's all pretty sick, if you ask me.

I don't know why cartoonists pick on frogs. Do they do as many jokes about cattle being turned into hamburgers? Or fish showing up in a soup? I don't think so. I guess that in the quirky world that determines what is humorous and what is not, frogs are funnier than cattle or fish.

In modern gastronomy, the legs of this web-footed amphibian are not so uncommon at some of the finer tables, especially in Europe, where they are an expensive delicacy. Although many of the frogs consumed in Europe are raised in Yugoslavia, more are imported frozen from Cuba and the United States, where the meat has not found a great audience, except in the southern states, where midnight frog hunts produce a key ingredient for stew. Nor are they popular in England, where when the esteemed Auguste Escoffier was chef of the Carlton Hotel in London, he craftily sneaked them onto the plate of the Prince of Wales only by calling them *cuisses de nymphes aurore*, legs of the dawn nymphs.

Why the rejection? Who knows. Maybe it's because frogs are funny looking and the subject of all those jokes. With their moist, hairless, feather-less, scale-less skin and large blinking eyes, wide mouth, an ability to live happily in both water and on dry land (where they hop rather than walk), and their deep, croaking voice, perhaps they are just a little too odd to consider. (Although when it comes to looks, I think chickens are funnier.) Perhaps, too, because they are so small and like song birds they are overlooked because it takes so many to make a meal. Kermit the Frog from *Sesame Street* probably doesn't help much, either. In any case, they are not easy to find in supermarkets, although they may be found in specialty shops in tins that are, like the legs on a menu, usually wildly overpriced.

Another mystery lies in the belief—endorsed, wrongly, by *Larousse Gastronomique*, the French encyclopedia of cookery—that only the legs are edible. While it is true that this is where most of the meat is, in many parts of the world the entire frog is eaten happily and healthily.

The French encyclopedia also would have us believe that preparation of the legs is somewhat complex. First, the frog is skinned then cut at the hips so that the legs remain in pairs. After the feet are removed (to disguise the meat's origin and make them look like small chicken legs?), they are soaked in cold water for twelve hours, with a change of water every three or four. This causes the flesh to whiten and swell as it absorbs the water.

They are then cooked in a variety of ways, marinated and grilled on skewers, dipped in flour and fried, sautèed in butter and chopped onion, or form the basis of a soup seasoned with shallots and a sweet white wine. In fine restaurants in Thailand, where they are sometimes euphemistically called "paddy chicken" because they came from the rice farms in the north, the legs are cooked in a wok with peppercorns, red chili peppers, palm sugar, basil, and galingale. They may also be served in a curry, with tomato sauce, and boned and included in egg frittata.

In much of Asia, Africa, and Latin America—there are 3,500 species found virtually everywhere in the world, except in arctic regions—the preparation is simpler and less wasteful. Here, frogs are not farmed as they are in Europe and North America, but caught in the watery woods, swamps and rice fields where they range freely, by villagers who stalk the creatures at night, following the sound of their throaty voices, "blinding" them with a light so that they freeze in place. They catch them with sharpened sticks, nets, or their hands and carry them home in sacks, where they are kept alive until the next day, when they are gutted and washed, then skewered on bamboo sticks and grilled for a hearty meal with rice and perhaps a spicy dip. They also are seen in open markets, hopping like mad by the dozens (hundreds?) in large pans with a wire mesh cover, strung like garlic or peppers on a long string, or grilled on bamboo skewers and sold ready to eat. Deep-fried, they look like men in suits—bloated plutocrats?—and disappear almost magically in the mouth, like cotton candy. Never are the legs removed, the rest wastefully thrown away. Here, they are consumed, completely and entirely, bones and all.

Where wetland rice is grown, the frogs are most numerous during the summer rainy season, thus they become a staple protein source, steamed and served cold in a salad with lemongrass, fresh coriander and hot chili peppers. If the frogs are large enough, they may be stuffed, chopping one frog and pounding it with a choice of seasonings, then stuffing the meat into the second frog, being careful to maintain its shape. The frog is then grilled or steamed.

Oh, yes, as is true of so many other "strange" foods, they, too, have a delicate flavor not unlike chicken.

Toads are another matter. If the frog makes some wrinkle their noses, it's fellow amphibian, the toad, probably makes them go googley-eyed and consider removing your card from their Rolodex if you dare to offer them. Again, I think it has to do with appearance. Where the frog is smooth and moist, most toads are dry and covered with warty bumps. Also, in recent years, one species of toad, found in the Sonoran Desert in the southwestern United States, acquired a nasty reputation for secreting a liquid that is dangerously hallucinogenic when dried and inhaled. ("It tasted like model glue," one woman who went "toading" told a newspaper reporter. "I took a few really deep breaths and got it into my lungs. You feel it immediately creeping down your spine. Within a minute, I was on the ground, thrashing around. I had no control of my coordination and a total loss of muscle control. I couldn't speak or anything. It was great.") Toads also have shorter legs, thus less meat.

All that said, many species are edible and if it is necessary to put five or six pairs of legs on the plate, instead of the recommended three or four for frogs, so be it. Preparation is basically the same.

Finally, a word about toad wine. Just about anything from the worlds of insects and reptiles—and let's not forget genitalia—has been used to flavor whisky and wine, usually in the belief that the combination of the two—gecko plus rice wine, snake plus corn whisky, etc.—will generate some medicinal benefit, usually connected to longevity and sexual potency. Thus there was in 1995 a fad that swept across Cambodia that nearly wiped out that small country's toad population.

So great was the demand for the wine, a stout-like liquid that was cheaper than beer or whisky, Dr. Mok Mareth, Cambodia's Environment Minister, appealed to toad hunters to halt their killing as they were upsetting the balance in the ecosystem. Chay Seang Y, a traditional healer in Phnom Penh, said that unlike gecko wine, which is believed to have originated in China and Vietnam, toad wine was entirely Khmer. In the recipe he recommended, the toads were dried, fried, crushed and stirred into white wine along with some herbs, including black sugar cane, producing a drink almost thick enough to require the use of a spoon.

What was the attraction? A belief, unproven, that consumption of toad wine would cure syphilis and a number of other kinds of sexually transmitted diseases, as well as promote appetite and good sleep. A tough combination to beat.

Undersecretary of State for Environment, Pou Savath was unimpressed. "I'd sooner see toads catching harmful insects that destroy crops in the field," he said.

Spoil sport.

Sources
Frogs from Rana Ranch, 1880 Jackson, Twin Falls, ID 83301, phone (298) 734-0853; Special Care, 5 W. Prospect Ave., Pittsburgh, PA 15205, phone (412) 928-9433, fax (412) 279-2913.

Opposite, above: When it comes to frog meat, the bigger the better: a frog-seller in Singapore's Chinatown market shows off two prize specimens.
Opposite, below: The small town of Mae Sariang in the far Northwest of Thailand is famed for its "mountain frogs" as they are locally known.
Opposite, right and this page: The preparation of a giant frog in Northeast Thailand for a spicy soup known as *om kob* begins with cutting the ventral side from throat to tail and pulling the skin off in one piece, after which the frog is lightly grilled over an open fire. The meat and accompanying spices and vegetables, including chilis, bay leaves, ginger, lemongrass, and fish sauce, are then ready to place in the pot with water.

shark

Shark Fritters

1½–2 cups chopped or grated shark meat
½ cup flour
2 eggs, beaten till foamy
1 small carrot, finely chopped
½ small onion, finely chopped
2–3 tsp. green onion, finely chopped
Salt and pepper to taste
Dash of monosodium glutamate (MSG)
1–2 drops of yellow food coloring, if desired

Optional:
¼ cup any combination of the following: sliced Chinese peas or string beans, slivered gobo (burdock), chopped water chestnuts, chopped Chinese parsley

Combine all ingredients. Batter should be stiff, but should drop easily from teaspoon. If not, add more flour or moisten with water as needed. Deep fry at 350°F until evenly browned. Drain on paper towel. Serve with tartar, tempura, or soy sauce.

University of Hawaii Sea Grant College, 1977

People who keep track of such things say that the chance of being hit by lightning is one in two million, of dying from a hornet sting one in five million, of being struck by a falling piece of an aircraft one in ten million. The chance of being killed by a shark is one in three hundred million! And more people die each year by choking on toothpicks than have been killed by sharks in the last decade in North America.

Thus the shark has an undeserved reputation when it comes to fine dining. Most people think it dines on you, when the opposite is far more common. The truth is, shark meat is regarded as a culinary treat in some parts of the world and in other areas, fish and chips.

Yes, it is true that sharks are nasty creatures when crossed. During the four hundred fifty million years sharks have patrolled the world's oceans, they have evolved into skilled predators who are at the top of the food chain among marine life. A shark can pick up sound waves in a three-mile radius and home in on the source to within a square yard, even in zero visibility. It can smell blood in the water at five miles, detect increased electrical current in the bodies of wounded fish or panicking humans, even hear their heartbeats. It can move at forty miles an hour, plus. It has no dental problems; if a tooth breaks off, another automatically takes its place. Is it any wonder that Steven Spielberg made a name for himself when he spawned a series of movies called *Jaws*? Can anyone forget the blonde teenybopper who left the beach party, slipped out of her clothes and swam off into the moonlight in that classic 1975 film? The music built to a crescendo and suddenly the water around the teenager foamed, we heard the sound of a human body being ripped apart and the screams of the girl before she disappeared amid gurgling noises into the depths.

Such scenes have occurred, of course, but rarely. Paddling surfers resemble a favorite shark meal, the seal or turtle. A woman who is menstruating may also be at risk if a hungry shark is nearby. Injured victims of maritime accidents are recovered infrequently. Yet, today, more often it is man who is the predator, as the hunter has become the hunted. Nowadays, shark meat may be eaten more widely in South America, Europe, Africa, and Asia than in the United States and Canada, but even those reluctant markets are expanding rapidly because of a trend toward eating more broiled and grilled fish, as the supply of tuna and swordfish shrinks. Shark meat also is praised for its high protein content and it contains almost no fat or cholesterol. One-third pound of raw shark meat yields about four ounces of lean, cooked fish, with more than an ounce of high-quality protein and only about one hundred calories.

In a pamphlet published by the University of Hawaii Sea Grant Marine Advisory Program as early as 1977, the shark was called not a swimmer's nightmare but "a chef's dream" whose "bland flavor allows it to conform readily to many tastes, with the use of sauces, herbs and spices, and flavorings. The boneless, all-meat fillets turn perfectly white when cooked, and this fish cooks easily and quickly." The flesh of the mako, which grows to twenty feet, was compared favorably to swordfish; in fact, even today, although restaurateurs may not admit it, some serve shark and call it swordfish, while others offer it under the names "whitefish" or "greyfish." Because the taste is indistinguishable from some other firm, pale fish, it is infrequent that anyone notices.

With demand growing, it is estimated that between one hundred million and two hundred million sharks are taken from the sea each year worldwide. Yet, while a number of sharks are threatened—the elephant fish, the lemon, some hammerheads, and the star of *Jaws*, the great white, all are on the endangered lists—many species are not. And they are found in great numbers virtually everywhere, with the world's main suppliers of high quality fins in Africa, Australia, Mexico and Indonesia, and the best meat thought to come from the waters between China and the Philippines.

Usually, they are caught on "long lines" with baited hooks, three hundred hooks on a heavy nylon line that may be up to nine miles long. Nets are destroyed by the sharks and because they don't swim in schools, they prove economically inefficient anyway. Once in the boat, sharks must be cleaned immediately. If the blood is not drained from the system right away, a shark's urea deteriorates into ammonia and gives the meat an unpleasant odor and taste.

To clean a shark, the University of Delaware Sea Grant Marine Advisory Service suggests putting it on ice (after gutting and bleeding it), then at the dock cut the shark's head all the way around and make a cut from the head to the tail on both the top and bottom sides. Using a pair of pliers in one hand and holding the head or tail in the other, skin the shark. Then cut the head and tail off, remove the underlying layer of dark meat, and cut the shark into fillets. Wash thoroughly and package the shark for freezing or cooking as you would any other fish.

Once ready to cook, the options are as numerous as for any other fish. A hasty check on the Internet shows there are many shark connoisseurs offering recipes for Shark Hors d'Oeuvres (deep-fried and served with Creole mustard), Shark Kebobs, Broiled Shark with Anchovy and Caper Sauce, Cape Shark in Essence of Fennel, Shark Tacos, Shark Amandine, Oven-Fried Shark, Shark Marseillaise, Shark Curry—Bengal Style, Crispy Shark with Sweet and Sour Sauce, Shark Teriyaki, and Poached Shark Remoulade. To insure good flavor, a quarter teaspoon of vinegar or lemon juice per pound of shark meat may be added to any recipe during cooking to eliminate any residual ammonia.

The University of Delaware offers more tips for preserving shark. Double-wrap the meat before freezing, wrapping only enough in one package for a single serving. Smoking does not preserve shark—it only

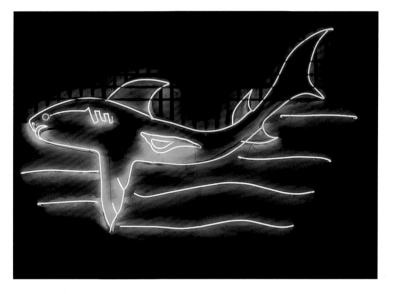

A neon sign advertises a shark's fin restaurant.

enhances the flavor. The salt for salting and curing shark should always be non-iodized; iodized salt will turn the flesh black or it will spoil. To salt shark in a crock, glaze the inside of the crock or the salt will leach the crock and cause the shark to spoil. Plastic containers work well for salting shark. Before salting shark in a plastic container or crock, soak the shark in a brine solution overnight to remove all blood. Then wash the meat with clear water, lay flat, and let drain. After one to two hours, place the shark in a container and layer with salt, covering the final layer with about one inch of salt.

Shark Leftovers

Besides the meat and fins, shark skin is used for leather in making wallets that cost up to US$200 and handbags priced as high as $1,300. The oil from the shark's liver—which constitutes up to twenty per cent of the body weight and was pressed into service as lubrication for fighter planes during World War Two—now is used in treating minor aches and pains and in hemorrhoidal medications. Shark corneas may be implanted into human eyes and shark cartilage, which makes up the shark's skeleton, is used to create artificial skin for burn victims.

There is, however, no evidence at all that the various cartilage creams and pills commercially available can cure cancer, arthritis, bursitis, carpal tunnel syndrome, acne or any other of a wide variety of ailments claimed by the manufacturers; one distributor even hinted that it might be effective against AIDS!

This page: At the Sze Lee Shark's Fin Company in Hong Kong, workers tenderize the tough fins by scraping, boiling, and even soaking them in hydrogen peroxide, a procedure that takes several days.

Opposite: Even after the lengthy process in preparing the shark's fin for use, it takes a long time and many stages to prepare sharks' fin soup. First soaked for at least three days with several changes of water, the fin is then simmered for up to five hours. The sandy skin is removed, as is the decayed bone hidden in the meat at the tip. The fin is then cooked for a further 10 hours in stocks that are regularly discarded to remove any smell from the curative process.

In a category all its own, of course, is the venerable shark's fin soup, a medium- to high-priced delicacy that has become a symbol of the world's most extravagant banquet fare and is believed by many to be an aphrodisiac. So profitable is this market that many nations have passed laws banning "finning," the cruel practice of catching sharks, removing their fins, then releasing them to drown, in much the same way a rhinoceroses is slaughtered for its horns, an elephant for its tusks.

This soup is made from the noodle-like, amber-colored gelatinous strands extracted from the dorsal "comb fin" or the two ventral fins of any of a variety of sharks. Some historians say it has been consumed in China since the Han Dynasty began two thousand years ago. Others contend it didn't come into vogue until the Song Dynasty, beginning in 960 A.D. Either way, it has a long, savory history, closely linked to the Mandarins.

According to a sixteenth-century *materia medica*, shark fin "opens the stomach," meaning it is an appetite stimulator. Thus, said one food writer, "it may start a meal, or served at the peak of a banquet, it readies you for the onslaught of dishes to follow."

This is a specialty that costs more than most if not all other soups (save those made with birds' nests) because, well, because it's made from shark, of course, but also because it is not prepared quickly or easily. In fact, on reading the instructions in Bruce Cost's *Asian Ingredients* (1988), a book hailed by Craig Claiborne of *The New York Times* as "by far the most comprehensive guide to the essential ingredients for Asian cooking ever published," I'm compelled to ask why anybody bothers cooking the dish in the first place. Only the status attached to its consumption, along with the hope that it will bring sexual stamina, could create such a market.

To prepare shark's fin, Cost says, it was necessary to soak the fin for twenty-four hours, changing the water several times, then after a vigorous scrubbing, the fin was to be boiled, drained, and then soaked again. A stock with wine was then poured over the fin. Steaming for three hours followed. Then the liquid was discarded and after more rinsing in several changes of water, it was—finally!—ready for use in most recipes.

It is no surprise that shark's fin soup rarely is prepared from scratch at home, but rather is purchased frozen, dried, or in tins or, most often, enjoyed at exorbitant prices in Chinese restaurants. There also are "instant" soups vacuum-packed in plastic trays that may be stored at room temperature for what the manufacturer calls "a long period of time." What would the Mandarins think?

The really odd thing about shark's fin soup is that after all the soaking and boiling and rinsing, the fin is rendered nearly tasteless, contributing only a gooey thickening to the dish. By itself, it is remarkable only for its blandness. It's chewy and it has a pleasing texture, but it is the crab meat, roe, shrimps, sweet-smelling mushrooms and other vegetables, ginger, bamboo, thinly sliced ham, shredded chicken, ginseng, and other ingredients that give the soup its flavor.

Steven Spielberg probably never goes near the stuff.

fugu

A giant reproduction of a puffer-fish lantern hangs over a Tokyo street to advertise a fugu restaurant. The real lanterns are made from the dried skin of the inflated fish.

When I was young, spending my summers on an island off the New Jersey coast, my brother and I greeted the fishing boats in the morning as they were rolled up onto the beach on logs. The fishermen sorted their catch, throwing the ones they didn't want over the side to the dozen or so of us who gathered there most days. For the fishermen, and the shops to which they sold their catch, the discarded fish were trash. For us, it was lunch or dinner.

One of the unwanted species was the blowfish, so called because it was able to inflate its abdomen like a balloon, a defensive talent used to frighten away predators who might be intimidated by the sudden increase in size. Some of our friends told us the fish was inedible, even poisonous, but my brother and I believed it was thrown away because it offered so little meat, only two small finger-sized strips along both sides near the tail. To get a meal, you had to catch and clean quite a few of them.

It wasn't until many years later, when I was living in Hawaii and exposed to Japanese nationals on holiday, that I heard about another species of blowfish, a deadly toxic variety generally known as *fugu*. I was told that the Japanese regarded it as a delicacy and that there were in Tokyo alone, hundreds of restaurants specializing in the dish. For those who could afford the price, and were willing to take the risk, fugu was an essential treat, a sort of ultimate edible.

How risky is it? Estimates range widely, but some say as many as twenty diners die each year, mostly from fish improperly cleaned at home. Whatever the figures may be, care must be taken and fugu chefs are meticulously trained and must serve a long apprenticeship before being licensed and permitted to work under strict government supervision. So rigid are the tests, in fact, that fewer than a third of the applicants pass.

Actually, the word fugu is a general name for what my brother and I called blowfish and others know as

the puffer, globe, or swell fish. When inflated and dried, it frequently is sold as a souvenir and may be seen in seaside restaurants in many parts of the world, hanging from the ceiling with a light bulb inside. There are nearly a hundred different kinds worldwide, thirty-eight of them found in the waters surrounding Japan and the rivers emptying into them. Most are quite safe to eat. However, those containing tetrodotoxin (TTX) are riskier. A pinch of the poison, the amount found in a six-pound tiger fugu, is enough to kill more than thirty persons. The lethal dose for an adult, one to two milligrams, could be put on the head of a pin. Scientists say its molecular structure is unlike anything else in organic chemistry, making it 250 times deadlier than a comparable dose of cyanide. And like curare, a poison with which it is closely compared, there is no antidote.

(The California newt and eastern salamander also possess TTX in lethal quantities, although no one has added them to their menu, yet.)

Over the years, many well-known names have either described or been exposed to the fish, going back to 1774 when Captain James Cook ate a bit after catching one in New Caledonia. J. Reinhold Forster and his son, George Forster, the naturalists for the expedition, sketched it before it was prepared for dinner. "Luckily for us," Captain Cook wrote in his journal, "that only the liver and roe was dressed of which the two Forsters and myself did but just taste. About three or four o'clock in the morning we were seized with an extraordinary weakness in all our limbs attended with a numbness or sensation like to that caused by exposing one's hands or feet to a fire after having been pinched much by frost. I had almost lost the sense of feeling nor could I distinguish between light and heavy bodies, a quart pot full of water and a feather was the same in my hand. We each of us took a vomit and after that a sweat which gave great relief. In the morning one of the pigs which had eat the entrails was found dead."

Years later, in Baja California, the writer John Steinbeck reported he and a friend tried to buy a puffer from a boy they met on the beach, but the boy refused, "saying that a man had commissioned him to get this fish and he was to receive ten centavos for it because the man wanted to poison a cat." Finally, it wasn't a cat but a spy who was poisoned, no less a figure than James Bond when Ian Fleming's novel *From Russia With Love* (1997) ended with Agent 007 being kicked in the leg with a boot containing a poisoned dart. "Numbness was creeping up Bond's body... Breathing became difficult...Bond pivoted slowly on his heel and crashed headlong to the wine-red floor." Bond survived, of course, and in the next novel, *Dr. No* (1997), it was revealed that he had been poisoned with fugu. "It comes from the sex organs of the Japanese globefish," a neurologist told Bond's chief. "It's terrible stuff and very quick."

The toxin works by blocking the nerve impulses, quickly shutting down the entire nervous system. The onset of poisoning ranges from twenty minutes to two hours following consumption, thus often strikes while the diner is still at the table. The first hints that there may be trouble are numbness of the lips and tip of the tongue, spreading to the extremities, followed by headache, stomach pain, a tightness in the throat, facial flushing, dizziness, and nausea.

The violent vomiting that is characteristic in some cases may permit the victim to expel enough of the poison to survive, as happened with Captain Cook and his naturalists, but for those who do not regurgitate, the prognosis is grim. Convulsions hit, followed by fatigue, feelings of doom, and a wish to lie down. It

---

Death of a National Treasure

The story of one death is told frequently in Kyoto, where restaurants specializing in fugu may be identified by the picture of an inflated fish, or a lantern made from one, displayed over the entrance. In 1975, Mitsugora Bando VIII, a Kabuki actor of such stature in Japan that he was described as a "national treasure," visited a fugu restaurant with a group of his fellow actors and insisted upon eating the liver. It is in the liver, intestines, gonads, ovaries, and other internal organs in which the toxins are concentrated and it is illegal to serve these organs. The actor was told no, deferentially. He asked again, and then again.

After a time, the chef relented and served each actor one small serving. Those who ate one piece survived. However, three of the men declined and Bando ate their portions as well as his own. In less than an hour he collapsed in convulsions. His final words were "I have eaten the death number." In Japan, the number four is considered cursed.

This page: At three o'clock in the morning at the beginning of October, at a dockside warehouse in Shimononseki, Japan's fugu season begins, with thousands of freshly caught fish awaiting auction.
Opposite: After filleting, the heads of young fugu are displayed for sale in the main fish market in Shimonoseki, in the extreme west of Japan's main island of Honshu,

becomes difficult to speak. Breathing is labored. Blood pressure and pulse accelerate, then fall as paralysis sets in and the skin takes on a bluish tint. Death follows within two to six hours.

Why, one wonders, would anyone want to take such a gamble and pay such a high price for taking it? Fugu is one of the most expensive foods in Japan, and in Japanese restaurants elsewhere, from Hong Kong to New York. A single kilogram can bring as much as $130 wholesale and when served in a restaurant in a variety of ways, as much as $400 for a four- or five-course meal.

Millions of people take the chance, betting their lives each year; it is, they say, no more dangerous than flying—a tragedy when a plane goes down, but don't most passengers arrive at their destinations safely? More important is the status attached to paying the high price and experiencing what is, after all, both hazardous and avoidable. For males in a macho society, it is a way of proving one's mettle far more admirably than singing in a karaoke bar. Even some foreigners are willing to put their lives on the line. And for a rapidly expanding tourist population in search of thrills, it requires far less effort than mountain climbing or white-water rafting.

In the Haedomari Market in Shimonoseki, where most of the country's catch is sold, the fish are auctioned in a peculiar manner. As the auctioneer describes the catch, buyers approach him and slip a hand into a long black sleeve that covers the seller's hand, grasping the auctioneer's fingers in a code that reveals what they wish to pay. The auctioneer may keep track of as many as ten secret handshakes before announcing the winning bid. In this fashion, more than two tons of fugu may be sold in under an hour.

As is true in many Asian restaurants serving seafood, the fish is kept alive until it is prepared. The customer selects his meal, the chef slaps it onto a nylon carving block, holding it firmly in place with one hand, then with a sharp, triangular knife, removes the toothy mouth, the pectoral and dorsal fins, and

Did the Bible Warn of the Danger?

The consumption of fugu dates back to 2,700 B.C., when identifiable symbols of the fish first appeared on Egyptian tombs, inflated and used as a ball in an early game. It's also thought that because the poisonous Red Sea porcupine fish—a related species—had no scales, it may have inspired the Biblical warning: "These ye shall eat of all that are in the waters: all that have fins and scales shall ye eat: And whatsoever hath not fins and scales ye may not eat; it is unclean unto you." (Deuteronomy 14:9–10)

No one knows precisely how long fugu has been consumed in Asia, but in Japan's medieval era, the Tokugawa shogunate regime banned it. It regained its popularity in the mid-nineteenth century. Despite this, as late as the early twentieth century, the Meiji rulers said it could not be sold in certain districts. Today, it is the only food that cannot be served to the emperor and his family.

tail. Mouth, fins and tail are placed on a black tray for additional preparation. Next he slices the fish from gills to tail on both sides, removing the skin and adding it to the same tray. Now his demeanor becomes that of a surgeon, as he cuts away the gills, placing them on a red tray, where all the dangerous bits go. He then slits the belly to remove the ovaries and roe if it's a female, the gonads if a male, the heart, and then the liver, kidneys, gall bladder and intestines. All join the gills on the red tray, as do the eyes and a thin membrane from the abdominal cavity. Finally, the fugu is thoroughly rinsed in cold water, patted dry, and cut into two fillets. There are thirty steps required by law, taking up to twenty minutes for a practiced chef, compared to less than a minute for other species.

It is served only between October and March and thought to be best from December to February. Many diners happily settle for an order of *fugu-sashi* (or *sashimi*), cut into almost transparent slices that are beautifully arranged (typically in the shape of a chrysanthemum or flying crane), and served on a large round plate or tray with a slightly sour sauce for dipping (usually soy), chopped chives and grated radish.

Some diners will order a full meal, with fugu prepared in a number of ways. *Hirezake* is strongly flavored, toasted fugu fins soaked in hot sake. *Fuguchiri*, or *chiri-nabe*, is a one-pot dish with pieces of fugu, assorted vegetables and thin noodles, boiled together; this may be cooked at the table, with the diners adding the ingredients as desired. Fugu *sosui* adds rice and egg to the liquid remaining in the *fuguchiri* pot. The fish may also arrive at the table whole, deep-fried in a light batter. And for those who wish an aphrodisiac, the pulverized genitals may be mixed with hot sake—although, as noted, the organs may only be served illegally, something that rarely is done except, perhaps, for a customer of long standing, a friend of the chef or restaurant proprietor, or an insistent and persuasive celebrity.

The fugu's bland taste—aficionados prefer the word "subtle"—and dense, chewy texture may be explained

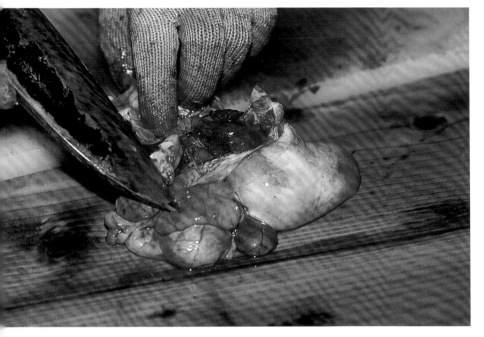

by the fact that the meat is without fat. When the poisonous organs are removed, they may leave a slight tingle behind, spreading delicately throughout the skin and the meat. This may cause a slight buzzing sensation in the lips and tongue, adding to the thrill of the meal, inasmuch as these are among the first symptoms of fugu poisoning.

When Japan's economy slid toward recession in the early 1990s, many fugu restaurants closed, as white-collar workers no longer could afford the luxury. Still, fugu remained big business, with fishermen catching the fish during the spring spawning season and raising the hatchlings in huge cages in the sea. Some of the cages hold as many as thirty thousand fish. The Japanese also have learned how to reproduce them through artificial insemination. In 1996, ten thousand tons were consumed in Japan. A cooperative agreement between the U.S. Food and Drug Administration and the Japanese Ministry of Health and Welfare ensures fugu is properly processed and certified safe for consumption before export.

The fish called fugu are not without their own risks in life and many die as violent a death as the feckless or reckless seafood fancier. The puffer is a tough and aggressive fish known for biting the tails of other fugu, rendering them helpless. In addition, the fugu is raised on a fresh seafood diet of mostly sardines and, ironically, because the fish lacks a proper stomach, one of the primary causes of death is indigestion.

Some people call that justice.

Opposite: Auctioned fugu are gutted and cleaned before sunrise by experts, who must remove the liver (shown in close-up) and ovaries, which harbor the toxin.

This page: One hundred tiny slices of raw fugu, shaved paper thin, are arranged in the traditional design of a chrysanthemum flower, with a tassel of fin and skin. The transparency of the flesh makes the plate itself an important part of the meal, and fugu restaurants have special and valuable designs on which to display this costly dish. Depending on the market price and the status of the restaurant, each slice on a plate like this will cost the diner the equivalent of between one and two U.S. dollars.

jellyfish

This page: Once the poisonous tentacles have been removed, the cap of the jellyfish finds a place in several Asian cuisines for its crunchy texture.
Opposite: Jellyfish salad, garnished with sliced shallots, bell pepper, chives, arugula, and spring onions, nestles in a cup made of two lettuce leaves. The spring onions are here given a Thai decorative treatment: partly sliced lengthwise with a number of incisions and dropped into cold water, causing them to curl into flower shapes.

In their natural state, as they go bobbing merrily (or malevolently) along, carried by the wind and ocean tides, jellyfish offer an unlikely source of food. Like so many other food sources in this book, in addition to an unseemly appearance, many species have a nasty reputation for painfully intruding on human lives, in this case, stinging swimmers and waders enjoying the sea.

It's no surprise that many people think jellyfish are a strange thing to eat. The beast itself floats to a different drummer. They have been on the earth for more than 650 million years, going back pre-dinosaur and shark (and, some might say, rudely, given all that time, they still haven't developed much talent or personality). It gets its name from its "jelly bag," a sort of skin filled with a gelatinous secretion that makes it more than ninety-five percent water—human beings, one of the other wettest creatures on earth, measure a little more than seventy percent—and it has no heart, brain, or bones, being held together by muscle fibers. Its stomach is connected directly to its mouth, the only opening in its body. This means that food enters here and the waste passes out there, too. Jellyfish also use their mouths to swim, taking in water to fill their stomachs, then pumping it out to propel themselves forward. The tentacles are there to help move prey toward this all-purpose mouth. Their favorite foods? Small, drifting animals called zooplankton, which include other jellyfish, juvenile fish, baby seahorses, and larval crustaceans. There are two hundred different species ranging in size from the tiny, spherical thimble jellyfish of the Caribbean to the Arctic "lion's mane," with a bell nearly nine feet across and tentacles that stretch half the length of a football field.

Those tentacles, used to paralyze and move food to the mouth, can be something to worry about. The umbrella-like form of some adult jellies are called a "medusa," so named because of its resemblance to the Medusa of Greek mythology with hair of writhing snakes. The small Portuguese man-of-war, with its colorful pink sack that floats on the ocean's surface to catch the wind and its luminescent blue trailing tentacles has pestered bathers and beach walkers with nasty stings for thousands of years. Australia's box jellyfish's toxin is more potent that cobra venom and can kill in minutes. Statistics show that more people are killed by jellyfish than by great white sharks. I doubt a good movie could be made about a jelly. As I said, they're totally lacking in personality.

Is it any wonder that many don't think of this as food?

That said, there is a small listing in *Edible Plants and Animals* (1993), a compendium of bite-sized descriptions of "unusual foods from Aardvark to Zamia" published by the respectable Facts on File, and, once you get away from Euro-American publishing and consult Asian authorities, jellyfish is as commonly

seen on the dinner plate as it is on the beach following a storm. It appears on restaurant menus from Tokyo to San Francisco to Lima, usually but not exclusively in Japanese restaurants. According to industry figures, nearly three hundred sixty tons of edible jellyfish were sold in 1997 by Tokyo wholesalers alone. I've even been served jellyfish salad by several Asian airlines.

The really weird thing about jellyfish—putting aside their peculiar looks and dubious renown—is that the edible ones have no taste. None. If it isn't served with a light soy or sesame oil dressing, for example, or as part of a salad that also offers chicken or fish and vegetables, the question arises: why is this considered food? Some people go so far as to complain that it's like eating rubber bands.

That's part of it. Its crunchy, chewy texture gives it much of its appeal, just as the tactile nature of many foods contribute to their attractiveness. Jellies also offer a fat-free protein related to albumen, the egg white protein, providing vitamins A and B. Like so many other exotic foods favored in the Orient—from snake blood to bird's nest soup—it's also believed to bring long life, lower the blood pressure, and cure a number of common ills, and, in fact, is now being used in responsible clinics and labs for cancer research.

Jellyfish in its natural form is off-putting, but so are many other delicious foods. Once harvested—besides Japan, Malaysia and the Philippines are prime sources—and the tentacles are removed, and the large, flat tops are dried, it looks no more threatening than a large, dried mushroom. The most popular species reaches fifteen to twenty inches in diameter and when dried is sold in one-pound bags. Preparation requires soaking them for about eight hours, changing the water two or three times. The blubbery flesh is then parboiled quickly and rinsed under cold water, and sliced thinly.

"It's a nuisance to some people, but a delicacy to others," Charles Blume, executive director of the Apalachee Regional Planning Council in Blountstown, Florida, said when announcing a plan to establish the state's first, authorized jellyfish harvest in 1997. The Asian market for the delicacy was growing, he said, and the fishing industry in Florida, as elsewhere, was in need of a new cash crop.

Reason enough, many agree, for any odd food to find new fans.

Jellyfish Salad

½ lb. salted jellyfish
1 large cucumber, julienned
1 tbs. creamy peanut butter
1 tbs. soy sauce
1 tbs vinegar
1 tbs. sugar
1 tsp. sesame oil
Dash of hot chili oil

Wash jellyfish. Rinse under running water for 20 minutes or until it is no longer salty; cut into strips. Put in boiling water for 5 seconds and rinse in cold water; drain. Arrange cucumber on serving plate. Place jellyfish on cucumber. In a bowl, combine remaining ingredients; mix until smooth. Serve with salad.

"The Electric Kitchen," Hawaiian Electric Co., Honolulu

The Jellyfish as Pet

Perhaps the oddest thing about jellyfish is a fad that hit urban Japan in 1998, when they escaped ending up on the dinner plate by becoming pets. Right. Pets. They don't slobber or bark or claw the sofa or leave any unwanted smells and mess around. Nor do they have to be taken for walks. They stay in their aquarium, undulating, like living lava lamps.

"It relaxes me to watch them float,' Mik Koyama, a 28-year-old office worker told the Associated Press about her two donut-sized jellies, recently installed in a tank in her Tokyo apartment.

"Jellyfish never disturb you," said Hironobu Fujii, an employee at a Tokyo pet shop. "If you leave the house for a week, it doesn't matter to them. I think that's why they are popular with women who live alone and want a pet."

And if you tire of all the floating and undulating, of course you can always turn Mr. Jellyfish into Mr. Salad—something you likely would not do with your pet dog, cat, or parakeet.

snails & slugs

"I have eaten several strange things since I was twelve, and I shall be glad to taste broiled locusts and swallow a live fish. But unless I change very much, I shall never be able to eat a slug. My stomach jumps alarmingly at the thought of it."

Thus begins an essay by Mary Francis Kennedy Fisher, better known by her initials M.F.K., arguably the best writer about food in English in the twentieth century.

"I have tried to be callous about slugs," she continued. "I have tried to picture the beauty of their primeval movements before a fast camera, and I have forced myself to read in the *Encyclopedia Britannica* the harmless ingredients of their oozy bodies. Nothing helps. I have a horror, deep in my marrow, of everything about them. Slugs are awful, slugs are things from the edges of insanity, and I am afraid of slugs and all their attributes.

"But I like snails. Most people like snails."

In this essay, first published in 1937, called "Fifty Million Snails," Fisher said that once, when she was living in Dijon, France, she ate so many she was dizzy for two days when the snails "changed into old rubber boiled in garlic." No matter. She still loved them, as did most other residents of France, who consumed, she said, fifty million snails each year.

I like snails, too, although I'm not sure why. (The truth is, I think I'd eat anything dipped in hot butter, even pieces of the rubber sandals I wear in Bangkok, where I live.) Nor am I sure why history reports that snails were among the first animals to be eaten by man, a claim more or less verified by evidence in the piles of shells found in prehistoric caves. Perhaps it was because they were so easy to catch.

The Romans are believed to be the first to cultivate snails as a food, fattening them on wine and grain, and Pliny the Elder wrote in the first century, in his thirty-seven-volume *Natural History*, of grilled snails eaten with wine as an appetizer before supper or as a snack between the feasts and orgies for which his countrymen were notoriously famed. While the Gauls in what is now France served them as a dessert and in the Middle Ages the Church permitted consumption of snails on days of abstinence. Usually they were fried with oil or onion, cooked on skewers, or boiled.

One of early acclamations to this culinary tidbit appeared in 1394 in a French newspaper, *Le Managier de Paris*: "Snails, which are called escargots, should be caught in the morning. Take the young small snails, those that have black shells, from the vines or elder trees; then wash them in so much water that they throw up no more scum; then wash them once in salt and vinegar, and set them to stew in water. Then you must tick these snails out of the shell at the point of a needle or a pin; and then you must take off their tail, which is black, for that is their turd; and then wash them and put them to stew and boil them in water; and then take them out and put them in a dish to be eaten with bread. And also some say that they are better fried in oil and onion or some other liquid, after they have been cooked as above said; and they are eaten with spice and for rich people."

By the seventeenth century, the consumption of snails declined and in much of Europe for centuries afterward, they were regarded not as a delicious food, but as a garden pest. Which indeed they were, wickedly reproducing in great numbers and eating virtually anything that was green. In France, they made a fashionable comeback when Talleyrand had some prepared for a dinner he hosted for a Russian czar. Since that time, France has been the snail's gastronomical champion.

In England, they were still detested for the agricultural damage done and shunned as a food. In a curious little book called *Why Not Eat Insects*, published in London in 1885, the author Vincent M. Holt devoted twelve pages to this edible mollusk (including it because he believed it was, like most insects, another example of diet prejudice that failed to recognize an abundant and available protein source). In the small book, he argued that "Something could be done by force of example. Masters might prepare savory snail dishes, according to the recipes used in all parts of the Continent and in course of time the servants would follow suit." One stumbling block, he said, was that many thought only one species was edible, when the only superiority of this particular snail over its fellows was its superior size. To the contrary, Holt insisted, all species were edible.

Holt further reported that in Italy and elsewhere in Europe, many households raised snails in a sort of "snail-preserve, or *escarcogotieres*, consisting of odd corners of gardens enclosed with boards and netted over the top. In these enclosures hundreds of snails are kept and fed upon wholesome vegetables and such herbs as to impart to their consumers an agreeable flavor. I should like to see a simply constructed snail-preserve in every cottage garden in England."

Holt's arguments fell on silent ears, but if England and the other developed countries still failed to embrace insects as a food, the snail found its slow and methodical way to the dinner table when France muscled its way to the world's culinary lead. In some areas of France today, the mollusks are starved for a week or longer to eliminate any toxins or unpleasant taste that might be in the flesh because of what the snails had eaten. In other regions, they are put on a diet of thyme or other herbs to flavor them. And then they are made into a broth; simmered inside their shells with white wine or garlic butter, a chili-flavored gravy, and chives; shelled and cooked with a white *roux* using butter and flour or garlic-flavored mayonnaise and bernaise sauce; or sprinkled with salt, pepper, thyme, and crushed fennel, then grilled. Served with farmhouse bread and red wine.

If these and numerous other snail recipes have found favor—mainly in upscale restaurants; escargot is still considered a dish for the rich—the slug remains, as it was for Ms. Fisher, at the bottom of the food chain as well as on anyone's list of desirable mealtime treats. It may be said that, lacking the pleasing, symmetrical shell, the common garden and sea slugs are, comparatively, somewhat unattractive. But so are many other foods "on the hoof," including the crab, the lobster, and the oyster.

In fact, the only significant difference between a snail and a slug is the shell. While most mollusks are invertebrates whose bodies are protected by a hard shell, the slug remains in the same scientific classification, along with squids and octopuses, but has no protective armor. There are more important similarities. Like the snail, the land slug dines on vegetation, usually at night, thus it, too, is regarded as a pest. While the sea slug, resembling its air-breathing cousin closely, feasts on coral or other animals in the sea.

If the land slug has failed to draw a hungry audience, the capture and cooking of the marine slug has a long and exuberant following, from China and Japan to the Eskimos of the frozen north. There are some visual differences between the two. Land slugs appear in many colors, from red to gray to yellow to black, and while they vary in size according to species and age, most sea slugs are black or gray and are far larger, weighing as much as two pounds.

Over time, it also has received some poor notices, dating back to a pre-fifth century fragment of a Chinese work called *The Canon of Gastronomy*, where it was called *hai-shu*, or "sea rat" and was described as "looking like a leech, but larger." In time, its status improved and it came to be called *hai-shen*, or roughly, "ginseng of the sea," as it was believed to have the same restorative properties as ginseng. So popular was the sea slug in China, the emperor sent huge fleets as far as Africa and Australia in search of an adequate supply. In what is now Sri Lanka in 1415, a war was fought over the lowly slug when the local king ordered the fleet away; in response, the Chinese dispatched an army, captured the king, and continued to harvest the sea and its shores.

Sources
Dried sea cucumber by mail from Enterprises Ondine Inc., 195 rue Bellevue, Sainte-Anne-des-Monts, Quebec, Canada, email <Ondine@glo-betrotter.qc.ca>.

One of the reasons for its lionization and renown was its supposed ability to enhance male virility, a reputation explained, perhaps, by the fact that it has a long, thick, muscular form that swelled to the touch. A document surviving from sixteenth-century China reported that when the slug was not available, "take the penis of a donkey and use it as a [gastronomical] substitute."

In 1913, a woman named Elie Hunt was interviewed in her native Kwakuitl language in what is now Alaska, recounting the details of how the sea slug was caught and cooked. The hunter, always a man, waited for low tide, when he paddled his canoe over the tidal pools and captured the plentiful animals with a forked stick. "He takes the sea slug, takes his knife, and cuts off the neck. Then he squeezes out the insides, and he throws it down hard into his canoe, saying as he is throwing it down, 'Now you will be as stiff as the wedge of your grandfather'."

Back on shore, the slugs were steamed for two days, then boiled over an open fire. Because the water of the slugs almost always boiled over, the Kwuakuitl woman said, the man threw handfuls of dirt from the floor of the house into the water, the only way to halt the boiling over. They were then washed a final time and served as is.

Today, the sea slug—sometimes called a "sea cucumber," again because of its shape—generally is dried and soaked for several days, then boiled in several changes of water until its original spongy texture returns. The slug is praised by nutritionists, if not for its aphrodisiac properties, for its zero cholesterol, saying, also, that pound for pound, it has four times the protein of beef.

Because it is fairly tasteless, but known for its satisfying crunch when eaten—similar to bamboo shoots or jellyfish—the Chinese usually cook it with chicken, pork, seafood, or vegetables, or add it to a soup. The Japanese sometimes eat them thinly sliced and raw in vinegar at sushi bars.

As for the garden slugs, the ones that Ms. Fisher found so off-putting, a cuisine has yet to be devised.

Opposite: A Laotian dish of *hoi khong*—apple snails—prepared simply by boiling and serving with a basic dipping sauce known as *jaew som,* made from pounded garlic, chilis, fish sauce, and coriander leaves. Traditional steamed sticky rice is the accompaniment. *This page:* Creamed slugs on toast make use of a mushroom cream sauce, garnished with sesame seeds. Lacking the protective shell of a snail, slugs protect themselves with a tougher skin on the upper body and a coating of slime. In order to remove the slime completely, the animals must be simmered with several changes of water, before being arranged on the slice of toast.

worms

Earthworm Patties

1¹/₂ lbs. ground earth
    worms (purified)
¹/₂ cup butter, melted
1 tsp. lemon rind, grated
1¹/₂ tsp. salt
¹/₂ tsp. white pepper
2 tbs. soda water
1 egg, beaten
1 cup dry bread crumbs
2 tbs. butter
1 cup sour cream

Combine earthworms,
melted butter, lemon rind,
salt, and pepper. Stir in
soda water. Shape into
patties and dip in beaten
egg, then in breadcrumbs.
Place in heated butter and
cook for 10 minutes, turning once. Place patties on
hot serving dish. Serve
with heated sour cream
on top.

Courtesy of Matthew Stewart,
The Incredible Edible Wild

As I was growing up in the United States, I remember that when someone felt rejected and angry they told their parents, "I'm going to go eat a worm!" I suppose they figured that by making such a nasty threat, the parent would give in. It never happened. And I don't know anyone who actually ate a worm, either.

Today I listen carefully when someone says that worms may be the meal of the future, or at least part of it—along with other life forms I once never thought were edible. I know now that worms are good to eat and so numerous as to be an answer to the food shortage that soon the entire world may face.

Like too many other great foods, worms have an unfortunate reputation, at least in the language and culture that shaped my childhood, when girls were made of "sugar and spice and everything nice" and boys were made of "worms and snails and puppy dogs' tails." Later in life, I heard people insult one another by calling out, "You worm!" And to use dubious means to accomplish or escape something was to "worm your way" into or out of it. The only positive thing I can think of referred to ambition and reward: "the early bird gets the worm."

When I was growing up, worms were what you put on a hook when you went fishing, captured in the early morning after a rain, when the "nightcrawlers" were still sliming around in the rectangle of crab grass we called our front yard. Later, in biology class, I learned that they were the earth's great composters and recyclers, transforming decaying organic matter and everyday dirt into worm "castings"— excrement, if you want to be frank—turning the soil over like tiny underground plows, giving the soil valuable nutrients. In just one acre, there can be a million or more worms, eating ten tons of vegetation a year, turning over tons of soil. Gardeners and farmers welcomed earthworms like sunshine and rain.

It is for such reasons that a sizeable earthworm industry exists today. All over the world, small businesses are selling worms by the bucket for what is called "vermicomposting." Just throw some of the critters into a box with some dirt, add lawn clippings and the kitchen garbage—apple cores, coffee grounds, that sort of thing—and the worms will quietly turn it into rich potting soil. There's not even any smell. Or, just add them to your garden and besides adding nutrition, they leave tunnels behind to let in air and water.

There also are dozens of entrepreneurs selling start-up kits and instructions telling how to join their ranks. The idea is: you buy some worms and "bins," or propagation boxes, that serve as "farms," then just sit back with a can of beer, watch the sunset, and let the worms reproduce. Then you sell them, either by mail (the post office and most couriers accept them), in a shop, or door-to-door in your neighborhood, although that last choice may get you some odd looks.

As desirable as this creature may be to farmers, home gardeners, and fishermen, very little credit has yet been given in the developed world to the earthworm as a food, and a shame it is, too, because earthworms are seventy to eighty-two percent protein (the

---

Another Odd Critter to Behold

The earthworm is a strange creature and that may explain, at least partly, why so many humans continue to think it's only good for bait and putting nitrogen back into the earth. The front end and rear end are hard to differentiate. They are slimy, moisture playing a key role in their survival. Although their gastrointestinal system is comparable to a human's—mouth, esophagus, intestine, anus, etc.—the worm has no legs, brain or lungs, but has five "hearts." It also is capable of producing sixty percent of its body weight per day in urine.

In addition, some species of night-crawlers can regenerate themselves when cut in half, occasionally creating a worm with two tails or two heads. There's one species found in South America that is eight feet long, making it clear why a movie starring Fred Ward and Kevin Bacon called *Tremors* is about huge, man-eating earthworms. Names like Red Wiggler and European Nightcrawler don't help lighten the image, either. Finally, worms have both male and female reproductive organs, making them hermaphroditic, although it still takes two to make a baby worm.

scientific findings vary) and the taste is pretty good, as well. Worms have always been only one step away in the human food chain via birds and fish, and in the case of Australian aborigines, New Zealand's Maoris, and some Chinese, it was and is a direct food source.

It should be understood, by the way, that many creatures called "worms" are not. Mealworms, for instance, are larvae that turn into beetles, and the "worms" in bottles of the popular Mexican booze, mescal grow up to be moths. Earthworms, on the other hand—and there are about six thousand species—are found in all regions of the world except in deserts and frozen areas.

Like larvae, worms should be purged before eating, an easy task: just put them in a container of moistened cornmeal for forty-eight hours as soon as you catch them or receive them live in the morning post. Then they can be washed and cooked right away, or washed and frozen for later use. To wash worms, rinse them vigorously in cold water, then blot dry on paper, removing any that have died. (They're the ones that aren't moving.)

Most often, worms are boiled or baked. Two pots of boiling water are used, transferring the worms from the first to the second after cooking for about fifteen minutes, then boiling again for another fifteen minutes—to remove the mucus. More boiling is okay if any mucus remains. To bake earthworms, they must be frozen first (so they won't wriggle off the baking pan), then defrosted and put on several layers of paper toweling on a baking sheet. Thirty minutes later, yum.

The baked worms may be eaten as snacks, perhaps with some salt and other seasoning; ground into a meal for use in a cake or bread; or included in any other dish that calls for meat. The Aztecs in Mexico and other primitive peoples usually baked them over a fire or in the sun, then pulverized them for use in a simple bread or stew. *The Worm Book* (1998) by Loren Nancarrow and Janet Hogan Taylor takes a more modish approach, suggesting recipes for Vermicelli with Earthworm Meatballs (adding earthworm flour to

ground beef), Oatmeal Earthworm-Raisin Muffins, and Caramel Earthworm Brownies. In another book, *Urban Wilderness: A Guidebook to Resourceful City Living* (1979), the author, Christopher Nyerges, suggests coating the worms with flour, browning them in butter, adding bouillon and simmering, then mixing in sautéed onions and mushrooms, and covering with sour cream.

And...they are cheap. If you don't have any in your yard or don't feel comfortable wandering around the public park or school yard after dark with a bag and a flashlight, there are dozens of sources where you can get up to a thousand large ones for only US$25; snack-sized "cups" of twenty-five go for about a dollar.

So far, the worm has not made many inroads as a food. Only a few are championing the wriggler's edibility. In Butler, Pennsylvania, in 1998, however, students in a Knoch High School eleventh grade class fried worms, coated them with chocolate, took deep breaths, closed their eyes and swallowed as part of an experiment in alternative food sources.

"I did it 'cause it was cool," said student Josh Murdoch. "It's really not that bad."

Sources

Worms and worm-raising equipment from Worm World Inc., 12425 NW CER 231, Gainesville, FL 32609, phone (352) 485-1235, fax (352) 336-3680; VermiCo, P.O. Box 1134, Merlin, OR 97532, phone (541) 476-9626, fax (541) 476-4555, email: <vermi-co@cdsnet.net>; Solana Recyclers Inc., 137 N. El Camino Real, Encinitas, CA 92024, phone (760) 436-7986, fax (760) 436-8263, email <solana@adnc.com>; New York Worms, 7 Germaine St., Glen Cove, NY 11542, phone (516) 759-3538, fax (516) 671-0917; Flowerfield Enterprises, 10332 Shaver Rd., Kalamazoo, MI 49024, phone (616) 327-0108.

A History with Twists and Turns

Worms have been around for about 120 million years and weren't always shunned by society. In Cleopatra's time, Egyptians believed they were sacred, and Socrates, usually credited with knowing what he was talking about, called them "the intestines of the soil." Charles Darwin studied them for nearly four decades, saying, "It may be doubted whether there are many other animals in the world which have played so important a part in the history of the world." He even wrote a book about them, *The Formation of Vegetable Mould Through the Action of Worms With Observations on Their Habits*. (Why is it that academics have such a hard time with titles?)

Loren Nancarrow and Janet Hogan Taylor write in *The Worm Book* (1998)—now there's a title I can live with—that most earthworms were killed in North America during the last ice age and that they were reintroduced by early European settlers in the seventeenth and eighteenth centuries. "Most worms arrived in the soil clinging to the roots of favorite plants brought to settle the new land,' they said. 'The settlers' ships also used soil as ballast, and this was off-loaded at ports once it was no longer needed. The soil contained many earthworms, which gradually spread out from the many ports. Some farmers, after seeing plants in the port cities do better with the earthworms, deliberately introduced the earthworms to their land."

fish eggs

Iranian beluga caviar served in the traditional way at London's Caviar House Restaurant: a spoonful on a freshly made blini.

I joined the Japanese women squatting at the ocean's edge at low tide, reaching cautiously into the tidal pools to lift sea urchins from the bottom. For every half-dozen to dozen gathered, each of the women seemed unable to resist eating one. The sea urchins—in Hawaii, where I lived at the time—were at the largest only three inches in diameter, each one a fragile, crustaceous dome covered with spines that looked like the pincushion my mother had in her sewing kit, with all the pins reversed and standing on end, sharp ends pointing out. To step on or handle a sea urchin may be painful, and their harvest is an activity defined by caution.

The women were gossiping, watching the sea for incoming waves, carefully turning the urchins over, the spiny top held in a gloved hand, to open them from the bottom with the unprotected fingers of their other hand or a knife, deftly breaking the invertebrate's shell, extracting the digestive system to get at the orange genital glands and eggs, attached to the top of the shell.

This is the edible portion, called "the coral." They then raised the broken shells to their mouths and sucked the eggs into their mouths. They gave one to me, along with a protective glove. I mimicked their opening ritual awkwardly, but was able to get to the eggs. The taste carried the tang of salt, mixed with a hint of iodine. The texture was similar to caviar, or sturgeon eggs. As it should have been. These, too, were eggs from the sea.

The women were showing me how to harvest the small, spiny creatures that they would serve, raw, with crackers that night to their husbands with the customary sake after work, or serve on balls of moist rice, a kind of sushi (called *uni*). But the roe tastes so good fresh from the sea, sparkling with brine, the women couldn't resist. They had to eat a few. It was like eating affordable caviar.

The sturgeon that swim in the Caspian Sea, adjacent to Russia, the fish that produces the "real" caviar today, may soon be declared a threatened species because the worldwide demand has overwhelmed the number of fish. (More about caviar in a minute.) If this is so, and the supply can't meet demand, or regulations cut back the capture of the fish, urchin roe could take up some of the commercial slack. It's an expensive delicacy for what is usually no more than a canapè, but compared to the least expensive caviar, urchin roe is a bargain. There are about seven hundred species of sea urchin in the world and all are delicious. Both the males and females bear edible eggs. It's best to use the roe within twenty-four hours and to keep it refrigerated until used.

Served in a sushi bar, atop the ubiquitous nugget of rice, or on a whole-grain cracker with finely chopped onion, lime juice, salt and pepper—as is popular in Chile—urchin roe is a perfect hors d'oeuvre. The classic recipe in Japan calls for *kanten* (agar-agar), which is processed from sea vegetables, not animal protein, to be added to the eggs. It jells more firmly than conventional gelatin, although that may also be used. This makes the dish more economical, while holding the crumbly eggs together, preventing them falling off the rice.

It may also be turned into a main course. In South America, the urchin, or *erizo*, grow large—some species up to ten inches in diameter—and are cooked in omelettes and other dishes. In France, where they are called *oursins*, or sea eggs, they may be boiled in seawater and eaten with the fingers. The eggs may also be crushed into a paste to flavor sauces, soufflès, and to accompany seafood. A paste called *neri uni*, sold bottled at most Oriental groceries, may be blended with eggs to make a glaze for boiled fish.

The food encyclopedia *Larousse Gastronomique* offers no fewer than five recipes where what is called in France a "sea chestnut" or a "sea hedgehog" is the key ingredient. Added for its rich taste—the champion flavor in a hearty soup with green crabs and rockfish, in an omelette, in a sauce with butter and eggs for fish, in a purèe with hollandaise sauce that is used to fill puff pastries, and in a mixture of diced tomato, chopped shallots, peeled shellfish, heavy cream, whipped butter, cognac, and white wine, which is returned to the empty, cleaned urchin shells and baked. Sprinkled with chervil leaves. Served with a good French wine, of course.

On to caviar, a dish that both Russians and Euro-Americans perceive as a delicious luxury food. The legend and lore surrounding caviar, the eggs of the sturgeon, goes back to at least to the days of Aristotle, who wrote about Greek banquets that ended with a trumpet fanfare introducing a heaping platter of caviar garnished with flowers. The Persians called the eggs the *Chav-Jar*, meaning "cake of power" and, later, in England the sturgeon was called the "Royal Fish of England" when King Edward II decreed that all sturgeon caught had to be given to feudal lords.

But it was in Czarist Russia where caviar hit its zenith. Nicholas II taxed sturgeon fishermen what amounted to a total of eleven tons of top-grade caviar each year, to be served at royal feasts. So passionate was the Czarist appetite, the favored species, the sterlet sturgeon, is virtually extinct.

A hundred years ago, it was plentiful, not only in Europe, but also in waters near North America, where along the Eastern United States it was set out on the bars in saloons much the way peanuts and popcorn are today, a salty snack that was believed to increase the patrons' thirst. Until the 1900s, the United States produced 150,000 tons a year, mainly in New Jersey. So common was it in some waterways—for example, the Delaware and Hudson Rivers—a serving of the best caviar was bargain-priced at five U.S. cents. Increased production in Europe drove the price down in France, to forty centimes for a kilo, little more than the cost of a loaf of bread.

But all good things don't last and as the number of sturgeon rapidly dropped, and the source of the prime caviar, the Caspian Sea, was isolated by two world wars, the price of the eggs went up again, until only the wealthy could afford them.

This is when much of the ritual was instituted, in the same way that the "right" way and the "wrong" way to drink expensive wine developed. For the connoisseur, caviar was never mixed with chopped egg, onion or sour cream and always was served either on toast points or a bland, unsalted cracker. It was never to be served with a metal spoon, as it would contaminate the flavor; instead, spoons made from bone, tortoise shell, or mother-of-pearl were used. The preferred drinks? Frozen vodka to honor the Russian heritage, of course, or a very dry champagne, or when the caviar snobs wanted to go slumming, a sparkling or a dry white wine.

There was also argument about "grades" of caviar. Beluga, produced by the largest species, was regarded by many as the best, thus was the most expensive. This was light to dark gray in color with large granules and a delicate skin. Osetra caviar had smaller grains a dark brown to a golden yellow in color; it has its champions, too. While Sevruga, a product of the smallest sturgeons, which are most prolific and give small gray eggs, is the cheapest.

There is, in fact, a fourth grade, "pressed" caviar, a thick, marmalade-like spread that is made from the ripest and broken eggs by pressing them in cheesecloth to remove the moisture. Some say the result is too salty, but many Russian caviar fanciers insist it is the best.

While most who can't afford it, or don't like the saltiness (in much the same way that anchovies and other highly salted foods are shunned) or reject the 'idea' of eating any eggs that didn't come from a chicken, caviar is dismissed.

Yet, in the Caspian Sea and some Russian rivers, it continues to be a major industry. Here, the sturgeon are caught in large nets and the females of egg-bearing age

Sources
Caviar House, 161 Piccadilly, London W1V 9DF, phone: +44 171 409 0445, fax: +44 171 493 1667, and all terminals of London Heathrow and Gatwick airports

La Fayette International Trading Inc., 1 Northwood Dr., Suite 4, Orinda, CA 94563, phone (510) 254-3447, fax (510) 254-3390, email <MrCaviar@ix.netcom.com>. Not for budget diners: overnight shipping in the United States costs US$25–35, and $75 for Canada, Europe, Australia, Japan and other Asian countries.

are stunned by a blow to the head with a wooden club. They are taken ashore, where they're given another knock, then cut open. The egg sack is removed and the "berries" are rolled gently across a grate to separate the eggs by size. After washing, a "Master Salt Blender" grades the caviar and salts it, depending on the quality of the eggs and the final product desired. The salt acts as a preservative and curing agent, causing the eggs to become firm. Borax may be added for the European market to give them a softer, sweeter finish—in the United States, borax is regarded as an undesirable additive—and after all excess liquid has been removed, the eggs are packed in lacquer-coated tins. The caviar may also be pasteurized for longer shelf life, and sold in jars.

For those who like fish eggs, and cannot afford caviar, there are numerous alternatives. (Technically, roe refers to the reproductive glands of both the male and female fish; the eggs are called "hard roe," the sperm or "milt" of the male "soft roe.") Salmon roe, the large, bright-red eggs from the Atlantic salmon, is prized for its decorative qualities as well as its flavor, while the golden whitefish produces tiny yellow eggs with a delicate taste used primarily as a garnish. The eggs of the cod (often smoked), Grey mullet, tuna, mackerel, carp, and lumpfish may also be used. In Japan, the roe most commonly served in a sushi bar, after *uni* and *ikura* (salmon roe), are *tobiko* (flying-fish roe), often served with the bright yellow yolk of a quail egg on top, and *masago* (the roe of capelin, a kind of smelt), while *kazunoko* (herring roe) is prized as a traditional New Year's dish.

As with sea urchin—and the caviar snobs with their dry toast points and mother-of-pearl spoons be damned—fish eggs go well with dozens of dishes. They can be used as a topping on scrambled eggs or wrapped into an omelette, mixed with sour cream and used to stuff baby red potatoes, stirred with softened butter to top grilled or poached fish, added to egg salad, or used as a garnish with beef tartare, broiled oysters or clams, cold soups and open-faced cucumber sandwiches.

Finally, there is shellfish roe, most notably and commonly, the red-orange eggs found in pregnant female crabs. In some parts of the world, the eating of female crabs is banned and those that are captured must be returned immediately to the sea to insure a continued crab population. In other areas, the eggs are so cherished that in markets the females have a portion of their abdomens cut away to show the presence of roe. And they command a higher price.

birds

birds

One of the most popular protein sources the world over today is a bird: the chicken, a domestic fowl that is easily digested, lending itself to preparation in hundreds of enticing ways, from soup to chop suey to paella to McDonald's and KFC. Other feathered species are popular as well—including turkey, duck, goose, and guinea fowl in the farmyard category, and among the numerous game (or hunted) birds, pheasant, grouse, quail, partridge, and wild duck.

There are many more species that find their way to the dinner table today less frequently, or at least in limited distribution and geography. Ostrich and emu, for example, are just now winning an audience outside their natural habitats in Australia and South Africa. While songbirds are a common dish in much of Asia, Africa, and Latin America, in the west they are almost completely overlooked.

Birds have much to offer. The meat has less fat than red meat and it is rich in proteins and B vitamins. And, birds are everywhere to be found, most species usually in abundance.

The smaller birds offer far less meat than is found in domesticated fowl, but if the game is young, the strong, fragrant aroma of the flesh more than compensates. Because so many are small, the bones (even the heads) often may be consumed as well, depending on how they're cooked.

Although wild birds have a culinary history that goes back to when the first human figured out a way to catch one and make it a part of the meal—something to fill in when mammals were unavailable—today they play a relatively small role in much of the world cuisine. Today, birds are regarded in Euro-American neighborhoods as something to watch hop around on the lawn, sing in the trees (or in cages), and lend a beauty to the world that can only come from their inimitable ability to fly. What's not given credit is that they're also a delicious treat.

Many birds taste like what they eat, their delicate flesh flavored by juniper berries, grapes, or other fruit, and they may be prepared in the same way as quail—grilled; sautéed in butter; braised with grapes; stuffed with ham, truffles, forcemeat or chicken livers—or a mixture—and roasted on skewers; poached and glazed; jellied; in a casserole dish (sprinkled with brandy before serving); made into a light paté; or cooked in pies and terrines.

Birds are also valued for their eggs; a perfectly balanced food, fairly low in calories, providing all the amino acids essential for human nutrition, and easy to digest, although they contain a high level of animal fat, which is found mainly in the yolks. What makes an egg "strange?" It is in what happens to it on the way to the mouth. Some are halfway hatched before serving, so that there are little bird embryos inside. Others are, by a simple process turned green or black. And cherished, every one of them.

ostrich & emu

Some years ago, while staying with a family in Capetown, South Africa, I found myself alone in the kitchen, foraging for something to eat. I opened the refrigerator door and saw, for the first time, an ostrich egg. It was about the size of an American football, somewhat fatter in the middle and rounded at the ends, and it occupied nearly half an entire refrigerator shelf. Before the day was out, it became the centerpiece for a meal, an omelet for ten, equal to about twenty chicken eggs. I was impressed. In the 1970s, the ostrich was not commonly regarded as a protein source, at least not outside its usual habitats, mainly in Australia and South Africa. Times have changed.

I'm drawn to ostriches. Like many people, I'm attracted to the physical oddities in the animal world. Giraffes, duck-billed platypuses, elephants, that sort of thing. Animals that look like they've been made out of spare parts for several species, or are too large to be practical or believable. They appear to be Mother Nature's private jokes, like dinosaurs. Ostriches, with their long, skinny necks and legs, their bulky bodies covered with feathers, and such big adorable eyes, must be liked as well as gaped at. Is it not for this reason that Big Bird is such a favorite character on television's *Sesame Street*?

That said, the ostrich's image in much of the world is that of a long-legged, long-necked, cowardly creature that sticks its head in the sand to avoid confrontation. This impression may be based on the fact that when the bird is resting, it sits on its haunches and extends its neck so it can look out for danger. This means all anyone sees from a distance is the ample bulk of its body with a head held close to the earth. In fact, the ostrich is not cowardly and can be quite aggressive. When a bird up to eight or nine feet in height weighing as much as 300 pounds, with a ground speed of up to forty miles an hour takes a disliking to some intruder into ostrich territory, that

someone or something is best advised to escape by any means available, preferably by horse or car. *The Guinness Book of Records* calls it the world's largest and fastest bird. Its egg is also the largest.

The ostrich originated in the Asiatic steppes during the Eocene Epoch, forty to fifty million years ago, and once ranged through much of Asia, Europe, and Africa. Ancient Egyptians trained them to pull carts and over two thousand years ago, the Egyptian queen Arsinoe rode an ostrich with a saddle. Teams of ostriches sometimes were used in Rome to pull chariots.

The ostrich's history as a food is long, going back to the days of the Roman empire, when strange foods—even for the time—seemed to be almost mandatory cuisine for emperors. Vitellius, considered the greatest glutton in all history by Robert Ripley, the world-famous collector of oddities, was known to favor ostrich brains, alongside the livers of parrot fish and the tongues of nightingales.

More recently and commonly, and certainly more affordably, the ostrich has been captured, butchered, and cooked by the Aborigine in Australia and the Zulu in South Africa. (The latter group's tall, fearsome warriors also included the feathers as part of their battle dress.) Until modern times, these birds were never farmed, but killed in the wild, usually with spears and traps.

Ostrich farming really began in the last half of the nineteenth century and by the early 1900s, it had spread from South Africa and Australia to Algeria, France, and the United States when there was a demand for the plumes used in feather dusters, as decorations on women's expensive hats and feather boas, and as accessories on showgirl costumes. Sally Rand, a famous fan dancer, star of the vaudeville and music hall stages in Europe and America in the 1920s through the 1940s, performed naked using a large ostrich feather fan to mask her nudity from the audience.

When the feathers—and fan dancers—eventually went out of style, so did ranching. Today, it's back, big-time, and not just for the feathers, but largely for the leather and meat. When diners around the world began to look for low-cholesterol alternatives to beef, ostrich farms popped up from China to Holland to Israel to North America. By 1997, there were approximately 70,000 birds in Australia. The same year, just two years after China imported its first eight birds, there were four-hundred farms across twenty provinces, with a total population of about 80,000. While South Africa was home to more than a quarter of a million birds, and the United States boasted 10,000 ostrich farmers with as many as 500,000 birds, located primarily in the South and Southwest where the climate and environment most closely resembled their natural habitat. Even in wintry Canada, there were thriving (heated) ostrich ranches in almost all the provinces.

How this happened is a tale in modern-day marketing. In a report in *Ostrich News* in 1993, the owners of the Day-O Ranch in the United States said they were intrigued when asked to invest in "a 400-pound chicken that has red meat that tastes like a cow, but with less fat, cholesterol, and calories than chicken or turkey; a fourteen- to twenty-square-foot hide that brings $40 to $50 a square foot wholesale for boots, briefcases, wallets, etc.; feathers for dusting new cars and computer components; and lays a three-and-a-half-pound egg that equals twenty-four chicken eggs." But when told how much it cost to buy a pair of breeders, they laughed and bought a Christmas tree farm instead. Later, as the market for meat, oil, leather, and feathers increased, they changed their minds and now Day-O is one of the many farms spreading the ostrich gospel on the Internet.

By the early 1990s, ostrich became the investment flavor, or curiosity, of the week, in the same way that people once invested in mink and chinchilla ranches

for the anticipated profit from the sale of furs. In 1993, ostrich breeding farms were selling a pair of chicks to start-up farmers for US$600, two three-month-olds for $2,000, and two adult breeders for $25,000! In 1994, cost of a breeding pair of emu was even higher, as much as $100,000!

Though start-up costs were high, it was pointed out that a healthy female ostrich, on average, could lay up to fifty eggs a year in captivity and that the birds were ready for slaughter at around a year old. With the meat selling at premium prices, profit seemed assured. In New Zealand, one new rancher named his first two birds Cash and Flo.

However, patience was required, along with the beginning bank account. "You need to wait two or three years for a good return," Raymond Lam, managing director of Global Ostrich Investments, Ltd., told me in 1997. His was one of several companies that sold ownership of birds that were raised on farms in Australia—the idea being that investors owned the birds and let the farmers do all the work, then reaped a share of the profits when the birds began to reproduce.

The concept of buying what might thus be called "ostrich futures" was not without its critics. Chas Dale, the general manager of the Australian Ostrich Company Ltd., in a phone interview disparaged the scheme. He told me that his company, formed by a non-profit ostrich farmers' association to market the leather and meat, would accept the $4,000 to $5,000 it believed a pair of proven breeders was worth, but warned that some investment companies charged the investor double that figure, or more.

"We believe the market will grow slowly," he said, "and part of the reason is that the meat is expensive. We're emphasizing the health aspects. We're targeting upmarket restaurants that will offer it as a superior meat. When you order lobster, you expect to pay for it. It's the same with ostrich."

Mr. Dale was right and when the market grew too slowly for some investors, the cost of a pair of breeders dropped to about half in just three years. But interest in

Sources

Live ostriches from Global Ostrich, Inc., 5131 Brand Rd., Dublin, OH 43017, phone (614) 764-1685, fax (614) 798-9899; HCR 1, P.O. Box 64F, Willcox, AZ 85643, phone and fax (520) 384-0033; and Rooster Cogburn Ostrich Ranch, P.O. Box 1087, I-10 and Exit #219, Red Rock, AZ 85245, phone (520) 466-3265, fax (520) 466-3634.

All cuts, from steaks to liver and heart, from B.C. Meats, Ltd. Co., P.O. Box 36, Ferris, TX, 75125, phone (972) 842-2219, fax (972) 544-2291, email <ratites@connect.net>.

More great variety, from tenderloins to soup bones (with marrow) to paté to jerky to mousse, by mail from Ostrich Purveyors of America, Ltd. Co., 3987 N. Beltline Rd., Irving, TX 75038, phone (214) 659-0810, fax (214) 257-1506, email <dgray@connect.net>.

This page: Like any other egg, those of the ostrich should be kept in the refrigerator if not being used immediately, although not in the usual rack in the door. *Opposite:* Lionel Wongawol and Adrian Tressider monitor emu eggs at the Wikina Emu Farm.

the industy continued to grow. Meat started appearing on selected restaurant menus worldwide. The distinctive tan hides with the evenly spaced dark dots were made into boots, shoes, belts, wallets and purses, seventy percent of the leather going to Japan. Ostrich oil became an ingredient in cosmetics and drugs. The feathers were discovered to be free of static electricity, so that when you brushed something with them, the dust was cleaned off completely; consequently they were used on cars before they were spray-painted, and also in the assembly of computer disks to brush away dust before the two sides were joined.

The meat market was given a boost when "mad cow disease" crippled the European demand for beef in 1996. In the search for alternative protein sources, ostrich was one of the big winners. It looked like beef and tasted like beef and was—guaranteed—"mad cow" free. Because of its lower interior and exterior fat deposits, it ranked lowest in calories when compared in a study to eighteen other meats, including pork, rabbit, chicken, and duck. Ostrich flesh also was higher in "good" cholesterol levels and lower in the "bad" cholesterol count. And a drumstick could weigh as much as fifteen pounds.

For a time, British Airways served ostrich medallions in its first class cabin and today, ostrich is offered in upscale restaurants from Dallas to London to Singapore, for as much as US$55 for a top loin or tenderloin plate. Once upon a time, ostrich (and emu and rhea) were cooked simply, chopped into steaks and roasted on a spit over an open fire. Those days are gone, along with the feather boas and hats. Now, the bird is served like any other gourmet meat. The Australian Ostrich Co. Ltd. distributes a glossy brochure full of recipes that includes such treats as (take a deep breath) Coriander Green Curry Ostrich Served with Cardamom Scented Rice and Cucumber Riata...and (take another breath) Bengal Five-Spiced Ostrich with Moroccan Couscous and Tomato Salsa.

song birds, pigeons, & doves

Pigeons with Bacon

4 young pigeons
2 oz. butter, unsalted
Salt and pepper
Winter savory
4 oz. fat bacon
1/2 lb. small onions
1/2 lb. carrots
1 lb. small potatoes
1 small head cauliflower

Pluck, draw, and wipe the pigeons. Put a knob of butter in each, worked with salt and pepper and the savory, chopped fine. Cube the bacon and sweat it in a casserole until the fat runs.

Meanwhile, peel the onions (tiny ones are the best and can be used whole) and chop them. Peel and slice the carrots. Scrub the small potatoes. Divide the cauliflower into small florets.

Preheat the oven to 375°F.

Turn the birds in the hot bacon fat until they sizzle. Tuck all the vegetables around in the casserole and add 2 tablespoons water. Sprinkle with salt and pepper and a little more chopped savory. Bring swiftly to the boil. Cover tightly, sealing down the lid with flour and water. No steam must be allowed to escape.

Stew in the oven for an hour. Unseal the lid at the table. The gardener has his revenge. No other accompaniment but good Belgian beer.

Elisabeth Luard, *European Peasant Cooking*

I'm an early riser, usually up before dawn, and on the morning of my first visit to Hanoi I noticed something odd: there were no birds singing. I looked out my hotel window. I saw no birds. Well, I thought, maybe it's the neighborhood. All day, I continued to look for birds on the street and in the trees, but I didn't see any. At the end of the day, I asked someone why there appeared to be no birds in Hanoi.

"We ate them," she said, matter-of-factly.

There are many foods that often are called "survival" foods and I suppose the birds of Vietnam's capital fell into that category, just as rats did in Paris during the Revolution and again during World War Two. In various places during times of famine people even ate tree bark and grass or anything else they could find. When I visited Hanoi, Vietnam had only recently emerged from the embargo imposed by the United States and during that twenty-year period, the country experienced extreme poverty and deprivation, when food, along with just about everything else, was scarce. So of course the Vietnamese ate the birds in the trees.

This is a story with a happy ending. Most people in Hanoi now have enough to eat, the birds have returned, and my mornings there sound like mornings anywhere else. At the same time, Hanoi is a city where you can order a delicious entrée of pigeon, dove, and a variety of songbirds in restaurants too numerous to count—birds that are frequently farm-raised. Birds have returned to the "legitimate" menu, leaving "survival" behind.

Over the millennia, "bird-catchers" supplied the gourmand and peasant alike with a wide variety of birds known not only for their splendor and song, but also for their succulence. The ancient Greeks hunted wood pigeons, jackdaws, owls, and seagulls, importing flamingos from Africa, while the Romans stuffed wild boar with thrushes before roasting. In sixteenth-century France, doves were cooked with other birds—curlews, wood pigeons and egrets among them—and, according to *Larousse Gastronomique*, "were more highly prized by some than beef, veal, and pork." Tits, lapwings, warblers, curlews, plovers, thrushes, robins, finches, sparrows, larks, and jays—all made wonderful meals across England and the European continent. Remember the children's rhyme about "four and twenty blackbirds baked in a pie" that dates back to the nineteenth century? Even the noisy crow was cherished in soups and stews. Of course, the most popular wild birds for eating have always been the larger game birds—the heron, the duck, the pheasant, the grouse, and among the smaller ones, the quail. But the song birds, the ones that did not greet the Hanoi dawn a few years ago, have long been welcomed at meal time and they are served in many parts of the world today.

In much of rural Southeast Asia, small rice birds known for their silky gray feathers, part of the sparrow family, are grilled until crisp and eaten in one or two bites, head and all. In 1995, a group of Australian Aborigines revived a centuries-old yolla bird industry that once harvested one-million birds during the annual five-week season, offering a range of new products from health pills to paté. About the same time, some four-hundred blue peacocks were introduced to the press in Yunnan province in China by a private company that said it planned to increase the number to 20,000 by 1999, with an eye to the gourmet market. Meanwhile in Spain and elsewhere along the Mediterranean, birds were still caught by small boys and sold, strung together in garlands, by black-clad old women at the entrance to villages.

"When the birds are cooked with the powerful aromatics so beloved of the Mediterranean palate," Elisabeth Luard wrote in *European Peasant Cookery* (1988), "there is not much difference in flavor between the farmed and the wild." She was talking about quail, but said it was the thrush that she had in mind when she included in her book recipes for Grilled Small Birds, Stewed Small Birds, and Small Bird Paté. She said she made the substitution because her book was published in England, where the thrush is protected and may not be killed. In other European countries and North America, the bird exists in great numbers.

Birds usually are caught in cages, or when they are moulting and unable to fly, baited with grain. They are prepared in much the same way as other animals, though they are usually plucked and cooked with the skin on instead of being skinned, the feathers to come off just before cooking time and never before. Fred Smith, a popular TV chef known as the Frugal Gourmet, warns that carrion eaters may be prone to infection, lice, and ticks, and says that they, along with old crows, blackbirds, and parrots, are best boiled. The young specimens can be stuffed with herbs and fruit and roasted. Fish-eating birds, he says, don't keep fresh longer than a day and should be skinned to avoid the fishy taste.

Of all species of song birds, pigeons and doves may be the most commonly eaten, in part because they have existed in such great numbers over so much geography. Pigeon stew was enjoyed in ancient Egypt and in imperial Rome, chefs clipped the birds' wings or broke their legs, then fattened them on chewed bread before cooking. During the reign of Louis XIV in France, it was fashionable to serve pigeon in a stew with peas. While menus for ordinary households in eighteenth- and nineteenth-century Europe and America frequently called for "potted pigeons," a sort of casserole, and "palpatoon or pupton of pigeons," a kind of hot paté.

Today, cage-raised pigeons under a month old, called squabs, may be found in Chinese poultry markets in many large cities, and commonly in Asian ones, frequently sold alive. Bruce Cost, in his book *Asian Ingredients,* noted that "plucking them is a hassle—unlike a chicken you can't scald them to loosen their feathers." (Although he said chilling them for a few hours in a refrigerator tightened the flesh, so there was less danger of tearing during the plucking process.) Once cleaned and dressed, the author said, they could be seasoned and roasted, grilled, or fried, Chinese-style, or like duck, seasoned and steamed or fried. "At around one pound apiece," said Mr. Cost, "they're an ideal size and have many times the flavor of a Cornish game hen."

Ms. Luard credits the Belgians for being excellent gardeners, numbering the Brussels sprout and Belgian chicory among their contributions to the vegetable markets of the world, but it is the battle between the sower of seed and those the farmer sees as seed-stealers—the birds—that inspired a recipe in her book where pigeon was cooked with the gardener's vegetables.

Pigeon eggs are a cherished food, as well, but here the price is dear, both in the retail cost to the customer, who may have to order the eggs—you rarely see them in shops—and to the birds themselves, who lay only two eggs a year, and if both are taken, sometimes stop laying. Like eggs of other small birds, such as quail, usually they are hardboiled and added to other dishes.

A final word about pigeon. The birds that proliferate in urban areas —called "street squab" in some

2,000-Year-Old Flamingo

One of the classic cookery books of history is *The Art of Cooking*, more commonly called *The Roman Cookery Book*, which was written during the first century by Gavius Apicius. Although modern editions of the book appear to have been expanded and much changed over time, his instructions for the preparation of flamingo may still resemble the original text:

"Pluck the flamingo, wash, truss, and put it in a saucepan; add water, dill, and a little vinegar. Halfway through the cooking make a bouquet of leek and coriander and let it cook [with the bird]. When it is nearly done, add defrutum [must or wine reduced by a half or more by boiling] to give it color. Put in a mortar pepper, caraway, coriander, asafetida root, mint, rue; pound; moisten with vinegar, add Jericho dates, pour over some of the cooking-liquor. Put it in the same saucepan, thicken with corn flour, pour the sauce over the bird and serve."

Flamingos used to be seen in large flocks along the southeastern United States, but now are nearly non-existent in the American wild and are seen only in zoos. They continue to thrive in large numbers in South America and East Africa.

cities—belong, like the song birds of post-war Hanoi, in the survival category. In London in 1996, there was a small scandal when more than a thousand pigeons disappeared from beneath Admiral Lord Nelson's imperious nose atop his statue in Trafalgar Square. The birds, which perched in and around Nelson's towering column, were as much a part of London's life as the ravens at the Tower of London. Well, it turned out that two bird-snatchers were scooping up the tourists' feathered friends in batches of thirty or forty at a time and carrying them off in a large box. One of them, a seventeen-year-old named Jason Lidbury, when arrested said he had caught at least 1,500 pigeons in various London locations over six months and sold them for US$3 apiece. To restaurants? Mercy, no. To people who raced pigeons as a hobby, a popular English passtime. He said.

Pigeons raised on farms for restaurants are plumper and cleaner that street pigeons, of course, and if prepared properly taste somewhere between chicken and fish. Some that I've eaten, in Bangkok, were fried to a delicious golden-brown, with enough fat sticking to the skin to keep the meat succulent. The birds were surprisingly meaty—I've had other small birds that seemed to be mostly frail skeletons—and flavorful enough to indicate they had not been subjected the kind of hormonal tampering that produces the large, bland chickens available in most markets.

Technically, there is little scientific difference between a pigeon and a dove, except that the dove generally is regarded as smaller. In fact, some say the rock dove, still thriving in parts of Europe, is the ancestor of all modern species of pigeon. There are several varieties of dove today, many taking their names from their appearance, such as the ringed, collared, and spotted doves, describing feather patterns and coloration. The mourning dove, so named for its plaintive cry, is the most plentiful game bird in North America today and is usually found on farmlands, cleaning up the grain left behind by modern harvesting machines.

birds' nest

"Trial and error" must explain the way many edible foods were discovered. As in: "Oh, that little round thing on that bush over there looks cute, I think I'll eat it." Then, if the courageous or foolhardy caveman or cavewoman who ate it didn't get sick or die, word spread that this little round thing, or berry, might be considered food.

In this manner it must be that a lot of strange stuff got moved from "what the hell is that?" to "oh, boy!"

After all, how delicious do snails, oysters, even chickens look? You can't help wondering how it was that they, along with other commonly eaten dishes—frogs' legs, sharks' fins, ants, and so on—ever found their way to the world's dinner plate.

One of the most puzzling may be birds' nest. How, I wonder, did anyone ever climb to the top of a dark Asian sea cave, look at a bird's nest made largely from saliva that was stuck to the side of the cave, and say, "Hey, I bet that messy piece of housekeeping would make a yummy soup"? One may also wonder why anyone today would be willing to pay a small fortune for a bowl of it.

Bird's nest soup is one of the true culinary enigmas, a high-priced delicacy that is made from the nests of swifts, found in bat-filled caves in Southeast Asia. The nests are made of seaweed, twigs, moss, hair, and feathers glued together by the birds' saliva and the spawn of small fish. Is this something you would pay up to US$300 a bowl for?

Why so expensive? Well, first of all, it's considered by many to be an aphrodisiac, a word—some say myth—that is driving many animal species to the edge of extinction. For centuries, Chinese have given their children the soup, believing it will help them grow. Others consume it to improve their complexion and defeat lung problems, or as an all-purpose tonic.

In addition, its cost is a status symbol. Factor in the physical effort and risk involved in harvesting the limited crop of nests—and the shooting wars being waged over the caves where they are found today—and it is no mystery why the dish is the soup world's most expensive as well as the most mysterious.

There may be no answer to the question why birds' nest soup is believed to be a sexual supplement. Rhino horn, at least, resembles an erect penis, more or less, and it is not too long a reach to think that tiger penis soup might convey the strength and stamina of what

The Guinness Book of Records calls the most dangerous man-eating animal on earth. Why the nests of birds who, just before their breeding season, feed on gelatinous seaweed that makes their salivary glands secrete a thick, glutinous spit, with which they construct their nests, should be added to this aphrodisiac list cannot be fathomed.

So be it. There are tens or hundreds of thousands, perhaps millions, of people—most of them living in Asia or born of Asian heritage—who think birds' nest soup is good for your appearance, sex life, general health, and social status. That is reason enough to make this dish one of the most exalted in modern Oriental cuisine.

The impact on the environment, and to the ultimate survival of the birds, is debatable. Some harvesters insist they have protected the species from extinction by collecting nests only after the baby birds have fledged. But there also are poachers who take the nests early, whether or not there are eggs or chicks in them.

Add to this the impact on the poachers themselves. No one knows how many poachers are killed in the nest wars each year. Best estimates run into the dozens, forgetting those who die when they fall from precariously erected bamboo ladders that may extend as high as three hundred feet. In the wide and amazing world of food stories, the bird's nest soup story surely is one of the most remarkable.

The origin of nest harvesting is, like so much of life, unclear. Dr. Yun-Cheung Kong, professor of biochemistry at the University of Hong Kong, says nests have been part of the Chinese diet for 1,500 years, as good a guess as any. He also notes that early in the Ming Dynasty (1368–1644 A.D.), a Chinese admiral made seven voyages through the "Southern Ocean" and it's believed that one of his missions was to find new sources for the nests, although no documented record has been discovered to confirm this. However, documents do exist showing that fleets of Chinese junks sailed the same waters yearly during the eighteenth and nineteenth centuries, not only to deal in

nests, but also in pepper, sharks' fins, and other items of exotic gourmandise for culinary and medicinal use at home.

An account of the nest-gathering appeared in 1928 in a book published in Sweden, *Forest Life and Adventures in the Malay Archipelago.* It was written by Eric Mjoberg, who was one of those wanderers drawn to the remote corners of the world and determined to share their experiences with the stay-at-homes, a large publishing milieu during the early twentieth century. He said the nests at that time appealed largely to "the almond-eyed sons of the Celestial Empire," a racist remark also typical of the period. He added that the natives he met in Borneo paid a yearly tax of £300 to the Raja of Sarawak for the right to collect the nests, selling them, in turn, for

£4 a kilo. They were harvested, he wrote, with "four-branched, spear-like implements—fixed to a handle several yards in length—and provided at the top with a lighted candle-end. Holding fast with his left hand to the ladder, he gives the nest a poke with his long tool and loosens it from its support, then hauls it down, takes if off the spiked fork and lays it in a rattan basket fastened around his waist."

The harvesting methods have not changed but the fees and earnings have gone up. Today, in Thailand, in the caves of the Rangnok islands, located near the Malaysian border, the Rangnok Laemthong Swallow Nest Company Ltd. has had a monopoly on the collection of nests since 1958. This company, headquartered in Bangkok's Chinatown, in 1994 was granted a five-year concession for which it paid Thailand's government nearly five and a half million U.S. dollars, a concession that was renewed before the expiration date, extending its monopoly through 2003. The amount paid this time was not revealed. It is believed to be twice the previous figure, counting in all the bribes paid for the continued exclusivity.

The search for the nests usually begins in March, when the birds begin mixing their regurgitated spittle with other handy building materials, a process that may take two to four weeks to create a nest that looks like half a tea cup and is affixed to the roof or wall of a cave. The collectors for Rangnok Laemthong insist they do not harvest any nests until the eggs have hatched and the chicks have left the nests, but the extraordinary high prices paid for the new nests has thrown the claim into doubt. It is at this time that they are the most translucent and least contaminated by bird droppings and feathers, thus sell for as much as US$2,000–3,000 per kilo! There are two other harvests, in May and August, by which time the quality of the nests has fallen, but even by the end of August, the price starts at $1,000. These prices then double or triple when sold to Hong Kong, Singapore and to Chinese restaurants in North America and Europe.

Rangnok Laemthong and companies in other

Bird's Nest Capital of the World

"The overall appearance of the place is that of any provincial boom town in Southeast Asia, but actually there is no place quite like Hat Yai anywhere in the world. Southwest from Songkhla Lake, it calls itself southern Thailand's major tourist center, and the brochure issued by the Tourist Authority lists sites like the Southern Culture Village and the Elephant Tusks Waterfall among its chief attractions. But the busloads of Chinese tourists who come over the border from Malaysia—only 37 miles away from the city center—do not all come for the sightseeing. Nor do they all come for the shopping. The two magnets which the tourist brochures do not mention are massage parlors and bird's nest restaurants, and it is these that explain the preponderance of males in those group tours from Malaysia.

"Hat Yai is the bird's nest city par excellence, the place with surely the world's highest concentration of bird's nest retail outlets and restaurants. Here, in any one of dozens of restau-rants, you can have bird's nest in a sweet soup, or in a savory one; served hot, or served cold; braised with shark's fin, or simmered with shredded chicken; flavored with almond and coconut, or mixed with pigeon's eggs and honey.

"What is so extraordinary about this peculiarly Chinese cult is that the bird's nest itself does not actually taste of anything. But this is of no concern to the millions of Chinese who pay through the nose for it; hypochondriac to a man, these people could only think of all the good that it is doing them, and all the afflictions that it is keeping at bay—the digestive troubles it is preventing, the phlegm it is dissolving, the aging process it is retarding, the loss of vigor its tonic qualities are remedying. While not exactly an aphrodisiac, the delicacy is thought to have a bracing effect on masculine vigor, and it seems only right that massage parlors should be interspersed among the bird's nest restaurants in the streets of Hat Yai."

Lynn Pan,
Sons of the Yellow Emperor, 1990

areas—in Java, the Moluccas, Borneo, and Myanmar—argue, logically, that it is in their best interest to preserve and protect the birds, thus insuring future sales. However, it's no surprise that in a region where income is minimal, the nests represent temptation for poachers who have no regard for the survival of the species, only their own survival. The first nests often are gathered even before eggs are laid—which actually is permitted as the adult birds then build another—but later, eggs and baby birds often are thrown away, which is illegal. The poachers, some of them former employees who know the cave locations, bribe the armed guards hired by the companies to safeguard their contracted rights by making them partners in the late-night theft.

The guards patrol the islands with automatic weapons and over the past few years, many poachers as well as innocent fishermen seeking shelter from storms have been killed. In 1992, ten were gunned down in one incident in Thailand and in 1994, more than twenty men were shot. Villagers who saw the bodies said one of the men was found with a Buddha image in his mouth—the victim having put it there, hoping to ensure his safety—while others were lying with their hands together in the *wai* posture, as if knowing they would be killed. The gunmen were found innocent by the Thai judicial system, claiming self-defense.

Many nest gatherers, legal and illegal, also have fallen to their death from the flimsy bamboo climbing ladders. Yet, the risk has not deterred the Dyak tribesmen or Moluccan aborigines or descendants of Muslim Thai fishermen from pursuing the trade for hundreds of years, even though what they are paid represents a tiny percentage of the harvest value. Seasonal nest gatherers in Thailand are paid a monthly salary of about US$80–100, supplemented by an additional $100 for each of the three annual seasons, while long-time workers may earn a bit extra. It is telling that the guards are paid more, about $110 for each season, with subsequent bonuses of $140 per harvest. In a region

where subsistence fishing may offer the only alternative, such income is considered excellent.

The problem is no one knows how many swiftlets and swallows are left. According to a World Conservation Union estimate, the demand for nests has reduced the population by a third. The Convention on International Trade in Endangered Species (CITES) has asked all countries in the region to conduct more scientific research in order to promote the sustainability of the harvesting through management programs. The birds are not considered endangered yet, but few studies have been instigated.

In Thailand, this is blamed on a general disregard for wildlife investigation, but also because the nest harvesting is not in the hands of the Forestry Department, whose job is to oversee wildlife. The responsibility goes instead to the Finance Ministry's Revenue Department, which collects all the fees and taxes, and it is believed that the profits made may form a barrier against such a survey or a review of harvesting practices.

However, there has been some examination made regarding the nutritional value of the soup. The news is not good. Birds' nests have occupied a prominent place in Chinese cuisine and medicine for centuries, but all the reports indicate that it's a waste not only of nests, but also of money and lives. Although the untreated nests have been found high in a water-soluble protein—fifty to sixty percent of volume that could

This Page: A street stall in Bangkok's Chinatown offers birds' nest soup both hot and cold.
Page 128: Brown-rumped, or edible-nest, swiftlets nest 500 feet up a sheer wall of the Gomanton caves in Sabah, Borneo. The nests, woven purely from the bird's saliva, adhere to the surface of the rock, enabling the birds to inhabit locations which are difficult for predators to reach—but not impossible for man!
Page 129: A bowl of sweet birds' nest soup garnished with watermelon balls at the Golden Island Bird's Nest Restaurant in Hong Kong. A tin of cleaned, dry bird's nests is in the foreground.

promote cell division within the immune system, a good thing—it's also been discovered that preparing the nests for consumption removes all but a fraction of one percent. The gluey stuff also contains small amounts of calcium, potassium, and phosphorus, but not in sufficient quantity to do any good, so claims about the soup treating and preventing illnesses is now regarded, officially, as bunk. In 1998, the Nutrition Research Institute at Thailand's Mahidol University compared bottled bird's nest soup with eggs and milk. Twenty-six bottles of the stuff costing a total of about US$100 offered the protein found in one egg, priced at six cents, while 36 bottles were required to match the protein in a fifteen-cent carton of milk.

Such negative notices apparently have little effect. Those who consume the revered soup have not changed their minds about its value, as if to say, "That bowl of soup cost me a small fortune, so it must be good for me." Such is the value that both buyer and consumer may attach to tradition, or superstition.

Nor is there any agreement in the manner of preparation. There isn't even any accord on how the dried nests should be soaked before cooking. Bruce Cost wrote in his book *Asian Ingredients*, "Some feel it's best to soak it overnight in cold water, then clean it, removing feathers and other foreign matter with tweezers, and finally to simmer it for ten minutes in water or stock, and drain it before using it. A quicker method calls for soaking it for one hour in warm water, cleaning it, then soaking it for five minutes in a bowl of hot water in which a little baking soda has been dissolved; it should then be rinsed thoroughly in cold water and squeezed dry."

And this is before the actual cooking begins, when a variety of ingredients—minced chicken and egg white, ham and wine, chrysanthemum petals, or lotus seeds—are added for flavor and texture. Mr. Cost reported a soup that was baked in a pumpkin, another that was steamed with rock sugar. Another source tells of an elegant recipe called Phoenix Swallowing the Swallow, calling for a chicken to be stuffed with bird's nests and double-boiled in a porcelain pot to produce a clear consommé. Still another suggests soaking the nest in hot water for several hours, then, when the strings of the nest begin to unravel, some vegetable oil is added; the goop is then stirred and more hot water is added, bringing the oil and impurities to the top. This process is repeated several times and the noodles are then boiled in chicken or beef stock, along with rice, vermicelli, and lotus seeds. It all sounds like too much work to me and it's no wonder that the soup is rarely prepared at home and is left to the kitchen staff in expensive restaurants.

Birds' nests may, of course, be purchased in Asian groceries and Chinese herbal shops, where it costs upwards of US$300 for a small packet weighing about an ounce—making it literally worth its weight in gold. With so much money changing hands, it is no surprise that a common crime in Hong Kong is the burglary of shops that sell nests, while some street vendors sell phony nests made from *karaya gum*, a harmless plant extract. Back in the gathering grounds of Thailand, a large black market has developed for nests that have either been stolen or skimmed from the official count.

Also for sale in shops today are a number of products containing birds' nest, including an eight-ounce can of liquid manufactured in Hong Kong whose ingredients further include water, sugar, and white fungus. No ingredient percentages are given and the expiration date that was claimed to be printed on the bottom of the can that I bought was missing. As is true when you consume many exotic foods, when you eat (or drink) birds' nest, you get what you get and you have no grounds for complaint.

Until 1950, China was the biggest importer of the nests. Today it is Hong Kong, currently consuming about a hundred tons (worth US$25 million) annually. Chinese communities in North America rank second, accounting for about thirty tons. The soup is offered throughout Asia, as well as in cities around the globe, wherever there are Chinese restaurants and rich Chinese who believe it is good for them.

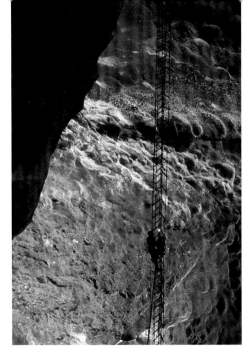

Opposite, above left:
Collectors leave the main
island of Koh Phi Phi in the
south of Thailand for a
day's work in the cave on
nearby Koh Phi Phi Lae.
Opposite, above right: In the
main lower section of the
Gomanton Cave in Sabah,
Borneo, a rattan ladder
measuring over 500 feet in
length is the only means to
reach the upper walls, where
the cleanest nests are found.
A collector climbs
slowly upwards.
Opposite, below: The entrance to Payanak Cave on
Koh Phi Phi Lae, festooned
with lianas and bamboo
scaffolding used for reaching the lower nesting sites.
This page, above left: A
prized nest, part of the collector's haul, is made purely
of the swift's saliva.
This page, above right: In
the Bangkok warehouse of
the Laem Thong Company, a
manager weighs nests.
This page, below: On the
same premises, women
scrub the valuable nests
clean before packing them.

balut

Ray Bruman is an American with an Internet web site called "Ray's List of Weird and Disgusting Foods." In his introduction to a long list, he says, "I have a theory that many (all?) cultures invent a food that is weird or disgusting to non-initiates as a sort of a 'marker.' The kids start out hating it, but at some point they cross over and perpetuate it (perpetrate it) on the next generation. Then they nudge each other when foreigners gasp."

That sounds like balut to me.

Balut is, or are, sixteen- to eighteen-day-old duck or chicken (traditionally duck) embryos, soft-boiled. They are eaten by opening the narrow end of the egg in much the same way a soft-boiled chicken egg is opened. Some aficionados add a sprinkle of salt before sucking out the mush and juices. This is the easy part of the experience. Next you carefully remove the remaining shell, revealing the unborn bird, veins, bones, eyes, beak—a scrawny little thing that looks precisely like what it is: a wet, warm, feathered fetus. More salt may be added, with perhaps a spritz of vinegar, then you just pop the little critter into your mouth and chew, little bird feet and all. Yum. Or so the connoisseurs insist.

While in Manila, I hired a taxi to take me to the balut capital of the world, a neighborhood called Pateros, once a rural suburb, now a part of the city. On the way, I asked my driver if he ate balut.

"Every time I make love to my wife, I eat balut," he said, giving me the thumbs-up sign. "Have five children. Pregnant with number six!"

Pateros became the center of the egg embryo universe many years ago, before it was incorporated into metropolitan Manila, when it was home to many duck farms. As urban sprawl overtook the neighborhood, the duck farmers moved away, mostly to provinces to the north. They still provide the eggs, but to avoid the long commute in heavy traffic, the freshly laid eggs are trucked to Pateros for processing and easy distribution once they are ready to eat.

Following instructions from someone selling balut on the street, we went to an address on Pateros Avenue and walked down a driveway past an ordinary clapboard home to a structure in the rear about the size of a large garage, which it might once have been. Five wooden boxes filled the room, measuring approximately three feet in height, five in width, and twenty in length, separated by narrow aisles. Each of the containers, looking like large, deep planter boxes for growing vegetables, was filled to the top with rice hulls, except for a dozen duffle bag–sized holes in

1,000-Year-Old Eggs

Related to balut are "salted eggs" and "thousand-year-old eggs," neither of which offer embryos, but both of which bring a pucker to the diner's mouth. Imagine encountering an egg that is black (or purple) that tastes sort of like salt and mud. Hard-boiled.

Salted eggs are easy to prepare. The uncooked eggs—usually duck—are immersed in a super-saturated solution of salt, created by adding salt to warm water until salt no longer dissolves in it. The eggs are placed in a crock or large jar, covered with the salty water, and there they remain for at least two weeks, and up to a month and a half. Before serving, they are hard-boiled and, if sold in markets or on the street they also are sometimes colored red so that buyers will not be surprised.

Salted eggs may be peeled, quartered and eaten with hot rice or *congee*, rice porridge that is a popular breakfast dish in many parts of Asia. They also may be sliced, added to cut tomatoes, and served with slivers of preserved ginger root, sprigs of fresh coriander or basil, and green onion. If a salad dressing is used, it should be light, or just a little oil and vinegar, or olive oil by itself.

They may be stored in the fridge if not all are used immediately.

The first thing that should be said about thousand-year-old eggs is that they are not that old—they just look that way, as if discovered in some long-dead Chinese emperor's tomb. Usually they are covered with what appears to be a dark brown or black paste that's dried. This is what makes them appear to be antique, an appearance that comes from being buried in a mixture of mud, alkali, and lime ashes for at least two months. Inside, the whites are a dark green and the yolks are almost black. The Thais, who seem to adore them, call them "horse-piss eggs," but that is to deride a food that actually has an enticing taste. However off-putting the appearance, the flavor is delicious, reminiscent of over-ripe Camembert, and they go well with pickled Chinese vegetables or ginger.

each box lined with burlap. These holes were filled with eggs and on top was a burlap bag also filled with husks, forming a sort of lid, replicating, more or less, the dark, warm comfort of a laying mama duck. Light bulbs in the low ceiling and a total lack of ventilation pushed the temperature well above one hundred degrees Fahrenheit. Men stripped to the waist bathed in sweat told me that some processors used mechanical incubators that made for better working conditions, but, they insisted proudly, balut produced in this "natural" manner had a better taste.

On the floor was a primitive sort of light box, with egg-sized holes. A hundred-watt bulb inside permitted the men to take an egg and hold it in the hole and "x-ray" (their term) the eggs from time to time during incubation to see that the semila, or "life of the egg," the embryo, then a shadow in the center, was forming on schedule. Then, after sixteen to eighteen days—the duck normally would hatch in twenty-eight—the eggs were removed from their nests and rushed to markets and street vendors all over Manila, where they were heated and sold for about US$0.25 apiece. I asked how many eggs the men in this garage produced. One of the men said, "Forty thousand." Weekly. And this was one of dozens of similar operations.

As Filipinos have migrated to other parts of the world, they have taken their cuisine with them, so it is now possible to buy balut from Hong Kong to Canada. In fact, a balut farm in California now exports some of its product to the Philippines, where it has been well received, just as some California wines made from cuttings from Europe find grudging approval in France. (It should be noted, apologetically, that like many other things from the U.S., the American eggs are larger.) The duck embryo is also a treasured dish in Vietnam, where it is called *ho bit long.*

Most balut in the Philippines is sold on the street by vendors and eaten as a between-meals snack. However, with the arrival of upscale restaurants and trendy nouvelle Philippines cuisine, some menus are now offering balut in specially prepared dishes. A pricey restaurant in Manila's financial district, Makati, prides itself on its Balut Bisque and I heard but never was able to track down reports of balut being used in a paté and a soufflé.

I confess that however much I pride myself on my sense of culinary adventure, I don't like balut, and I find the salted and "thousand-year-old" eggs are most palatable when eaten with other foods. M.F.K. Fisher was probably right when she said that if we didn't start early enough, some foods may never be embraced. After my visit to where most of Manila's balut was incubated, in Pateros, my driver suggested we give the local treat a try right there on the street. When in Manila with a cab driver, as the old saying about Rome sort of goes, you do what the cab driver does. He loved it and I silently promised myself that I'd never eat balut again.

I didn't want any more children, anyway.

Sources

Balut and salted eggs from Metzer Farms, 26000 Old Sage Rd., Gonzales, CA 93926, phone (800) 424-7755 fax (408) 679-2711, web site <http://www.metzerfarms.com>.

Duck and chicken balut; salted duck eggs from Tuazon Holdings Ltd. (9724 27th Ave., Edmonton, Alberta, T6N 1B2, Canada, phone (403) 450-6103.

The Monster Egg

The following has nothing to do with balut or other salted eggs, but it is an egg recipe, so this seems the right place for it. I first spotted the recipe in the estimable *Larousse Gastronomique* and since have seen variants reprinted or paraphrased in many other texts. The recipe calls for twelve to twenty-four eggs, two clean pig bladders, one of them small, the other large, and a very large pot for boiling water.

The eggs are broken and the whites are separated from the yolks. The yolks are then beaten and tied up inside the smaller bladder and boiled in a pot until hard. Once cool, the solid ball of yolk is removed, the unbeaten whites are placed into the larger bladder, and into this the ball of yolk is placed. (It will float to the middle automatically.) The larger bladder is then tied tight and boiled until the white hardens. After a second cooling, the gargantuan egg is removed and sliced.

Larousse suggests eating it cold sprinkled with vinaigrette or browned in the oven with bechamel sauce.

Balut, the national snack of the Philippines—at least for men—is sold and consumed on the street. The duck embryo inside the egg, which has been allowed to go more than half term before cooking, is believed to enhance virility.

insects

insects, spiders, & scorpions

Insects have played an important role in the history of human nutrition in Africa, Asia, Australia, and Latin America, and were an equally important resource for the Indians of western North America, who, like other indigenous groups, expended much organization and effort in harvesting them. Spiders and scorpions have contributed much to the world's cuisine as well, and although they are from another scientific order, I include them here because they and insects seem to look alike and elicit the same response from most diners in the so-called west.

In Euro-America, most may regard these creatures as emergency food to ward off starvation; that's what they're called in United States Army and England's SAS survival manuals. Millions more disagree, including insects—in the larvae, cocoon, pupa and adult stages—and other creepy-crawlies as a planned part of their diet throughout the year or when species are seasonally available. In fact, the Yukpa people of Colombia and Venezuela prefer some traditional insect foods to fresh meat to such a degree that when mopane caterpillar (larvae) is in season, the sale of beef is seriously affected. While in some countries in Africa, the enjoyment of eating caterpillars is so commonplace, it appears in children's rhymes and songs.

For many in the developed world, insects are viewed as a culinary curiosity and while it is true that in some cases in undeveloped or still-emerging countries, people eat insects out of necessity, generally speaking it is the abundance, accessibility, nutritional value, and taste that makes insects popular as food, and not the threat of starvation.

Of the more than 800,000 species described by entomologists, thousands play a role in the human diet. Some of the more important groups include grasshoppers, beetle grubs and adults, ants and termites, moth and butterfly larvae and pupae, crickets and cicadas, and flies.

In Mexico, where many Indian tongues include no separate word for *insect*, people there consume at least 308 species. Insects comprise as much as two-thirds of the animal protein eaten in parts of southern Africa. The Thais fix a zesty hot-pepper sauce with ground-up water bugs. In Cameroon, a dish for special guests is palm grubs with salt, pepper and onion, cooked slowly inside a coconut. The Nepalese squeeze live bee larvae through cloth and fry the resulting liquid like scrambled eggs. In Venezuela and Laos, giant tarantulas are a tasty snack. On and on.

Kevin Krajick argued in 1994 in *The Food Insects Newsletter*, published quarterly by the Department of Entomology at the University of Wisconsin, that while the eating of insects "has never gained global acceptance, partly because ancient hunter-gatherer methods limit harvests, and because the only insect most Westerners eat is the accidental fly in the mashed potatoes...a growing number of scientists and businessmen [now] want to make insects a main course for the masses, using industrial-scale cultivation. According to recent studies by Third World entomologists, this most plentiful of creatures—rich in food value and agricultural potential—could substantially cut malnutrition in poor countries.

"The study of edible insects is a growing speciality: African and Asian researchers are documenting insects' role in human diets and pushing governments to promote them. Analyses of Mexican and African food species show that some contain sixty or seventy per cent protein, carry more calories than soybeans or meat, and offer vitamins and minerals lacking in plant-dominated Third World diets."

In the developed world, entomophagy—as the eating of insects is called, scientifically—is still largely a matter of fad. Trendy Australian restaurants serve witchety grubs along with emu steak and European and North American zoos hold annual insect cook-offs

Previous: Mealworm salad in cucumber cups—artfully arranged for a cocktail party—are prepared with peeled, cored cucumbers, and filled with lightly fried mealworm, chopped shallot, bell pepper, coriander leaf, and chives.

Sources
The Food Insects Newsletter, Department of Entomology, University of Wisconsin, 1630 Linden Dr., Madison, WI 53706; a contribution of at least US$5 is requested to be placed on the mailing list; back issues sell for $1.50 each.

and buffets with celebrity chefs (as fund-raising events). Tequila-flavored lollipops containing an embedded beetle "worm" sell as fast as they can be produced by their California manufacturer. Even Jay Leno had a good time with a presentation of insect foods by entomologists from the University of Iowa. Despite this high-profile exposure, deep-fried grasshoppers, ant egg salad, and mealworm bread are not replacing more traditional protein on many Euro-American dinner tables. Yet.

The odd thing is that we're all eating insects already. The Food and Drug Administration (FDA) in the United States and similar regulatory agencies elsewhere all permit a surprising number of "insect parts" in a given weight of packaged food because it is impossible to remove all of the insects during processing, especially in plants. For example, the FDA allows about four-hundred and fifty insect fragments per kilo in wheat flour, a staple used in dozens of foods, from bread to hot fudge sauce.

Some time in the future, the aversion to eating insects in the developed world may change, either because of a need for new protein sources, or when this or other reasons make it clear that big money can be made from their sale. Dr. Gene DeFoliart, former editor of *The Food Insects Newsletter*, wrote in 1992 that if insects "become more widely accepted as a respectable food item in the industrial countries, the economic implications are obvious. They would form a whole new class of foods made to order for low-input small-business and small-farm production. International trade in edible insects would almost certainly increase."

New York Entomological Society Centennial Banquet
Wednesday, May 20, 1992

At the Bar

Crudité with Peppery Delight Mealworm Dip

Spiced Crickets and Assorted Worms

Butlered Hors d'Oeuvres

Waxworm and Mealworm and Avocado California Roll
with Tamari Dipping Sauce

Wild Mushrooms in Mealworm Flour Pastry

Cricket and Vegetable Tempura

Mealworm Balls in Zesty Tomato Sauce

Mini Bruschetta with Mealworm Ganoush

Worm and Corn Fritters with Plum Dipping Sauce

Buffet

Chicken Normandy with Calvados Sauce

Rice Pilaf

Roast Beef with Gravy

Roesti Potatoes

Mediterranean Pasta

Melange of Vegetable Ragout

Mesclun Salad with Balsamic Vinaigrette

Assorted Seasoned and Cricket Breads and Butter

Dessert Buffet

Lemon Squares

Chocolate Cricket Torte

Mini Cannoli

Peach Clafouti

Cricket and Mealworm Sugar Cookies

Sugar and Tea

grasshoppers

Fried Locusts With Salt

1 lb. 1- or 2-day-old locusts
8 oz. groundnut oil or butter
1 pint water
Vinegar
Salt to taste

Remove the limbs and wings and place locusts in a heavy pan with the salt and water. Simmer for about half an hour, until they are soft. Then boil until the water evaporates, lower the heat, and stir in half the oil or butter. Cook over low heat until the insects are crisp. Spritz with vinegar and add salt.

Opposite, above: A Thai snack called *gai sam yang,* to go with drinks, featuring grasshoppers, fried chillies, chopped lemongrass, peanuts, small wedges of lemon, chopped shallots and diced ginger.
Opposite, below: A striped locust in Pakistan.

Entomophagists—students of insects as food—generally concede that next to ants, grasshoppers are the most popular six-legged edible bug, with a cuisine dating back at least to Old Testament times, when it is reported in Leviticus 11:22 that four bugs were an approved part of the ancient Hebrew diet: "Even these of them ye may eat; the locust after his kind, and the bald locust after his kind, and the beetle after his kind, and the grasshopper after his kind." Inasmuch as grasshoppers are locusts, at least in modern times, that gives this creature three out of four holy stamps of approval. (It was not specified what beetle was approved.)

Grasshoppers are found worldwide, wherever any vegetation grows, and range in size from one to five inches in length. The young are similar in appearance to the adult, but wingless. (Only the adult is eaten.) Some species undergo seasonal color changes, from green to red or brown, and many make chirping noises like their cousins the crickets, by rubbing their spindly, barbed legs against other parts of their bodies.

Mostly, over time, the locust has been known as a pest. Agricultural journals are full of stories of migratory swarms so vast and destructive they make many Hollywood disaster films seem tame. In fact, *The*

Guinness Book of Records calls the desert locust whose habitat is the dry and semi-arid regions of Africa, the Middle East, through to Pakistan and northern India, "the most destructive insect in the world." This arbiter of superlatives goes on to say "this short-horn grasshopper can eat its own weight in food a day, and during long migratory flights a large swarm will consume 20,000 tons of grain and vegetation a day and bring famine to whole communities. In the U.S., a swarm that once swept across Nebraska was reported to be one hundred miles wide and three hundred miles long—nearly half the size of Nebraska itself—and, in some places, nearly a mile high. In Ethiopia one huge concentration destroyed sufficient cereals in six weeks to feed a million people for a year."

The fight against such insect odds is not an easy one. The hordes of hungry hoppers that invaded Utah in the mid-1800s, for example, threatened to destroy the Mormon settlement at Salt Lake City as well as Indian villages in the region, prompting the Indians to counter-attack in an interesting fashion. Carleton S. Coon, in his book, *The Hunting Peoples,* told a story about a group of Indians who dug trenches a foot wide and a foot deep and thirty to forty feet long, covering the trenches with a layer of the dry grass on which the insects were feeding. Villagers then spread out in a line, beating the 'crickets' toward the line of trenches with armloads of grass. The insects hopped and crawled into the trenches, when the Indians set fire to the grass held in their hands and scattered it over the grass in the trenches, killing, and at the same time cooking, the locusts with the heat and smoke. The women then removed the toasted insects from the trenches by the handful, and carried them in baskets home.

The Indians ate the locusts, of course, while the Mormons prayed for help (history does not indicate any Mormon ate a single insect), finally getting it

---

Village torches in fight for grilled locust

HANOI *(Reuters)*— A meal in a remote Vietnam mountain village got out of control when a four-year-old's fight over a barbecued locust ended with 19 houses being burnt to the ground, local officials said yesterday.

Some 18 tons of rice paddy were ruined and two school classrooms razed in the incident, details of which took a month to reach Hanoi, officials in northern Lao Cai province told Reuters.

'The boy wanted to eat the locust, but so did his elder brother,' said the official. 'They started fighting as the fire flared up. It was during the dry season.'

The fire took place in a hamlet populated by members of the Thai ethnic minority. Total damage was put at 300 million dong (US$24,500).

Word on the boy's fate was not known, but he was not hurt in the blaze, the official said.

Nov. 22, 1997

when seagulls in the Great Salt Lake region began to feast. Today, a large statue of a seagull decorates the Utah capitol grounds.

Why modern Euro-Americans don't include the locust in their diet remains a mystery. Grasshoppers sure seemed fit to eat in other eras and in other parts of the world. Pliny the Elder, ancient Rome's greatest naturalist, said that they were much eaten by the Parthians and Herodotus, the Greek historian, described the method adopted by the Nasamones of powdering locusts, then baking them into cakes. Over millennia, they have been cooked in various ways—merely fried with their legs and wings plucked off, boiled, curried, and whatever other fashion suited the local palate.

Today, in Africa, they're eaten raw, fried, roasted, boiled, jellied, mashed into a paste, or cooked in salt water and dried in the sun. In many parts of Asia, they have been a culinary staple for more than a thousand years and may now be purchased inexpensively from street vendors from Bombay to Bangkok to Beijing. Usually, locusts are consumed in Asia as a snack rather than as part of a larger meal or as an ingredient in other dishes. I've eaten them on several occasions; the crisp outer portions and legs are crunchy and taste much like anything else that has been deep-fried, the softer insides creamy in texture and mildly sweet.

And, as mom always used to say—and in 1996 the *Journal for Appropriate Technology* agreed—they are good for you. High in protein (with between fourteen and twenty grams apiece), low in fat (under four grams), rich in minerals (calcium, phosphorus and iron) and vitamins (B_2 and Niacin).

A quiet warning may also be appropriate. Grasshoppers sold on the street nowadays are not harvested by people patiently driving them into trenches, setting fires to roast them naturally, but are killed with chemical pesticides. Of course, other chemicals and preservatives and who knows what are present in more traditional foods, so it remains the decision of the individual diner whether this should be a factor in deciding yes or no, just as it is with any other food.

Some people say it's also a good idea to remove the legs before eating, because they sometimes get stuck between your teeth.

Grasshopper Paste

1 lb. 1- or 2-day-old locusts
1/2 lb. peanuts or cashews
Vegetable or peanut oil
Salt and pepper to taste

Limbs and wings may be left on. Deep-fry in oil and drain when crisp. Then grind in a mortar, adding more oil and nuts until a paste the consistency of peanut butter is produced. Or, dry in the sun and add oil sparingly as the locusts are ground together with the nuts. Store in a jar and use as a spread for sandwiches or crackers.

This page, left: The roadside remains the prime location for cooked food in Thailand. On Bangkok's busy Sukhumvit Road, a vendor cooks up a mound of *takataen,* as the Thais call grasshoppers.

This page, right: Folded into a packet made from a rice paper sheet, fried grasshopper is combined with rice vermicelli, bean sprouts, and coriander leaves to make a Vietmanese spring roll. Eaten by hand, it is dipped into a *phuang nam* sauce made from equal quantities of fish sauce and rice vinegar, thinned with a little water, and blended with finely chopped chilis, ginger, and a pinch of sugar.

Opposite: A Thai girl bites into a crisp-fried *takataen.*

ants & termites

I once ate chocolate-covered ants, back when I was in college and you could find them in jars and tins in specialty shops. It was a sort of fad in the United States at the time, usually purchased as a sort of gag gift, if you'll forgive the pun.

I had no idea at the time, of course, that in many parts of the Third World—in Africa, Asia, and Latin America—ants were a valued source of cheap, fresh protein and a regular part of the local diet. Now I know. I live in that part of the world—Thailand—and there is a restaurant not far from my Bangkok flat that has Sweet Vegetable Curry with Ant Eggs on the menu. And just a few weeks ago as I write this, I had lunch at a restaurant in Singapore that offered Crispy Black Ants on Shredded Potato and Vegetable. At the same time, I know that in parts of "upcountry" Thailand (outside Bangkok), ants, along with a number of other insects show up at mealtime regularly, just as deep-fried grasshoppers and a selection of beetles and grubs are commonly sold on the street as a crunchy snack, to be consumed like salted peanuts or potato chips.

Of all the two million insect species, ants likely are the most popular—that is, their consumption is the most widespread. Perhaps this is because they are virtually everywhere on the planet, from the tropics to the arctic regions, and they are plentiful. It is unusual to see only one or two, unless they are scouts in search of something, which, if they find it, means that in minutes there will be hundreds more in orderly attendance, forming bridges out of their own bodies to cross a stream, building mud homes taller than a man, waging well-planned wars and carrying their dead home in their teeth, marching across kitchen cabinets, inviting themselves to picnics, and crawling up pantlegs.

There are five thousand or so ant species and all are prolific, as hungry as they are industrious, and always, always numerous. Many claim that ants are the best-organized species on earth (certainly more organized than anyone I know)—living in colonies, abiding by strict rules and divisions of labor, always accommodating the group, and humbly serving their queens. Ants also have served a medicinal need for man, with one species used three thousand years ago in India to close wounds; the live ant was held in position to bite the skin, whereupon the jaws locked and the rest of the ant was pinched off, leaving the jaws intact, and so on with other ants until the cut was sealed. More recently in China, the Nanjing Jinling Ant Research Healing Centre developed Chinese Ant King Wine on the basis of an ancient recipe and modern discoveries concerning the medicinal qualities of ants. It says the wine is effective in treating rheumatism, strengthening muscles and bones, boosting the immune system, and preventing senility.

Most often, ants are eaten mixed in with other foods, but also are eaten raw or cooked by themselves, by the handful. The *U.S. Army Survival Manual* recommends the ant as a food and it was, in fact, part of the emergency diet of Captain Scott O'Grady, the American pilot who was shot down over Bosnia in 1995, just as it has served as a protein substitute for other military men when the C-rations ran out. But it is in the tropics among native peoples where the ant is regarded not as an emergency food, but a relished and nutritious part of the diet.

It may be in Colombia, the South American country infamous in recent years for mass-producing a coca plant byproduct illegal in many countries, where the ant is at the center of a contemporary insect cuisine. Here, in the jungle in late spring and early summer, what the locals call the big-bottomed ant crawl from their earthen catacombs for a rare look at the sun. Waiting are peasants who rush them to the roadside marketplace, where they are sold either raw or cooked, bringing about US$3 a pound—about as much as can be collected in a morning, producing more than double the income that might be earned for an entire day harvesting other crops. In this region, many buses have ants painted on their sides and lottery shops are called "The Little Ant." In one town, prominently displayed in the mayor's office, is a statue of an ant.

Ants get no such official recognition in Thailand, but in the vast and poor northeastern part of the country, they play such an important role in the cuisine there are restaurants that have much of the menu devoted to them. One such is Satow Wan near Surin, a region also known for its large elephant population. Here, duck soup— including the bird's liver, meat and blood—is served with hundreds of the local red ants floating on top. This part of Thailand, closely identified with the culture and cuisine of neighboring Laos, also is known for a dish called *larb*, a crumbly sort of paté of beef or pork with fiery chili peppers and raw, chopped onions. Ants are included in the recipe at Satow Wan when larb is made from minced catfish. Ants also are added to curries and stir-fried with vegetables and served with rice. The ant eggs may also be steamed in banana leaves with minced pork, pounded shallots, chopped green onion and hen's or duck's eggs, seasoned with salt, black pepper, and fish sauce.

The ants used most often in Thailand are red ants that live in large mounds above ground, which are shoveled and thrown into the air. The ants separate from the dirt and are scooped into paper bags and transported to restaurants and local markets, where they sell for under US$0.50 a pound. Other species in the same region live in nests in trees and are collected in a long-handled net, the ant-catcher dumping both ants and eggs into a bucket half-filled with water. The ants drown, making it a simple matter to separate the eggs and edible winged females.

Of all the edible ants, one of the most interesting

may be the parasol, or leaf-cutting ant, so called because they cut out pieces of leaves and carry them back to their nests, where they chew the greenery into a sort of mulch, lining their chambers. Fungus grows on the mulch and the ants eat the fungus. These ants, in turn, are eaten by most of the Indians in the Amazon Basin and by others in Central America. The winged females are collected as they swarm from the nest by the thousands on their mating flights during the early part of the rainy season. They are easy to collect, as they leave their nests at dawn and can be drawn to a wood fire and caught in a basket. The part eaten is the abdomen, which when roasted tastes like crispy bacon.

Other ants taste like a tangy honey. These include, in Australia, a favorite of the Aborigines called the honeypot ant. Workers of this species gather honeydew from other insects, feeding it to other worker ants. They, in turn, store the sweetness in their stomachs and serve as a sort of larder from which other ants later dine. These helpless ants with their greatly swollen abdomen are kept in underground chambers, ready to regurgitate some of the nectar when solicited by hungry workers. These subterranean nests were as deep at two meters, but once discovered by the Aborigines, were easily dug out. Usually, the heads were pinched off and the remainder was eaten raw.

The honey ant served a similar role in dry areas of the western and southwestern United States, where they collected the sweet sap that oozed from large swellings, or galls, on oaks and other trees. Again, the "honey" was stored in the ants' abdomens and once found, the insects were popped into the mouth like a berry or small grape.

Other ant species are considered delicacies, as well. In Mexico, pupae of two species known as *escamoles* are on the menus of urban restaurants. They have a

---

Basic Insect Safety Test

Cooked insects are safer than raw ones.
Never eat bugs you find dead.
If it smells really bad, don't eat it!

Termites à la Bantu

1 pint termites
1 teaspoon vegetable oil
Salt

Remove wings and spread on a flat stone in the sun to dry. Smear pan or stone with oil and spread dried termites upon it. Toast over hot coals until almost crisp. Sprinkle with salt. Eat like popcorn immediately or store for future use—they can be stored for months.

Insect Fact and Folklore

delicate flavor and are usually served fried alone or with black butter (made from clarified butter and vinegar), or cooked with garlic and onions. Rural people who collect escamoles by digging them from their underground nests sometimes earn more during the collecting season than many rural workers do during an entire year.

People who study the eating of insects—entomographists—believe ants are one of the true bug feasts. The formic acid in some species pretty much disappears when they are boiled or fried, while other species—including the ever-present black ant—have a semi-sweet flavor eaten raw and may be used to sweeten tea. They may also be crushed and used to thicken and add protein to stews and soups, made into salads, and fried with eggs. Like many other insects, they are rich in protein, low in fat, and high in phosphorous, but include only trace vitamins.

A dish popular throughout Laos and northern Thailand, the large white eggs of the red ant known locally as *mot som*, or "sour ant," can be steamed, cooked in a curry, or made into a spicy salad. Part of their appeal is the texture—in the mouth, their delicate skin pops open to reveal a creamy texture like soft Camembert cheese.

Termites are a different species, but many look like ants with wings and they share many characteristics. They build tall homes made of mud, they consume paper and wood, they are prolific, and they are captured when they swarm and eaten soon thereafter. The only time I ate termites was when I lived in Hawaii and tentatively popped a few of the little guys into my mouth when they arrived in a small cloud at my desk on a roofed but open patio. They tasted okay, although I know now that I should have removed the wings, which tended to get stuck to my lips and the roof of my mouth. I also think I'd have preferred them cooked and sprinkled on rice or mixed with vegetables.

As is true of winged ants, termites are attracted to light and may be collected by placing a bowl of water under a light source. When I lived in Hawaii, some joker suggested an almost effortless way to get rid of the pesky critters was to turn on the swimming pool lights after dark. The termites will be attracted to the light and drown and in the morning all you have to do is scoop them up with the pool net. Of course, you have to have a swimming pool and a taste for chlorine, if you have dinner in mind.

The most widespread consumption of termites is in Africa, where they are a highly regarded food in nearly every sub-Saharan country. So common are they found in the markets, some longtime residents from developed nations are among the enthusiastic customers.

In his classic study *The Hunting Peoples*, Carleton S. Coon told a story about the harvesting of termites in pygmy Africa, where each man in the village staked out his own termite hill for later harvest. Then, as the swarming season neared, the villagers probed the mounds to see how high the insects had risen, so that they could be there when they emerged. Next, trenches were dug around each hill and a roof of leaves was erected over the top, so that when the termites began to swarm, they banged into the roof and fell into the trenches. The women collected them in covered baskets, serving them alive at the soonest mealtime, boiled or roasted them, or ground them into a paste. When boiling, the oil that rose to the surface of the water was put aside for cooking and used as a pomade, mixed with red wood-powder.

Mr. Coon said the women scooped them up in baskets. This is not unusual. When termites swarm, they have been known to darken the sky. Tropical termite queens can produce between eight thousand and ten thousand eggs a day; some Australian queens are believed to lay as many as three million a year. African queens, who may reach the size of a large potato—the world's largest termite, according to *The Guinness Book of Records*—may lay a hundred million in her lifetime. So this is hardly an endangered species, and every category in the colony is tasty and nutritious, including the eggs and queen.

Like ants, the taste for termites is not new. An analysis of digestive remains from a prehistoric dig in Mexico shows the residents of the region once ate winged ants and termites (also water flies and grasshoppers). Roasted, inch-long queens with swollen backsides are sold on the street in Colombia today, a custom that dates back to pre-colonial times.

There are about 1,700 species of termite, some of which live in rotting wood, others underground, others in elaborate if unattractive mounds that in Australia and parts of Africa rise up to forty feet in height and

Below: Honeypot ants in the "larder" chamber.

are 100 feet in diameter. If these small insects were man-sized and their homes were made proportionate to man-made buildings, these castles would rise many times higher than the Empire State Building in New York and measure five miles in diameter at the base.

One of the most avid proponents of termite cuisine is Frances L. Behnke, who wrote in her *Natural History of Termites* (1977) that the insects "destroy wood, distill an acid that eats through lead, manufacture liquid that will dissolve glass, and spread a substance that will rust metal, which allows them to bore through it. Yet, they are good to eat." Like ants, they can be eaten as a snack—roasting removes the wings—and ground for flour or oil for cooking. Ms. Behnke said chicken fried in termite oil tasted as if cooked in butter.

Another enthusiastic advocate was the late Laurens van der Post, the South African writer (and, late in life, a sort of guru to Britain's Prince Charles) whose book *First Catch Your Eland* is regarded as one of the finest about African food. He wrote that the taste for termites "existed all over Africa and is not to be despised if one is hungry in bush or jungle." As a child growing up in South Africa, he said he knew it as "bushman's rice" or "rice ants" because of their color and size. "They had a sharp tartaric flavor and, when fried, even in tinned butter, went down well with roast venison," he said. "In fact, some of the capitals of Europe today, specially prepared termites are on sale in tins and the Japanese in particular have developed a liking for them."

Termites, uncooked, taste sort of like pineapple and are higher in protein than an equal weight of chicken, fish, or beef. (Someone once counted the number of termites it took to equal a pound. Thirty thousand.) They also are a rich source of fat, thus high in calories. Gene Defoliart wrote in the *Bulletin of the Entomological Society of America* that a 3.5-ounce (100-gram) portion of fried termites "would go a long way toward meeting the daily requirement of 65 grams of protein recommended by the USDA and supply a nice ratio of protein to fat calories. One can even

visualize that the chitlin, which constitutes 5 to 10 per cent of the dry weight of insects, would provide sufficient roughage to help maintain the intestinal tone."

In Indonesia, older men eat the queens, believing they will strengthen their failing bodies and make them feel young again.

To listen to the humor, no picnic is complete without ants. In time, they may be not only be invited, but prepared at home and brought along with the rest of the lunch nesting in the Tupperware.

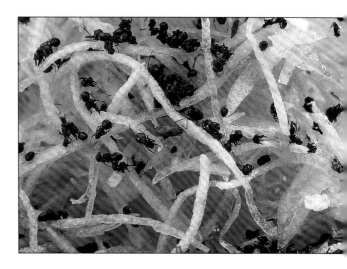

spiders & scorpions

Even beetles and grasshoppers pale next to this category of food, at least to most Euro-Americans. However, spiders and scorpions, like others in the creepy-crawly set, represent to others a rich source of protein and a tasty snack.

The first time I ate scorpion was in a highly unlikely setting, a very nice restaurant in Singapore just a two-minute walk from the fashionable Raffles Hotel. The Imperial Herbal Restaurant is a pink tablecloth sort of place known for its resident Chinese pharmacist and a menu that includes many special dishes and drinks aimed at fixing you as well as filling you. Deep-Fried Drunken Scorpions with Asparagus was one of them. At US$3 per scorpion, how could I resist? I was told they were small, so I ordered a half dozen.

The "drunken" part of the dish meant the scorpions had been marinated in wine, after which they were deep-fried, as was the small asparagus tip after being dipped in a flour paste. As usual, it was the *idea* that made eating the critter difficult. I have a theory that you can eat just about anything—perhaps including your socks—if it is fried in oil until it is crisp, then served with a tangy dipping sauce. That meal proved to me that at least it is true for scorpions. And, yes, you eat them whole, tiny claws and pointed tail, too.

There are about 350 different species of scorpion worldwide, but most live in dry, warm areas. They have four pairs of legs, a pair of claws, and a segmented tail that contains two venom glands connected to a needle-sharp stinger. The tail is brought forward over the scorpion's back when it stings, either to kill other insects it plans to eat or to defend itself when threatened (say, when you disturb it when it's sleeping inside your shoe). Most are nocturnal, hiding in dark places during the day. Only fifty or so are known to be dangerous to humans, a threat that is diminished by deep-frying them.

One of the species harvested in Singapore is the black scorpion, a glossy, blue-black creature that reaches six to seven inches in length and is found in public parks. The spotted house scorpion is smaller and more venomous. I don't know which I was served, except that they were awfully small, only about three inches from fried claw to fried stinger. Small usually means tender in the food world. In this case, I couldn't tell, as I had no larger scorpion with which to compare it. All I can say is that it crunched when I bit into it, it had a soft, sort of mealy center, and it disappeared quickly down my throat with a swallow of a decent Chardonnay. Perhaps my health improved. Who knows?

There is another way to eat a scorpion, available to everyone with a postal address. A company in Texas sells sugar-free toffee flavored candy that contains a real scorpion "cooked and prepared carefully."

Spiders are eaten more commonly than scorpions, most frequently by Indians in South America, the Bushmen of southern Africa, and the Aborigines, or native Australians. In China and other parts of Asia they are regarded not only as food, but also medicine. This is explained by the permanence of an undisturbed web, which the Chinese take as a sign of long life. Some believe that ten years is added to the life of someone who eats spiders. For common contagion, people in Old England—the word comes from Old English *spinnan*, to spin—were advised to carry a spider in a silk bag worn around the neck or in a nut shell in the pocket. Live spiders were also rolled in butter and swallowed, or eaten in molasses, or rolled in a cobweb and taken like a pill.

All spiders are "venomous" in the sense that most of them possess a pair of poison glands, the toxin used mainly to paralyze or kill their prey. However, of some fifty thousand different species, only a couple of dozen are known to be dangerous to humans. The notorious black widow spider—for which novels, movies, and murderers have been named—found in America,

Europe, and Australia, can paralyze breathing muscles, killing the victim by suffocation. Bites from other dangerous spiders can cause pain, blisters and local swelling, chills, muscle cramps, nausea, vomiting, fever, and loss of sight.

Still, most spiders are harmless and several make a lovely meal, even some of the more "threatening" ones. One such is the tarantula, also famed in humankind's scary fiction and film. Its bite is painful, but it will strike only if threatened and it can only knock out a mouse. People, generally, don't like spiders and this one can grow to the size of a human hand and it has hairy legs, which I guess puts people off. Nonetheless, in Laos and Cambodia, the blue-legged tarantula is toasted on a bamboo skewer over a fire and served whole with salt or sliced and mixed with chilies. Raw, they taste like something between (if you can make the leap) almonds and the marrow of chicken bones.

In this part of Asia, as in many undeveloped areas, foraging is a way of life and anything that crawls or flies will be served with the daily starch and vegetables. So it's not unusual to see women beside the road and at transport cafes bearing trays piled high with hairy, two-inch arachnids on wooden skewers. Passing motorists are the primary customers, paying, in 1997, just five hundred Cambodian reils (then worth about US$0.20) for a brochette of four with fiery green chilies.

Other tarantula fanciers are the Amazonian Indians, who lure the spiders out of their tunnels, deftly grab them by the thorax, fold the legs back and wrap them in leaves for transportation back to the village or camp. There, the abdomens are removed and stripped of eggs, which are stirred and wrapped in a leaf and roasted over a fire to produce a sort of spider egg omelette. While the bodies are thrown directly onto the fire to burn off the hair and cook the meat. When they're done, the legs and thorax are cracked open and picked at in much the same way you eat a boiled crab.

Spiders and scorpions differ from insects in several ways. They both have four pairs of legs, no antennae, and no wings. By contrast, all insects have three pairs of legs, one pair of antennae, and many adult insects have one or two pairs of wings. Spiders and scorpions are also meat-eaters, subsisting on insects, while the insects feed on nearly anything organic: plants, animals, wood, garbage, etc.

The thing they do share is dinnertime. Could it be *your* dinnertime?

Sources

Tarantulas from Spider Patch, where they are sold as pets, 10315 Avis Ln., Santee, CA 92071-4432, phone and fax (619) 596-8174.

Scorpion candy Nevada W&S Corp., 7 Switchbud Pl., #192178, The Woodlands, TX 77380, phone (281) 34-7048, fax (281) 367-7267, email <rodrigo@ onramp.net>

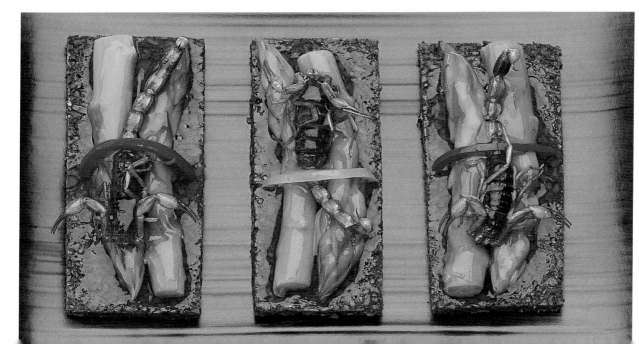

Below: To prepare scorpion and asparagus canapés, the scorpions are first deep-fried until crisp, while the asparagus spears are boiled in the normal way for five minutes. These are both arranged on slices of pumpernickel and decorated with thin strips of bell pepper. Each canapé is then carefully coated with vegetable aspic and chilled in the refrigerator until the aspic sets firm.
Overleaf: Scorpion candy, available by mail from the Nevada W & S Corporation (see **Sources**)

beetles

I'd already eaten ants, termites, grasshoppers, and silkworm larvae when I first watched Nittaya Phanthachat casually consume a bag full of what appeared to be huge cockroaches while drinking a beer in Bangkok. I was wrong about the species—they were water bugs, called *maengda* in Thai, the largest of the true bugs, reaching three inches in length—but at the time it didn't matter. I watched, both fascinated and repelled, as she removed the carapace (the hard outer shell), the wings and the legs to get to the edible bit in the center.

Later, I learned from Ms. Phanthachat that the large blue bugs were found wherever there was standing water and harvested most easily during the rainy season, when for reasons she couldn't explain, they tended to fly toward lights. Ms. Phanthachat worked as a chef and I assumed she knew what she was doing when it came to food. She told me that the Thai liked to eat the beetles marinated in fish sauce, roasted over a fire, steamed, pounded, and added to chili paste. She said it gave the paste a pleasant aroma.

All that said, when she offered me one, I blanched. Simultaneously, I knew my moment had come, there was no escape. Fortunately, I'd had several beers by then myself, which sometimes helps at such precarious times. So as she disected another water bug, I followed her lead, awkwardly picking off the outer casing, gingerly nibbling at the soft insides.

"Hey!" I said, grinning foolishly. "It tastes sort of nutty."

"Good for you," my friend said. She wasn't congratulating me. She was talking about my health.

Most beetles are good for you and according to A.D. and Helen Livingston's *Edible Plants and Animals* (1993), all 250,000 species are edible, offering protein in both the larvae and adult stages, eaten either raw or cooked. Most of the beetles I've encountered were being sold by street vendors in Southeast Asia and were either deep-fried or steamed. Most in the adult stage are somewhat nutty in flavor—although I know a Thai woman named Meo who is so practiced at this she insists that she can identify the plant the bug had been eating before it was caught and cooked.

It was Meo's friend Richard Lair who introduced me to (take a breath) buffalo dung beetles, a frequent part of his diet when he lived with elephant trainers in the jungle in northern Thailand. Named for their peculiar habit of burrowing into freshly deposited water buffalo dung, Mr. Lair said they were collected in the morning and left until the evening when the beetles re-emerged. The beetles are left overnight in a bucket of water to allow them to rid themselves of the ingested dung. They were then soaked in clean water for two to three hours until clean, then thrown into a covered pan and fried without oil with a little salt.

"The noise of their running inside the fry-pan is off-putting to some," Mr. Lair said, grinning devilishly, "but it doesn't last long."

The larvae of beetles are consumed in greater numbers than are adults, and usually consumed raw, roasted, or fried—from the dry aboriginal lands of Australia to the rice fields of Asia to the jungles of Africa and South America to the desert of northern Mexico. They also have a long culinary résumé, going back to prehistoric times when they were eaten, like anything else edible that could be found by the hunter-gatherers. According to Pliny the Elder, who published a thirty-seven-volume *Natural History* in 77 A.D., the ancient Romans fatted grubs on flour before eating them; the noted gourmet, Lucullus, had stag horn larvae fed for months on wine and bran before his chefs roasted them. More recently, those welcoming grubs to the meal included North American Indians, the Aztecs in Mexico, the Maori in New Zealand, and natives of the West Indies during Christopher Columbus's time.

One of the most popular today is the yellow meal

worm, often used as food for reptiles, thus it can be purchased from pet stores, biological supply dealers, aviary owners, and bait-and-tackle shops, or raised at home in an aquarium. The adult, a hard-shelled beetle, may lay as many as three-hundred eggs in her two- to three-month lifetime. Small, tough-skinned larvae hatch from the eggs and grow to about one inch long, when they may be eaten raw or cooked.

Stephanie Bailey, entomology extension specialist at the University of Kentucky, offers helpful hints on the Internet, urging buyers of mealworms to put them on a diet of bran or corn meal before consumption to purge them of impurities. After washing, she said, they could then be cooked or frozen for later use—baked in an oven and ground into a flour for bread, or used as thickening in a soup or stew.

Sometimes larvae are mistakenly called "worms." One of these is the so-called sago worm, a favorite in Indonesia, where they are sold live in the open markets and served roasted or in a sort of stew in small, out-of-the-way restaurants catering to local diners. The sago worm gets its name from its home, the sago palm, a tree cultivated in the tropics that at the end of the seventeenth century was one of the most popular sources of starch in the developed world, used for garnishing veal or chicken, for thickening soup, and for making soft rolls. Today in Europe it is only used for thickening and to make puddings, but from Papua New Guinea to India it is still used in a vast variety of dishes, from fritters to ravioli to jelly. As for the larvae, who offer the same pulpy taste, outside the tropics, they haven't been properly introduced.

Oddly, the sago worms are harvested "by ear." Collectors roam the forest and when they find a downed tree, they thump on the trunk as if knocking on a door, then stoop to listen. If they hear worms moving around inside, they hack away the tree's outer shell with machetes and claim their meaty reward, which are then eaten raw on the spot or taken back to the village for the evening meal.

In West Africa, another palm weevil is the most widely used. A cookbook on Cameroon cooking, *Le grand livre de la cuisine camerounaise* (1985), described a recipe for "coconut larvae" as "a favorite dish offered only to good friends." Coconuts at the half-hard stage are emptied of their milk, refilled with the larvae and condiments, then re-capped and cooked in water.

Different species of the same beetle family appear in Southeast Asia and the Western Pacific, as well as in Colombia, Venezuela, and Paraguay, where they are farmed in a process that Gene DeFoliart of the Department of Entomology at the University of Wisconsin calls "semi-cultivation."

"The cultivation and harvest procedures vary slightly from one region to another," he wrote in *Biodiversity and Conservation* (1995), "but, basically, palms are cut down and the logs left lying in the forest with the expectation that larvae will be ready to harvest from the decaying pith one to three months later."

Mr. DeFoliart has suggested that palm worms, which grew up to four inches in length, could be promoted as "traditional cuisine of gourmet quality, the kind of delicacy that could be promoted as tourist and urban fare by the best restaurants throughout the tropics and subtropics, and eventually, maybe, even as an item for export." So far, no one has taken his challenge seriously.

And so it goes around the world. The "banana grub" is found in many tropical areas in fallen banana trees. The larvae of the long-horned beetle, reported in much of Southeast Asia, Sri Lanka, and Papua New Guinea, are cooked in coconut milk. (Hunters may find as many as one-hundred grubs in a single, rotting log.) The larvae of the rhinoceros beetle—remember this one, able to carry eight-hundred and fifty times its body weight?—is eaten in India, Myanmar, Thailand, and the Philippines. The tiny flour beetle, sometimes found in the home flour sieve, are the same insects consumed avidly from South America to the Middle East to India, where they are mixed with other insects into an appealing paste. Metallic wood-borers and June beetles

Rootworm Beetle Dip

2 cup lowfat cottage
cheese
1 1/2 tsp. lemon juice
2 tbs. skimmed milk
1/2 cup reduced-calorie
  mayonnaise
1 tbs. onion, chopped
1 tbs. parsley, chopped
1 1/2 tsp. dill
1 1/2 tsp. Beau Monde
1 cup dry-roasted root
  worm beetles

Blend first three ingredients. Add remaining ingredients and chill.

Entomology Department, Iowa
State University

Sources

Live mealworms by mail:
Nature's Way, P.O. Box 188,
Ross, OH 45061, phone (800)
318-2611; Timberline Live Pet
Foods, 201 E. Timberline Rd.,
Marion, IL 62959, phone (800)
423-2248 or (618) 997-4692,
email <livefood@timberline-
fisheries.com>; and Grubco
Inc., phone (800) 222-3563 or
fax (513) 874-5878.

Tequila worm lollipops by mail
from Nevada W&S Corp.,
7 Switchbud Pl., #192178,
The Woodlands, TX 77380,
phone (281) 364-7048, fax
(281) 367-7267, email
<rodrigo@onramp.net>

are prized in Southeast Asia because they carry with them the taste of their own diet of tamarind, persimmon, plum, mango and custard apple tree leaves. And so it goes.

It seems appropriate to close this chapter with a note about what may be the world's best known grub, the white maguay worm, larvae of the *hesperiid*, a beetle that hatches out of large cactus in Mexico, being inserted into bottles of tequila, the alcoholic drink that is made from the same desert plant. In the United States, where until recently more tequila was consumed than even in Mexico, a test of manhood involved eating, or swallowing with a shot, the worm at the bottom of the bottle.

Today in Mexico, this "worm" is appearing as an exotic *hors d'oeuvre* in expensive restaurants as an essential part of *alta cocina*, the Spanish phrase for haute cuisine. As a writer for the *Los Angeles Times* put it, "What Wolfgang Puck did for the pizza, these chefs are doing for tacos, cactus leaves and worms." The crunchy, brown larvae also are being stuffed into tacos and washed down with a "designer" tequila that may cost as much as US$1,000 a bottle. Thus, Mexico's 3,000-year-old gastronomic heritage, once shunned by the middle and upper classes, is now becoming hip.

Finally, for entomographers with a sweet tooth, a sugar-free tequila flavored lollipop with a real "worm" inside is available by mail.

This page and opposite: Bamboo grubs—known colloquially as "fast cars" because of their rapid crawling ability—are fried with a little garlic by a Lisu hill-tribe woman.

This page: Their feet tied with rubber bands, live water bugs known as *maengda*, fresh from a Thai market, will be pounded into a spicy dip, then relished for their perfumed aroma and flavor.

Opposite: Mexican tradition holds that swallowing the agave "worm"—a moth pupa—aids virility, and one is now always added to a bottle of the national drink, mezcal.

crickets & cicadas

What do crickets and cicadas have in common? Well, they're really quite different, although both have six legs and are reputed to have good voices, and for me that's enough to let them share a culinary duet.

Both are popular snack foods in the Orient, but in the west, for a variety of reasons, they are shunned. Not only do most westerners decline to eat any insect, but when it comes to a cricket, there seems to be a lot of cultural baggage that gets in the way. After all, Pinnochio's best friend, and conscience embodied, was a cute little fellow named Jiminy Cricket, and for hundreds of years, a cricket chirping in the home or barn has been considered good luck. For many, the cicada, the bug that clings to the trunks of trees and make a loud chattering, buzzing sound during the mating season are just too unattractive to eat, resembling large cockroaches, measuring up to three or four inches long. Euro-Americans just don't eat cartoon characters, magic charms, and anything that looks like a cockroach.

Opposite: The famous Cricket Lick-It lollipops come with a cricket enclosed in each. The insects seem as if sealed in amber.

Crickets are much smaller than cicadas, with approximately 1,500 species ranging in length from under a quarter of an inch up to two inches, and all have outsized rear legs designed for jumping. Mostly they like to sing in warm, dry places (the hearth is a preferred "stage"), and in many cultures, most commonly in China and Japan, people have kept crickets in petite, finely crafted cages as pets. Such a cage played a small but key role in the film *The Last Emperor*, hidden in cushions by the emperor as a child and retrieved by him as an old, defeated man.

Mostly, crickets are found in and near homes, barns, or other buildings. And while some consider them pests—they are known to chew or damage silk, woolens, paper, fruit, and vegetables—many are deliberately raised at home, either for song or for food. The Entomological Society of Michigan at Michigan State University suggests that you grow them in a "large glass container with a screen cover. Place three to four inches of dry sand in the bottom and put three small shallow cups (about a half-inch high) on the sand. (Sea shells or inverted lids from small jars work well.) To one cup, add water and a cotton ball so the crickets won't drown. Keep it wet. To the second, add slightly moist (not wet) sand for the egg. Place small bits of food in the cup, not on the sand. Crickets eat almost anything, but very small nymphs prefer soft food such as banana, apple, or lettuce. Dry dog food is good for the larger crickets. Add some crumpled paper for hiding places. Discard dirty food and clean the jar occasionally to keep it free of mold."

In years past, crickets were raised for fighting, once a traditional pastime and the object of much gambling activity in China. In some Asian cities today they are still sold on the street in bamboo cages, but more often they are collected or raised for food. Filipino farmers flood fields to capture crickets as they rise to the water's surface; they are then cooked and may even be

---

Bug Bonanza Chirping up Local Menus

Phnom Penh (Reuters) — Residents in Cambodia's capital Phnom Penh are licking their lips over the arrival of a favorite local delicacy — crickets.

The seasonal invasion of the insects, during a full moon in the early part of the rainy season, is considered a bonanza, sparking a rush to capture and cash in on the bugs.

Walking slowly, crouched over in the glow of a street light, 35-year-old Bun Vitha, and his 10-year-old son are busy catching crickets.

"They're good food for us, you know, and they're delicious and not so cheap in the market," Bun Vutha said.

Bun Vutha pounces on a cricket, carefully picks it up and puts it in a bottle carried by his son.

"I'm sorry to do that, cricket, but you were born an animal, which is the food for human beings," he says.

Uk Heang sells crickets at Phnom Penh's central market.

The fifteen-year-old vendor said she buys the insects from cricket hunters who work in the countryside around the city. She sells about 2,500 of the insects a day, earning about 40,000 riel (US$12). Four members of her family are involved in the cricket business.

Chhum Him, enjoying a beer with some friends at a city restaurant, says he's a big fan of crickets — lightly grilled with a peanut placed in the abdomen.

"They smell delicious when they're properly cooked," he said.

July 7, 1998

found on restaurant menus. In Africa, the cricket is collected from tunnels beneath the earth and roasted over a fire or hot coals.

After capturing crickets, they should be kept alive and in a refrigerator to slow their movement. This will make washing them easier. After dry roasting them, or cooking them in a pan, you may want to remove their legs and wings before eating, although if they are deep-fried, the entire bug will be edible, crunchy on the outside with a soft mid-section.

In classic insect cookery, crickets probably are the most frequently encountered, and nowhere more prominently than in the premier guide to insect recipes, *Entertaining with Insects* (1992) by Ronald L. Taylor and Barbara J. Carter, whose home-tested recipes include Cricket Crisps, Cricket India, Cricket Patties Claremont, Chirping Stuffed Avacados, Hot Cricket-Avocado Delight, Pizza Hopper, Tempura Cricket with Vegetables, and Jumping Melon Salad. Leftovers are best when kept frozen.

Another kind of cricket snack is marketed by a company in Texas. This is the Cricket Lick-It, a translucent Crème de Menthe–flavored lollipop that contains a real cricket. Health-conscious diners should know that the item is sugar-free.

Cicadas are less commonly eaten. In Homer's time, the cicada was a popular theme for poets, both for its music and its flavor. Aristotle wrote of the Greeks eating the pupae, or chrysalids, as well as the females heavy with eggs. There are two thousand species, most of them tropical, although they are found in temperate parts of the world as well. In Japan, the seasonal buzz is often so loud, it competes with the roar of traffic, heralding their addition to selected restaurant menus, usually during the hot season in March and April. Even in the larger cities, tree trunks will be so thick with them they may be harvested by the bagful in just a few city blocks.

In rural areas, the capture is more relaxed. Following a heavy afternoon rain, as the sun sets, a blue lightbulb will attract the large flying bugs, which then can be caught in a net. The males are discarded—because of a somewhat offensive odor—and the females may be eaten raw, fried, roasted, or cooked on a bamboo stick over an open fire or grill. More often, they are steamed, and after the hard carapace is removed, they are eaten like a snack or served with cooked vegetables. The tender, nutty meat may also be pounded or mixed in a blender with chopped red chilis, diced onion, garlic, and sufficient lemon juice to form a thick paste, then spread on crackers or bread.

Crickets may be found at pet shops (where usually they are sold as food for reptiles and amphibians) and bait stores. Tell them you're taking the bugs home for your turtle.

Chocolate Chirpie-Chip Cookies

1/4 cup flour
1 tsp. baking soda
1 cup butter, salted (room temperature)
3/4 cup white sugar
3/4 cup brown sugar
1 tsp. vanilla
2 eggs
1/2 cup dry-roasted crickets
12 oz. chocolate chips
1 cup chopped walnuts

Preheat oven to 375ºF. In a small bowl, combine flour and baking soda; set aside. In a large bowl, combine butter, white sugar, brown sugar, and vanilla; beat until creamy. Beat in eggs. Gradually add four mixture and insects, mixing well. Stir in chocolate chips. Then drop by rounded measuring teaspoonfuls onto an ungreased cookie sheet. Bake for 8–10 minutes.

Iowa State University, Dept. of Entomology

Sources

By mail, Rainbow Mealworms and Crickets, P.O. Box 4525, 126 E. Spruce St., Compton, CA 90220, (800) 777-9676 or (310) 635-1494; Nature's Way, P.O. Box 188, Ross, OH 45061, (800) 318-2611; and Timberline Live Pet Foods, 201 E. Timberline Rd., Marion, IL 62959, (800) 423-2248, fax (618) 997-4692, email <livefood @timberlinefisheries.com>.

Cricket Lick-It: W&S Corp., 7 Switchbud Pl, #192178, The Woodlands, TX 77380, (281) 364-7048, email <rodrigo @ontheramp.net>

Opposite: The size, shape and crunchiness of crickets make them an ideal ingredient for cricket-stuffed baby tomatoes. Here, the tops of baby tomatoes have been sliced off, and the pulp and seeds scooped out with a teaspoon. They are then stuffed with humus and two crickets with a garnish of thin slices of green chili.
This page: Mealworms and crickets coated with brown and white chocolate as an after-diner accompaniment to liqueurs. Leaving the ends uncoated allows guests to eat without getting their fingers sticky.

butterflies & moths

During my first visit to Thailand, I stayed in a small village where I was introduced to an older woman who was sitting beside a wood fire outside her home. On the fire was a pot of boiling water and in the pot, floating, were what appeared to be a dozen or so yellow worms. One at a time, she removed them from the water with a bamboo stick, then with her fingers she began to pull a golden thread from them. These were silkworm cocoons, also called pupae, or chrysalids, the almost adult stage of the mulberry moth, which hold an extremely fine filament up to a thousand feet long. It is from such basic beginnings that dresses, shirts, suits, neckties, and various accessories are made.

Once she had exhausted the pupae's silk supply, the woman held the small golden corpse that remained up to my face and opened her mouth, her way of telling me to do the same. Thinking I might offend her if I refused, I did as she asked. I was happily surprised. It tasted like corn and I ate two more. Later, I learned they were regarded as a quick and easy snack for the villagers, much cherished by the children and sometimes added to stir-fried dishes with vegetables. Rarely were they discarded and, in fact, in Thailand, China, and other countries where there was a silk industry, the worms were collected and sold commercially and eaten boiled, steamed, baked, fried, or roasted, depending on the locality and individual preference.

In China, they may be pickled with salt or softened with water and fried with chicken eggs in the form of an omelette or simply fried with diced onion and a thick sauce. In Thailand, where in 1987 the Thai Ministry of Public Health included silkworm pupae on a list of local foods that could be used in supplementary food formulas developed for malnourished infants and pre-school children, they are fried and ground into a coarse powder, which is then added to curries and soups. From South Korea, they are exported in tins and sold in Asian groceries as far away as the United States.

Today there are many countries with silkworm farms—stretching from Asia to Italy—but a few hundred years ago, the silkworm center was in China, where, according to Marco Polo, the pupae were sold in the markets of Hangzhoo, the capital of China during what Westerners call the Middle Ages. Later, the French missionary Père Favaud, as quoted in *Larousse Gastronomique*, wrote that he witnessed and participated regularly in the consumption of silkworm chrysalids in China, describing them as an "excellent stomach medicine, both fortifying and refreshing and often a successful remedy for those in poor health."

Silkworm pupae represent one of three stages of the unborn—or more accurately, immature—insects: the eggs and larvae being the earlier stages of insect life, with most eggs looking like, well, tiny white eggs, and the larvae being what is commonly called a caterpillar. All three—eggs, larvae, and pupae—have a long and delicious history, moths and butterflies, or *Lepidoptera*, forming a substantial part of the diet in parts of the world.

Lepidoptera comprise a major order with species of about eighty genera in 20 families used as food, not only in Asia but in sub-Saharan Africa, where, in some areas, the large, spiny mopane caterpillar (the larvae stage of a giant silk, or emperor moth) is so popular that when they are in season, crawling all over village and jungle trees, the sale of beef and other protein meats is seriously affected. In the early 1980s, annual sales of mopane entering commerce were estimated by the South African Bureau of Standards at 1,600 tons, not including those collected privately. One company in Botswana with retail outlets in Johannesburg, sold what it called mopani worms (the word is spelled variously), turning a profit its first year (1983), selling them dried in large bags, much like any other dried food.

Found mainly in the bushveld from Mozambique

and Zimbabwe to Namibia and South Africa, where village women collect them in the early spring, often popping one into their mouths after deftly pinching out the pungent-smelling insides. Later, the women may stew them with tomato, onion, and a wild spinach-like green, or fry them, then sprinkle them with salt and lemon juice. Leftover mopane may be dried in the sun. Any way they are prepared, South African government researchers claim that just 20 of the protein-rich caterpillars will satisfy an adult male's entire daily requirement for calcium, phosphorus, riboflavin, and iron.

Gene R. Defoliart of the University of Wisconsin's Department of Entomology and the former editor of *The Food Insects Newsletter*, wrote they had become "a feature on the menus of some small-city restaurants and the trend appeared to be spreading." He also noted that mopane could be eaten like peanuts at cocktail time, with or without a sour cream dip.

The mopane are not alone. According to Prof. Defoliart, food use of *lepidopterans* reaches its maximum in Africa, "where more than 20 species are consumed in some countries." And they are not only tasty, they are good for you. There were, he wrote in an academic journal called *Biodiversity and Conservation*, "some 23 species of caterpillars analyzed by nutritionists who found that the crude protein content averaged more than 63 per cent, compared to beef's meager 18 per cent. The calorie count was about the same—200 to 300 per 100 grams for beef, depending on the fat level, and 265 for moth larvae—but where beef contained about 58 percent water, the caterpillars came in at a dry 4 percent. Thus, as noted by one entomologist, moth larvae are "good if you want to get into body building on a budget."

The consumption of butterflies and moths has a long history, dating to prehistoric mealtimes, but usually has eluded the blessing of Euro-American peoples. In *Swiss Family Robinson*, the account of a family shipwrecked and stranded on an island, published in 1813, moths were presented as a safeguard against

hunger. In 1885, when Vincent M. Holt published a treatise called *Why Not Eat Insects* he took that story and altering it to his own argument, lobbied enthusiastically to put moths on the menu. Alas, in vain.

Mr. Holt further said that "The Hottentots," a term used for natives of Africa at the time, collected and carried the caterpillars in "large calabashes to their homes, where they fry them in iron pots over a gentle fire, stirring them about the while. They eat them, cooked thus, in handfuls, without any flavoring or sauce. A traveller who on several occasions tried this dish, tells us that he thought it delicate, nourishing and wholesome, resembling in taste sugared cream or sweet almond paste."

At the same time Mr. Holt was waxing so eloquently in England, in the Cascade and Sierra Mountains of North America, Indian tribes harvested the large caterpillars of the pandora moth. "The full-grown caterpillars measure from two to two and one-half inches in length and are as fat as an index finger," wrote the author of *Insect Fact and Folklore* (1954). "Normally, these caterpillars live on the pine trees, far out of reach, but in order to pass into the pupal stage they descend in great numbers to burrow into the soil. Just before this takes place the Indians build fires under the trees and stupefy the caterpillars by the smudge. This causes them to loosen their hold on the trees and fall to the ground where they are collected in baskets. They are then prepared as food by being dried over a bed of hot ashes or by being boiled in water." These moths are rarely, if ever, eaten in North America today.

Of all the moth larvae likely it is the Australian witchetty "grub" that has found the most exposure to western tongues and tastes recently. Australian natives, known as Aborigines, have eaten many different insects for uncounted thousands of years. In a 1995 article in *Cultural Entomology Digest*, Dr. Ron Cherry claimed that they were the "most important insect food of the desert." The grubs were collected by digging up the roots of the acacia bush (also known as the witchety bush), and chopping them to obtain the grubs

Fried Silkworm Chrysalids

After the cocoons have been spun, a certain number of chrysalids are taken and grilled in a frying pan, so that the watery fluid runs out. The outer coverings come away easily, leaving behind a quantity of small yellow objects that resemble a mass of carp roe.

These are fried in butter, fat or oil, and sprinkled with stock. After cooking them for 5 minutes, they are crushed with a wooden spoon and the whole mass is carefully stirred so that nothing remains at the bottom of the pan. Some egg yolks are beaten, in the proportion of 3 to every 100 chrysalids, and poured over them. In this way, a beautiful golden yellow cream with an exquisite flavor is obtained. This is the way the dish was prepared for the Mandarins and the wealthy. On the other hand, the poor people, after grilling the chrysalids and removing their outer coverings, fry them in butter or fat and season them with a little salt, pepper, or vinegar, or even eat them just as they are, with rice.

Père Favaud

within. "Ten large grubs," Dr. Cherry said, "are sufficient to provide the daily [protein] needs of an adult."

Such indigenous foods are called "bush tucker" and one or more of the dishes found on trendy restaurants now offering this cuisine from Sydney to Melbourne to Perth includes this grub. Originally they were eaten raw or cooked in ashes and now they are prepared according to Euro-American tastes, roasted and served with a frosty can of Foster's lager, or stir-fried with vegetables, perhaps with a side order of kangaroo. "Tucker trips" are among the most popular expeditions for both domestic and overseas visitors throughout Australia's tropical north and the Outback around Alice Springs, where people pay an absurd amount of money to hunt and sample these larvae live.

While it is the larva, or caterpillar, stage of the moth (and, in rarer instances, the butterfly) that is

Opposite: Sericulture workers almost everywhere are familiar with the nutritional value of the pupae. In a Thai village specialising in silk production, the pupae are a regular snack consumed while spinning.

most popular, adults are eaten, too. The Australian Aborigines, like the stranded Swiss Family Robinson, also feasted on Bogong moths, harvesting them in large numbers during the winter months from the caves and rock crevices of the Bogong Mountains. By cooking them in hot sand and stirring in hot ashes, they burned off the wings and legs. The moths were then sifted through a net to remove their heads, kneaded into balls and roasted in open fires, or ground into a powder and with water made into a paste that was cooked into bite-sized cakes.

Obviously, a single moth or butterfly, or larvae from either one, will not fill an empty stomach, or even constitute a snack. Some effort must be made in harvesting. Yet, in parts of southern Africa one person can pick about five gallons of a single caterpillar species in a day if the bush is rich, and seven days' picking, if all are sold, can earn the equivalent of a month's salary for a general worker.

Pickers and traders today may travel several hundred miles during the regulated season, in November and December, the opening date intended to ensure that the caterpillars are large before harvesting, the closing date to ensure that there is enough "seed" for the next season. However, pickers arrive in such great numbers that officials now consider the pickers rather than the caterpillars a larger threat to the national forest because of the damage done to trees and undergrowth. It also is difficult to enforce the closing date.

As noted by one entomologist in *The Food Insects Newsletter*, "People find it very difficult to stop picking this sweet relish!"

Insects That Are Good to Eat

"I think it is in the *Swiss Family Robinson* that there is a clever account of some travellers, wandering at night through a forest by torchlight, being greatly annoyed by huge moths, which repeatedly extinguished the torches by their suicidal love of light. However, annoyance was turned to joy when, tempted by the appetizing smell of the toasted moths, the hungry travellers ventured to satisfy in part their hunger with the suicides, which they found as excellent in flavor as in smell. From what I recollect of the tale, I believe this was quite a fancy description, probably founded on the real habits of the natives which had been observed by the travelled author of the book. I well remember that, on reading that account, my youthful imagination reproduced without effort the appetizing smell of a plump baked moth; but it did not occur to me then to try such a tidbit. Lately, however, I have done so, to find the dream of my childhood fully realized as to the delights, both in taste and smell, of a fat moth nicely baked. Try them, ye epicures! What possible argument can be advanced aganst eating a creature beautiful without and sweet within; a creature nourished on nectar, the fabled food of the gods?

"Most of the commoner moths which flit in thousands by night, around our fields and gardens, have nice fat carcasses, and ought certainly to be used as food. Why, they are the very incarnescence of sweetness, beauty, and deliciousness; living storehouses of nectar gathered from the most fragrant flowers! They, too, voluntarily and suggestively sacrifice themselves upon the altar of our lamps, as we sit, with open windows, in the balmy summer nights. They fry and grill themselves before our eyes, saying, 'Does not the sweet scent of our cooked bodies tempt you? Fry us with butter; we are delicious. Boil us, grill us, stew us; we are good all ways!'"

— Vincent M. Holt, *Why Not Eat Insects* 1885

flies

According to afficionados, the dragonfly is a wondrous beast with a history that pre-dates the dinosaurs, an exotic beauty that sends those who eat them into cries of ecstacy as they catch them in their nets.

The ordinary fly, on the other hand, elicits not praise and nets, but curses, smelly sprays, sticky strips of paper hung from the ceiling, and rolled-up newspapers.

Both are good to eat, in the larva as well as the adult stage. Fly larvae? Isn't that...aren't they...maggots? Alas, it's true. But the maggot is unfairly maligned. The high protein content—about sixty percent—makes them especially desireable in areas where more conventional protein choices are limited. A report by the Zinhua News Agency in Beijing put the protein content at fifty percent, and claimed that the low-fat oil produced from them was effective in preventing heart disease.

"Some term other than 'maggot' should probably be coined for muscoid fly larvae when discussed as food," Gene DeFoliart wrote in *The Food Insects Newsletter* in 1994. "The natural habitats with which many of these species are normally associated conjures up rather unsavory connotations."

It is true that maggots and adult flies have a curious diet, at least by human standards. In fact, they will eat nearly anything: meat that's beginning to go bad, rotting fruit and vegetable matter, other insects, sucking whatever they find through what might fairly be compared to a syringe. (No adult fly can chew.) They then fly about, landing here and there, cleaning themselves and, it cannot be denied, spreading germs.

But as is true with cockroaches and other "loathsome," disease-spreading creatures in the insect world, not all flies are bad news. Flies are one of the major successes of the insect world, with at least 60,000 different species surviving happily just about anywhere, even in Antarctica. The common house fly is the one that humans see most often and with good reason it is to be shunned. It is always advisable when eating insects to get as far from humans as possible, in order to avoid pesticides and other contaminents so often associated with human development.

And so it has always been, with most stories about eating flies associated with primitive or indigenous groups in undeveloped areas. For example, snipe flies frequently laid their eggs on vegetation hanging over streams, where the females soon died. As more and more laid their eggs, the masses of insect corpses soon grew large, inspiring the Modoc Indians of California to dam the stream with logs, then shake the bushes, causing the dead insects to fall into the water. When the bodies reached the hastily constructed dam downstream, the Modocs merely scooped them out.

"As many as a hundred bushels a day could be secured in this way," according to *Insect Fact and Folklore* (1954). "The Indians used a basket to dip the flies from the water and to carry them to their ovens, where they were cooked. They were not taken out of the oven immediately, but were allowed to cool gradually. The Indians called this dish 'Koo-chab-bie.' When cold, it was about the consistency of headcheese and

An Aeronautical Impossibility

Members of an organization called the Dragonfly Society of America, whose members organize safaris with large butterfly nets, marvel at the speed and elusiveness that characterize the creatures they admire. With the sharp eyes of a skilled predator and aerobatic talent that the U.S. Air Force has tried to quantify, it is no wonder that they're called "mosquito hawks" and that the poet Alfred Lord Tennyson described them as "living flashes of light."

Aeronautical engineers are flying them through windtunnels and hooking them to strength meters, trying to figure out how they can go from zero to thirty miles per hour and then stop on a dime in a blink, hover like a hummingbird, and dart right, left, backwards, and upside-down in a manner that defies conventional flying theory. Of course, they've had three-hundred million years to develop, and those same engineers, following similar logic said it was impossible for the bumble bee to fly because it was too heavy for its wings.

Balinese youths hunt for dragonflies using a long thin strip of bamboo coated with the sticky sap of the jackfruit tree. This strip is inserted in the end of a long bamboo stick, which is then wielded to touch the dragonfly as it alights on a blade of grass. The legs and wings are removed, and the insect is then ready to cook.

Sources

Fly larva by mail from Nature's Way, P.O. Box 188, Ross, OH 45061, phone (800) 318-2611, fax (513) 737-5421.

Flightless houseflies and fruitflies from Mary Testa, P.O. Box 250, Yolo, CA 95697, phone (530) 666-0321, email <ladyfly@dcn.davis.ca.us>.

This page: Typically, the Balinese add dragonflies to a pounded mixture of coconut paste, fermented fish paste, garlic, chilis, tamarind juice, basil leaves, ginger, and the juice of a lime. This is then wrapped in banana leaf packets to make a variety of the common dish known as *pepes*. *Opposite:* Maggot fried rice, a variation of the one-dish meal, common throughout Asia, makes use of leftover cooked rice, dry-roasted maggots, chopped garlic, sliced peppers, and is seasoned with fish sauce, soy sauce, sugar, shallots, spring onions, and coriander.

was firm enough to be cut into slices with a knife." The Modoc Indians are long gone, but lake flies are still cherished in tropical Africa and mayflies are caught for food in Mexico. And the role of such insects in diet is now being studied by entomologists in several American and European universities.

Significant research also has been done in using soldier fly larvac to grow edible protein for livestock. University of Georgia entomologist Craig Sheppard estimates that the waste from a large commercial chicken farm (minimum of 100,000 birds) seeded with soldier fly eggs will produce sixty-six tons of animal feed larvae in five months. They can be cooked, dried, and mixed in with conventional animal feeds.

Similar preparation of fly larvae will do for us as well, even that found on decomposing meat. The meat is placed in a box with openings in the bottom corners. Containers for collecting the larvae are placed under the openings, the larvae crawl to the corners and fall into the containers. Once captured, they are washed in cool water, then cooked. They may be stir-fried with vegetables, added to fried rice with onions and chilis, or boiled and made into a stew or soup. They also may be roasted or grilled.

Near the Arctic Circle, a species of botfly deposits its eggs on the backs of caribou. When the eggs hatch, the larvae tunnel through the skin to feed, and as they grow in size, swellings that look like boils appear. When the larvae are full grown, they emerge through the skin and fall to the ground where they hatch. The Dogrib Indians in northern Canada, who raised caribou as beasts of burden as well as a food, learned to squeeze the swellings, forcing the mature bot to fall out. Usually, they were eaten alive and when a mature caribou was slaughtered, they were left alone and cooked along with the meat. Maggots also are eaten in Africa, dead or alive, when other large animals were found to be infested while butchering.

Dr. Ed Dresner wrote a letter to *The Food Insects Newsletter* (1994), telling how he came to eat Oriental fruit fly larvae while working on a control program in

Hawaii. "I and most of my hiking companions ate the fruits enthusiastically, not discriminating because of larval infestation," he said. "My impression is the larvae made the fruit a little less tart." While Tom McRae, retired chief of scientific research for the Entomology Department of the University of Queensland in Australia said in a letter to me that adult fruit flies were easily cultured in huge numbers, "so are an excellent bulk source of insect protein." Kill by freezing, he said, then wash and dry, and cook in a skillet with finely hashed onions, butter, and a pinch of ground ginger.

Fly larvae, sold mainly as food for for pets, are also bargain-priced—just US$5 for 500 by mail, a thousand for $7.50, delivered live to your door.

If maggots are easy to collect or purchase, flies are

not and most of those available commercially today are of the wingless variety, sold by pet shops for feeding reptiles.

Dragonflies are hard to catch, too, but highly prized. Dragonflies begin life underwater, clinging to a reed and consuming protozoa, even tadpoles and tiny minnows. At the end of a year, the nymph crawl out of the water onto a stem of a plant and dry off, as the wings and legs emerge. In another two to five hours, the creatures will be airborne and in search of a meal. Prey is caught in full flight and they are known to eat as many as three-hundred mosquitoes and other small insects a day.

Most are caught in nets, but because the dragonflies have a habit of sitting on the end of a stick or reed over the water, some hunters will put a sticky substance on the perch that catches them like ordinary flies on fly-paper. In Bali, where dragonflies are a special treat, hunters go out with long sticks "baited" with a gummy substance, and after picking off their legs and wings, grill their catch with rice, herbs and seasoning inside banana leaf wrappers.

Some dragonfly hunters raise the nymphs at home in aquariums. In prehistoric times, their wingspan equalled that of a modern hawk or large crow, but today's 5,500 or so species are far smaller, thus one or two will not go far toward filling an empty stomach.

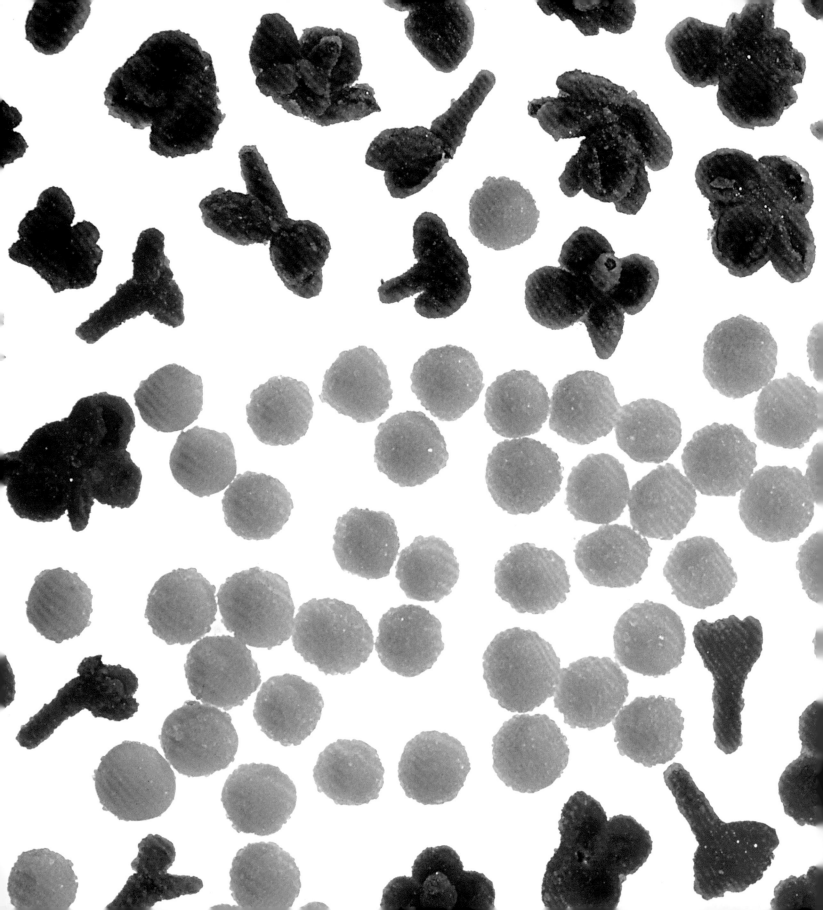

plants

plants

Plants are miracles that come from a combination of sunlight, water, and dirt, and they come in hundreds of thousands of varieties. To put it in technical terms, they are multicellular organisms that produce food from sunlight and inorganic matter by photosynthesis, with rigid cell walls containing cellulose. Most, but not all, are edible.

In fact, one of the chapters in this section is titled "Poisonous Plants," which explains how some foods must be processed in a prescribed way to remove the threat (or at least most of it) or consumed only in the minutest quantity. One wonders how such things were discovered and why anyone bothered to try when so many got sick or died in early experimentation. For example, manioc is deadly when left uncooked, yet today it is one of the world's top carbohydrate sources, after it has been properly treated.

Historians believe that, traditionally, it was the women who gathered the plants, while their burlier mates went out to hunt mammoth and other large game. "Hunting was a flamboyant business—the drama of the chase and the return in triumph are still enshrined today in the ceremonies of many primitive tribes—whereas gathering depended on quiet patience and the kind of perseverance that was continuous rather than (as with hunting) sporadic," wrote Reay Tannahill in her classic *Food in History* (1995). "But though there might be little excitement in the task, the foodstuffs women collected were more than just supplementary to meat. When the hunting was poor, they were what everyone depended on."

So much so that modern agriculture developed before the domestication of animals, with the cultivation of wild wheat and barley in what is now called the Middle East. Gathering still plays a significant role in many parts of the undeveloped world, but elsewhere farming is dominant, and plant life continues to play a monumental role in the human diet—even our meat sources depend on it.

As is true in other sections of this book, the plants considered here generally are ones that may be valued in one part of the world, but are denigrated or ignored in another. Some, like keluak, a fruit found in the Caribbean, is actually banned from import into the United States, because it is regarded as life-threatening, and the durian from Southeast Asia is forbidden by many airlines and hotels because its strong odor is considered offensive.

Another, cactus, has been associated for millennia in some areas or with specific groups such as native Americans, gaining only a small following outside those populations, perhaps because of their spines; and while flowers are turning up nowadays in the spring mix in select supermarkets, most Euro-Americans still regard them as something decorative rather than delicious or good for you.

In the 1960s and 1970s, accompanying a sort of back-to-nature movement nurtured by the hippies and a newfound interest in organic foods and medicinal herbs, wild plants as food attracted more attention. Books by Euell Gibbons, most notably in *Stalking the Wild Asparagus* (1987), and others became bestsellers. Niche markets developed and something called the "health food store" became a commercial generic. Thus, many new foods found new commercial success.

Previous: Candied flowers from the renowned food-store Fauchon in Paris include pink and mauve lilac, rose petals and mimosa.

Universal Plant Edibility Test

The following sounds like a lot of work — it is! — but that's because it comes from the *U.S. Army Survival Manual* as republished in 1994 as " a civilian's best guide for toughing it, any place in the world... a must for campers, hikers, explorers, pilots, and others whose vocation or avocations require familiarity with the wilderness or out-of-doors... "

1. Test only one part of a potential food plant at a time.
2. Break the plant into its basic components — leaves, stems, roots, buds, and flowers.
3. Smell the food for strong or acid odors. Keep in mind that smell alone does not indicate if a plant is edible.
4. Do not eat for 8 hours before starting the test.
5. During the 8 hours you are abstaining from eating, test for contact poisoning by placing a piece of the plant part you are testing on the inside of your elbow or wrist. Usually 15 minutes is enough time to allow for a reaction.
6. During the test period, take nothing by mouth except purified water and the plant part being tested.
7. Select a small portion of a single component and prepare it the way you plan to eat it.
8. Before putting the prepared plant part in your mouth, touch a small portion (a pinch) to the outer surface of the lip to test for burning or itching.
9. If after 3 minutes there is no reaction on your lip, place the plant part on your tongue, holding it there for 15 minutes.
10. If there is no reaction, thoroughly chew a pinch and hold it in your mouth for 15 minutes. DO NOT SWALLOW.
11. If no burning, itching, numbing, stinging, or other irritation occurs during the 15 minutes, swallow the food.
12. Wait 8 hours. If any ill effects occur during this period, induce vomiting and drink a lot of water.
13. If no ill effects occur, eat ½ cup of the same plant part prepared the same way. Wait another 8 hours. If no ill effects occur, the plant part as prepared is safe for eating.

It is further recommended that all parts of the plant be tested, as some plants have both edible and inedible parts. Nor is it to be assumed that a part that proved edible when cooked is also edible when raw.

It seems so much trouble, it'd be easier to starve.

poisonous plants

Opposite: A stinkhorn mushroom, so-called because of its putrid smell. This attracts insects, which then carry off spores on their feet.

When Sam Sebastiani Jr., a member of one of California's most prominent wine-making families, died in 1997 after eating mushrooms gathered near his home, the media went mad about mushrooms. Someone whose fortune and fame was founded in the growing of grapes had been felled by another plant. It was as if Henry Ford had been run over and killed by a Buick while jay-walking. How ironic—and how stupid—people said. While newspaper and television reporters dashed into the forest with their camera crews to photograph mushrooms.

Mushrooms, a type of fungus (a plant with neither chlorophyll nor flowers), have a reputation that most of them don't deserve. Nearly all are not only edible, but have greater food value than green vegetables. Consequently, dozens of varieties are staples in every supermarket produce section. On the other hand, some are deadly, the most infamous of these being members of the mushroom family collected by Mr. Sebastiani and his friends: the *amanita*. The *amanita* are a genus of mushrooms containing a few species remarkable for their toxicity. There are many edible *amanita*, but eating the wrong one can bring on cholera-like diarrhea, dehydration, vomiting, abdominal pains, delirium, cramps, or, as the young wine-maker discovered, death by liver and kidney failure.

The odd thing is that many people felled by this mushroom didn't mistake it for an edible cousin: they knew that this was the mushroom made famous by

Lewis Carroll in *Alice in Wonderland*, and they ate it deliberately. Carroll's wonderland, after all, was the result of eating the distinctive red caps with the big white polka dots, wasn't it? And if you didn't eat too many...you went on a wonderful trip. Yes? Yes. Many plants have been eaten over the centuries in order to get high and several of them have proved deadly when consumed in too great a quantity.

The *amanita*, along with a basket full of other mushroom varieties, is just one of many health- or life-threatening plants that are consumed as food, several of them matter-of-factly. The difference is, that even when cooked, some of the mushrooms can kill, while proper processing of several other poisonous plants renders them safe.

Some may reasonably wonder how such dangerous foods were discovered not only to be edible, but also palatable and, in many cases, nutritious, too? How long did it take to develop such long, complicated preparations as are sometimes required to make a toxic food safe? How many culinary pioneers, out of ignorance or curiosity, fell over dead or got sick before the proper preparation was discovered? In a phrase, how many cooks were spoiled by the stew rather than the other way around? History rarely answers such questions. These dishes were not created overnight; they evolved. However it happened, through perseverance, or possibly dumb, blind luck, someone eventually created from a dangerous plant a food that found its way into an exotic and cherished delicacy, or, in one instance, one of the world's most important sources of starch, the manioc. (Back to the mushroom in a minute.)

Manioc, also called the cassava and in Latin America the *yuca* or *mandioca*, is a white, starchy tropical tuber native to Brazil that was established as far north as the West Indies by the time Columbus arrived, then quickly spread to Africa and Asia, where it is now an essential food staple—the most common

Titanic Tapioca

In 1972, tapioca pudding threatened to sink a freighter off the coast of Wales when fire started in lumber stacked in the upper holds. The water thrown onto the flames by firefighters seeped down to the lower holds where 1,500 tons of tapioca pellets from Thailand were stored. The water swelled the tapioca and heat from the flames began to cook it. Firefighters said the ship's steel plates could have buckled if they hadn't reached the shore quickly, where some 500 truckloads of tapioca pudding were hauled away to the local dump.

poisonous plant, the one eaten over the greatest expanse of geography and by the largest number of people. It is easily grown in hot, humid environments, resists drought and insect pests, requires little cultivation, and provides a valuable source of carbohydrates for peoples who have difficulty raising other crops.

It also is used to make a food called tapioca, a starch for puddings and thickeners. When I was growing up in the United States, my brother and I called the little starch globules in the bowl of tapioca we sometimes got for dessert "fish eyes." We would have preferred ice cream.

Although there are many varieties there are only two main categories: bitter and sweet, and it is the former that is life-threatening, in its uncooked state containing lethal amounts of linamarin which releases hydrocyanic acid, more commonly known as cyanide. When I was a child, tapioca pudding was served frequently in my home and I had no idea. I assume my mother was similarly uninformed.

The manioc is a bushy plant that grows three to nine feet high, depending on the variety, with large flat leaves and green flowers that may also be eaten when cooked, like spinach. After six to twenty-four months, again depending on type of plant and location, the entire bush is dug up and the roots are harvested, like potatoes. The tubers vary in shape, number, color, and size, and may weigh as much as thirty pounds. The longer they are left in the ground, the more starch they contain.

The flesh beneath the rind is crunchy, like most root crops, and both varieties are calorie-rich (262 calories for one 3.5-ounce serving), as well as high in carbohydrates, but have only small amounts of proteins, vitamins, and mineral salts. This leads some to describe it a nice "filler," staving off hunger cheaply, but offering little else.

Commercially, manioc generally is processed within twenty-four hours of harvest to halt the loss of starch. First, it is washed to remove dirt and impurities, then it is peeled and rasped to reduce the flesh to a thick,

coarse mixture of pulp, juice, and starch called a slurry. Next, it is exposed to sulfur dioxide gas or a sodium-bisulfite solution to prevent discoloration and retard bacterial growth. Then the juice is extracted in much the same way soap is removed from clothing in a laundry, by repeated rinsing in clean water. Finally, the starch is dried with hot air, and sifted. The result is manioc flour, used to make cakes, soups, stews, and bread.

In native villages, the processing is handled more simply, of course. After peeling, slicing and grating, it is washed thoroughly and packed into a long cylindrical sort of woven "press" with loops at both ends. One loop is tied to a tree limb and the second is heavily weighted, causing the press to increase in length and decrease in diameter, much like a woven straw Chinese finger trap. This extracts the juice, which is collected in a vessel placed below. The paste that is left in the press may now be formed into patties much like a small tortilla or pancake and cooked on a piece of flat pottery or slate placed over an open fire. In some areas, they are cooked until crisp, in others they are only lightly toasted, leaving them soft and pliable. Pieces are then torn off, boiled fish paste is spread on top, and they are served like open-face sandwiches.

The leftover juice may be boiled and used as a thickening for soups. Additional boiling and sweetening in the sun produces what is called *casareep*, which is used as a flavoring that is especially popular in Guyana, where it appears in virtually every dish. In the West Indies, it is the foundation of that country's celebrated pepper pot.

The root may also be roasted like a potato, with the extreme heat removing the poison.

Alternatively, the root may be peeled, cut into quarter-inch slices, and dried in the sun for two or three days, then stored for later use. (Frequently, it may be seen drying on rural highways or urban sidewalks. I've seen the former in Vietnam, the latter in China.) It may be stored and when needed, the washing, grating and juice removal process is identical to that described above.

Finally, of course, manioc may be fermented to produce an intoxicating beverage. (Is there any botanical product in the world that can't be turned into booze?) The home brew—it hasn't been manufactured commercially yet—is produced in a manner that has gone unchanged over centuries. The sliced and grated tuber is fermented in water, with some chewed root added to assist the process. The liquor is then stored in gourds.

Manioc flour may be made at home by peeling the root, then grinding the flesh to a pulp, which is then wrapped in cheesecloth and submerged in a container of water. Then it is kneaded by hand until a white powder flows through the gauze and sinks to the bottom of the container. The water is poured off and the residue is dried in the sun for two or three days. The flour usually dries in lumps that can be rolled until fine with a bottle or rolling pin. (An interesting note: dry the paste in sunlight and it remains white, but if the weather is cloudy, the flour turns pink.)

The flour is sold commercially and is added in small amounts to rice flour to give Southeast Asian and Chinese pastries a translucent sheen and chewiness. Mixed with an equal amount of taro flour, it is used to wrap a filling of Chinese mushrooms, pork, dried shrimps and fish, Chinese chives, winter bamboo shoots and dried bean curd; these dumplings are then steamed.

As for that gooey, globular tapioca pudding I ate as a child, it is made from the same manioc flour, cooked with milk and sugar, then stirred with egg white and vanilla extract.

Another poisonous plant is the ackee, a bright red tropical fruit not recognized as edible in most of the places where it is grown—in parts of Central America, as well as in Antigua, Trinidad, Grenada, and Barbados. More ominous, its import into the United States is banned. Yet, it is a sort of "national dish" in Jamaica and to visit this Caribbean nation without eating it is akin to visiting Japan without consuming sushi or Kobe beef. And, it will kill you, if its poison is not neutralized carefully.

So why do people eat it? For the same reason they

eat anything, because it tastes good, and, for some foreigners the whiff of danger gives them an added thrill. Disarming the fruit is easy: all you have to do is wait for the fruit to ripen, then boil it. It is when it is not ripe, or eaten uncooked that you are playing Jamaican roulette.

Most often, it is consumed at breakfast with salted, dried fish, usually cod, though other fish such as mackerel may be used. Just bring the fruit to a boil in water for about ten minutes, simmer it down with the fish (or cooked bacon), cut-up onions, peppers, tomatoes, and seasonings, then serve with fried dumplings or roasted bread fruit (a tropical starch fried, baked or roasted like a potato), put on a Bob Marley record, and pour yourself a cup of Blue Mountain coffee laced with a tot of Jamaican rum.

Ackee is believed to have come to the Caribbean from West Africa on a slave ship in the eighteenth century. Its scientific name, *blighia sapida*, comes from Captain William Bligh, who took the fruit to England in 1793, one of his many important botanical contributions that were, later, overwhelmed by a famous disciplinary problem in the South Pacific called mutiny.

A Southeast Asian food that is deadly if eaten in its natural state is the *buah keluak*, whose very name translates as "the fruit that nauseates." In fact, it is not a fruit at all, nor a nut, as many of its champions insist. It is the soft interior of a hard seed case about the size of a small egg found within the fruit of the great kepayang tree. In its uncooked state, it is used in the Indonesian jungles to coat spear and arrowheads for hunting, providing a clue to its deadliness.

Yet, with the appropriate—and somewhat peculiar—preparation, it is transformed into a delicacy that many call the "Truffle of Asia." Usually it's found in a curry called *ayam buah keluak*, or chicken with keluak fruit. This is a cherished part of the cuisine of the Peranakan, the "native-born" Chinese who have lived for generations in Singapore, Malaysia, and Indonesia.

Its danger lies in the prussic acid contained within the flesh, a poison that can be removed only by burying it in the ground with ashes for at least thirty days and preferably for double that. It must then be soaked in fresh water for one to two weeks, with frequent changes of the water. Finally, it is boiled in hot water for ten minutes before opening each seed with a cleaver to see if the meat inside is moldy. One bad seed will spoil the dish and they must be removed. (How, I ask again, did anyone discover such a process to make this strange fruit edible?)

Connoisseurs argue over the ways to cook any special food, and so it is with buah keluak. Some eat the somewhat bitter flesh straight from the shell, once it has gone through the long burial and soaking process. Others prefer to scoop out the black meat and blend it with chopped pork, fish, prawns, salt and pepper, then stuff it back into the hard seed case before cooking. It may then be added to a chicken curry that contains ground onions, ginger, lemon grass, chili pepper, the skin and juice of tamarind, and a paste of mashed candlenut, which provides the required stickiness.

One final note: the flesh of the buah keluak is black and it dominates the dish, so if you think you might be squeamish about eating anything black, Singapore is also famous for its fried rice.

Rhubarb Fool

In researching this book, I was also surprised to discover that another meal from my childhood was potentially dangerous: rhubarb, which usually arrived at the table in my house as rhubarb pie, one of many ways the red celery-like stalks can be used in a dessert. Recipes spooned up from the pages of such magazines as *Bon Appétit*, *Gourmet*, and *House & Garden* magazines include such mouth-drooling choices as Rhubarb-Raspberry Jam; Lemon Ice Torte with Strawberry-Rhubarb Sauce; Scandinavian Rhubarb Pudding; Rhubarb and Pear Compote; Rhubarb Tart; Rhubarb, Onion and Raisin Chutney; Strawberry-Rhubarb Cobbler with Cornmeal Biscuit Topping and something called Rhubarb Fool.

The latter dish may carry the most weight (as a warning perhaps), if not the greatest number of calories: only the stalks of this buckwheat family member are edible and care must be exercised when harvesting to leave out the leaves and roots, which contain oxalic acid. Even the stalks, carefully culled, are unusually tart, needing sweetening from a sugary fruit, as the recipes named imply, or generous amounts of sugar. For good reason the ancient Greeks called it "the vegetable of the barbarians," and deer, who will eat almost anything, give it a pass. It doesn't just make your mouth pucker, it turns it inside out.

Opposite: As depicted in an illustration by Arthur Rackham in 1907, Alice's wondrous adventures include eating noxious mushrooms.

Finally, we return to Sebastiani and his final mushroom harvest. The fungus Sebastiani is thought to have eaten was an *Amanita Phalloides*, known as the "death cap" mushroom. It is the cause of ninety-five percent of mushroom poisonings worldwide, fatal in one out of every three cases. Toxins in its cap destroy the victim's liver and kidney by rupturing the cells.

At the time of his death, Sebastiani was one of three victims of *amanita* poisoning awaiting a possible liver transplant at the University of California Medical Center in San Francisco. Several of his relatives had volunteered to be donors for a partial liver transplant (in which part of the donor's liver is grafted onto the patient's liver, and the healthy liver often helps the damaged cells to regenerate), but a transplant was ruled out because his body was too heavily infected.

Welcome to Wonderland

Reduced to a height of three inches, Alice philosophized with a caterpillar smoking a hookah (while seated on a mushroom) and watched a baby turn into a pig; then after taking advice from a vanishing Cheshire cat, she had a wild tea party with the March Hare, the Mad Hatter, and the Dormouse; and after that, played croquet with the King and Queen of Hearts, using flamingos for mallets and hedgehogs for balls.

What had happened to her? Was it something she ate? Was it poisonous? "Go ask Alice!" as the rock band Jefferson Airplane sang in a hit song inspired by the tale in 1967. "Feed your head!"

flowers

Dandelion Wine

2 quarts dandelion blossoms, without stems
1 orange, peeled and sliced thinly
1 lemon or lime, cut into slices
1½ lbs. sugar
1 tbs. brewer's yeast
1 piece toast

Place blossoms in a bowl and cover with boiling water, stirring, then cover with a cloth and leave for 3 days, stirring occasionally.

Strain into a second vessel, add the rind of the orange, lemon and sugar. Boil slowly for 30 minutes, then leave to cool.

Add yeast spread on a piece of toast to the brew and let stand for 2 days. Then pour into a dry cask, well sealed. Leave for 2 months, then bottle.

In Hawaii, where I lived for a number of years, it was common in a hotel restaurant to see an orchid decorating a plate of fresh fruit, a sandwich, or a salad. It was something to give the tourists a small touch of tropical exotica, purely decorative. Many of the tourists had never seen orchids before and, thinking them part of the dish, ate them. Poor dears.

Garnishing a plate of food with uncooked blossoms and sprigs of fresh this and that is common and while many of the floral and green decorations, like parsley, are nutritious and edible, the orchid is not. In fact, most orchids don't taste very good. They don't even have much of a scent, contrary to what a lot of novelists say in their poorly researched books; for the most part, they are odorless, as well as sort of bitter. The diner is not the fool in this tale. The chef or restaurant manager is. No one should ever put anything on a plate that is not meant to go into the mouth.

Many blossoming plants are not only palatable, they add surprise and zest to a meal and elegance to a dinner party that guests likely won't forget. They also offer nourishment. The custom of eating flowers began at least five thousand years ago, when the Chinese began to consider herbal medicine and food as having the same origins (and flowers were an essential part of both), and continued right through history. The Roman chef Apicius sprinkled brains with rose petals, added sweet marjoram blossoms to an assortment of hashes, and made a sauce with safflower petals. The great nineteenth-century French novelist Alexandre Dumas, author of *The Three Musketeers* and *The Man in the Iron Mask*, created a recipe for herb soup *à la dauphine* containing marigold flowers. Today? Even some supermarkets in America include a few flowers in their produce section, not far from the artichokes and broccoli. (Which are also flowers.) As is true of many foods unknown or rejected in Euro-America, the pretty part of the plant recently has found a niche market.

In considering the ethnology of eating flowers, botanists discuss only the blossom itself. For example, the seeds of the sunflower are of no interest to them, but should someone sautée the buds with butter and lemon juice and then garnish the dish with fresh petals, the scientists will reach for their knives and forks.

The number of flowers and their culinary uses seem almost countless and a newcomer to flower cuisine may wonder where to start. In one of the best of recent books on the subject, *Edible Flowers: From Garden to Palate* (1995), the author, Cathy Wilkinson Barash, recommended a "Big Ten," based on taste, versatility, and ease of cultivation: the calendula (a member of the marigold family), chives, day lily, mint, pansy, rose, sage, signet marigold, squash blossoms, and nasturtium. Of these, mint, sage, and chives might be called somewhat commonplace. But how many in Europe and the U.S. put any of the others on their plate recently?

I ate my first nasturtiums in the 1960s, when my wife and I followed the back-to-the-earth crowd and bought a farm in California, where we planted and nurtured a garden about an eighth of an acre in size, adding a bed of nasturtiums near the compost heap to mix with chervil, oil, and lemon juice for a salad based on a recipe we saw in a book by Alice B. Toklas, the companion to Gertrude Stein who was better-known during the 1960s for her recipe for hashish brownies. (A food made from another flowering plant, familiar in our neighborhood at the time.)

Toklas was not alone in her appreciation of the nasturtium. The Greek historian Xenophon reported this ornamental plant was eaten by the Persians about 400 B.C. Louis XIV of France cultivated them in his garden, as did Thomas Jefferson, who used it as a seasoning. Even Dwight D. Eisenhower, not known for his gustatory sophistication, had the White House chef put nasturtiums in vegetable soup.

The name is Latin, combining two words, *nasus*, for "nose" and *torquere*, "to twist," the nose-twister, for its tangy fragrance and peppery taste. Some compare the flavor to capers, thus it is no surprise that Ms. Barash offers recipes for salmon with nasturtium butter or nasturtium vinaigrette. The flower may also be added to cloves, peppercorns, and garlic to produce a spicy vinegar, or stuffed with cream cheese. Most commonly, they are used whole as an accompaniment to salads, vegetables, pasta, and meat dishes.

Better known but also under-appreciated as a food is the rose. No other flower is wrapped in more legend and history. Its petals were used to make early Catholic rosaries, the white rose regarded as a symbol of the Immaculate Conception, the red representing Christ's blood. The same two roses were flown on flags of opposing armies in the War of the Roses. Today, songwriters call the rose the ultimate symbol of romance, a dozen of which, with long stems, may cost as much as dinner for ten and last just a little longer than the meal before wilting.

The rose is also one of the tastiest and most versatile flowers in the kitchen when and if it ever gets there. The fresh petals can be made into rose water, dried petals into rose tea. The petals may also be used to season butter; flavor ice cream (a favorite treat in India); make jelly, syrup, and jam; like the nasturtium, flavor a vinegar or vinaigrette; and bring fragrance to salads and vegetables. The buds can also be used in summer puddings or as a condiment when dried. The more fragrant roses offer the most flavor and the darker ones usually have the strongest taste.

If you've ever eaten Chinese hot and sour soup, you've eaten the dried petals of the day lily, as it is one of the key ingredients. The name comes from a blossom that blooms only a single day, but it has been eaten for thousands of years in China, where it is cultivated as a cash crop for export around the world. New York City imports more than two tons of the dried petals each year, nearly all of it sold in Chinatown.

The use is not confined to soups. The flowers can be cooked with duck, pan-fried with pork and onions, wrapped into pancakes, sautéed alone as a vegetable, and stir-fried with chicken or shrimp. The buds may also be dusted with flour, dipped in a batter and deep-fried, then served with an avocado dip, or blanched and frozen for up to eight months, allowing almost year-round use.

The calendula is the marigold's botanic name, derived from the Latin *calens*, meaning the first day of the month. Christians called it "marygold," honoring the Virgin Mary, because it was thought to be ripest during holidays. The signet marigold is generally agreed to be the tastiest of the large group, when bruised giving off a lemony scent. Enjoyed for their bright color, they once were called a "poor man's saffron," dried and powdered and used as substitute for that expensive condiment.

Early this century, the dried petals were sold in country stores, "out of a wooded barrel by ounce" as were other herbs. Leona Woodring Smith writes in her book, *The Forgotten Art of Flower Cookery* (1973), that "our great-great-grandmothers left us many recipes using marigolds in buns, rice stews, cakes, broths, 'drinkes', pickles, and 'possets and pottage.' Dutch chefs famous for their soups and stews acknowledge the marigold as their secret ingredient. Many wine and cordial recipes today use marigolds as the base." As versatile as the rose, the fresh petals can be cooked with quiche or eggs, and added to a custard, biscuits, or a sandwich spread, while the powdered petals can be mixed with flour, butter, cheese, and egg yolk, then baked on a cookie sheet.

Pansies offer a taste reminiscent of grapes if the petals are used, of peppermint if the entire blossom is added to salads and Italian dishes. Sage, mint, and chives are well-known as herbs; the point is to use the flowers, not the leaves. I've watched large yellow pumpkin blossoms being harvested by hill tribe villagers in Vietnam to cook with maize and garden greens. Xu Jian Chu of the Kunming (China) Institute

Sources

For seeds: The Gourmet Gardener, 8650 College Blvd., Suite 205IN, Overland Park, KS 66210, email <information@ gourmetgardener.com>; and the Bethlehem Seed Co., P.O. Box 1351, Bethlehem, PA 18018, phone (610) 954-5443.

For live plants and crystallization kits, as well as a book of recipes and a poster picturing thirty-nine edible flowers: Meadowsweets, RD. 1, Box 371, Middleburgh, NY 12122, phone (888) 827-6477; and Sudden Elegance Ltd., 3724 Cedar Dr., Baltimore, MD 21207-6356, email <sudden.eleg@juno.com>.

This page: Canned chrysanthemum drink.
Opposite right: Battered and lightly deep-fried flowers from the French countryside include angelica, elderflower, and nasturtium. The basket behind contains the same flowers uncooked, together with red clover and common mallow, also edible.
Opposite left: A young angelica flower growing wild. At this stage, just before the bud opens, the plant is perfect for eating.

of Botany told me that 150 different flowers were eaten in Yunnan province, among 1,200 plant species used country-wide for food and medicinal purposes.

Ancient Chinese folklore insists that if you add one chrysanthemum petal to a glass of wine, gray hair returns to its natural black. The blooms of borage, cornflower, and dianthus add brilliance to a soup or punch. Banana flowers, hanging in dense clusters in a purple pouch beneath the fruit, may be cooked and eaten like a vegetable or boiled and served cold with salads. Violet, lavender. and honeysuckle add a sweet flavor to salads or desserts. Mustard flowers lend a spicy taste to casseroles. Boiled rice cakes made from the powder of glutinous rice are stained yellow with dried, powdered camellia petals. Numerous blossoms are "crystallized"—dipped in beaten egg white, then in super-fine granulated sugar and dried—to decorate pastry or eat like candy. (Martha Stewart suggested them for wedding cakes.) Dandelion heads are made into coffee and wine.

Varieties of chamomile, jasmine, hibiscus, butterblossoms, gardenias, carnations (pinks), geraniums, gladiolas, peonies, primroses, johnny-jump-ups, orange and apple blossoms, sunflowers, tulips, hibiscus, daisies, and yucca blossoms, to name just a few more, are nutritious and tasty as well.

This does not mean that you can just buy some flowers at the local florist or nursery, or reach over your neighbor's fence when it's dinnertime. Not all blooms are edible and, in fact, many of the pretty things are toxic, including azalea, buttercup, several types of lily, rhododendron, morning glory, sweet pea, and hyacinth. It is also important to note that virtually all commercially available flowers likely have been heavily sprayed with pesticides and some have been hybridized to where there is only beauty left and little or no taste or nourishment.

B. Rosie Lerner, a consumer horticulture specialist at Purdue University in the United States, offers a few more words of caution: "On your first trial, go easy on the flowers. Eating too many blossoms can lead to

upset tummies, diarrhea, and stomach cramps. You might want to start out using flowers as a garnish and sample the flavors before trying more daring culinary delights. Or sprinkle a few flower petals over a salad to add color and flavor."

She also suggests picking flowers in the morning or late afternoon when water content is at its peak, unless they are to be dried, then midday is best. "Choose only those blossoms that are free of insects, disease, or other damage. Do not harvest from plants that were treated with pesticides, unless the product was labeled

for use on edible flowers and the harvest restrictions have been followed. Gently wash the blooms in water to remove dirt and allow to drain on paper towels. Once harvested, [most] flowers will not keep long—even when refrigerated so plan to serve within a few hours of harvesting."

The best advice comes from the chef who said that the key to happiness was to make time to stop and smell the roses...then eat them.

cactus

Cactus Juice, Jelly, Syrup, and Wine

"Now's the time to dig out those kitchen tongs and a plastic two-gallon bucket. Remove the ripe fruits with the tongs. Fill the bucket with fruits. Now wash those fruits with a garden hose. Allow the water to spill over... you'll want to wash the fruits twice. Allow the water to spill onto a plant that needs a drink. Dump the fruits into a large kettle and add two quarts of water. Bring this to a boil and then stab the softened fruits with a fork. This punctures the skin and allows the juice to escape. When the fruits are soft, they can be mashed with a potato masher. Dump the mashed fruits into a colander and allow them to drain.

"Now strain your juice through three layers of cheesecloth. You are now ready to venture into making cactus jelly, cactus syrup, or perhaps cactus wine.

"Here's a never-fail method of making cactus jelly. To one quart of cactus juice, stir in four cups of sugar. Bring this to a rolling boil and stir in two packages of powdered pectin. Slowly bring this to a boil and then remove it

(Continued opposite)

I swear this is a true story, the simple moral of which is to remove the thorns, or spines before eating. This seems an odd thing to say. After all, most animals are skinned or at least the hair is removed, ducks and chickens are plucked, fish are scaled, and porcupines, presumably, are de-quilled before consumption. But I had a friend once who saw a cow on the open range in the southwestern United States, munching on a prickly pear, the cactus that looks like a lot of green Mickey Mouse ears stuck together in a random pattern. (It has brilliant flowers blooming along the edges of the pads in spring or summer, followed by succulent, fleshy fruits, usually red or yellow.)

"I hear cactus tastes pretty good," he said.

I nodded my assent and asked if he'd like to take some back to the cabin for lunch. We began to harvest some of the flat, oval fruit and younger pads, or leaves, using a knife, carefully dropping them into a small knapsack. My friend glanced back at the cow who was also looking at us and still chewing and, apparently figuring what worked for the cow would work for him, he took a bite out of one of the leaves, failing to avoid the spines, piercing his lip.

"Cactus especially tastes good with blood," I said. "You damn fool."

My friend was right in one respect. Cactus is usually eaten raw, but only after it is peeled, which removes the spines to which the cow seemed totally oblivious. There are many ways to remove the glochids, or spines: by swatting the fruits with small, leafy branches while they are still attached to the adult plant, by rolling the fruits and leaves on the ground while wearing heavy gloves, or by wiping with a damp, rough towel. (Leather gloves are recommended, but even they are not impervious; some harvesters insist on using tongs when detaching the leaves from the plant.) Then cut off a slice from the bottom and top, make an incision lengthwise, and peel.

Inside is the gooey, sweet pulp that has been a part of the human diet according to ethnobotanists for about nine thousand years. You can also cut the fruits lengthwise in half and scoop out the pulp with a spoon, seeds and all, sprinkling the cacti with lemon or lime juice. Or, you can pick out the seeds and roast them for snacking, or dry them in the sun and grind them into a flour-like meal for cooking bread. The seeds may also be made into an oil. The fruit and leaves can be dried for later use, for making jellies and candy, and, with small effort, brewed into a low-alcohol drink.

In *The Hunting Peoples*, Carleton S. Coon described an unusual practice devised by the Indians of Baja California in Mexico, who feasted on the sweet pitahaya cactus in early summer, then carefully picked the seeds out of their excrement, to be roasted and ground and made into a bread. A Jesuit priest who was witness to this eighteenth century custom, Father Jacob Baegert, called it "a second harvest."

This odd custom aside, there is no question about the value of the cactus as a food. The question is now that several edible species, notably but certainly not exclusively, the prickly pear generally regarded as the tastiest, have spread from their native North, Central and South American origins to parts of southern Europe, North Africa, the Middle East, Hawaii, Australia, and parts of Asia, why aren't more people eating them? The plant may also be cultivated easily in gardens at home, and in pots, another reason to ask the question. If the home gardener wants a low-maintenance food crop, cactus is it. Just put it in the sun and forget about it. You don't have to water it very often; occasional rain or fog will suffice.

There are about two hundred fifty species of prickly pear, all of American origin. So much of the lore is American Indian, giving it an alternate name, "Indian fig." (The French snootily call it *figue de barbarie*.)

Navajos harvested the spiny pads with forked sticks, the Apaches used wooden tongs. Usually it was peeled and eaten raw, but it was also dried for later use. Sometimes it was ground with dried venison and fat, producing a dish that could be scooped up with the fingers or eaten as a spread on coarse bread. The Indians also roasted the unpeeled pads (the cooking removed the spines) or used them as an emergency source of water by peeling the "figs" and chewing the raw pulp for its high moisture content. The young leaves additionally were peeled, sliced, and boiled like beans, or fried in fat or oil with other vegetables.

The lowly but nutritious cactus still isn't eaten often in most areas where it grows, but it is consumed here and there in small, increasing quantities. In Mexico and the Southwestern U.S., the young stem segments (cladodes) of the prickly pear are sliced or diced and cooked with green vegetables, onions, chili peppers, cheese, eggs, spices and herbs to make fillings for tacos. They also may be added to salads, and chopped for omelettes. Park S. Nobel, author of *Remarkable Agaves and Cacti*, (1994), suggested harvesting the cladodes when they were a few weeks old, when under twelve inches in height and had no spines, using a potato peeler or knife to remove the small knobs where the spines would later grow.

"Simmer until tender, about 10 minutes, in roughly one-third their volume of water with salt and sometimes onions, garlic and cilantro," he wrote. "If any sticky material remains after cooking and draining, rinse with cold water. They taste like gherkins or green peppers, with a texture between string beans and okra."

In many parts of the American southwest and Mexico, where the cactus is called *nopal* and the food is known as *nopalitos*, a significant cactus industry has developed in recent years. This has put canned cactus in Mexican food stores as a vegetable, and candies and jams in tourist shops and supermarkets.

A cactus is a plant of the family *Cactacae*, green, fleshy, with typically leafless joints, very spiny, and remarkably resistant to drought. Besides its value as a food, several Indian tribes attached religious significance to the plant, using it to physically whip their new chiefs to imbue them with great power and luck in hunting. They also placed pieces of cactus at the corners of a new house "to give the house roots." In China, it is called the "fairy's hand" and is considered unlucky for pregnant women, although widely eaten otherwise. It's also found in salads in Greece, North Africa, and the Middle East.

Especially valued for its moisture, cactus sometimes provides the only source of water in a semi-arid or desert environment. Besides the prickly pear, there are three other species offering such relief. The pincushion cactus, a round, short, barrel-shaped plant covered with spines, is one; just slice off the top and dig in. Another is the Cereus cactus, a tall, thin plant with ridges running lengthwise, sharp spines, and protruding fruits. All parts are edible—and for water, all that's necessary is to break off the stem and scoop out the pulp. The third is the saguaro, sometimes called the "monument" or giant cactus because of its size; the central stem may be up to two feet in diameter and as tall as fifty feet, with branches that grow out at right angles and then turn upwards, as if a large green man were holding his arms up while being held at gunpoint.

The saguaro is about as close as the cactus world comes to an endangered species, with a range that includes only southern California, Arizona, and a swath of northern Mexico. When it was more plentiful, the Indians considered its sweet, red fruit a special treat and made jams and fermented syrup from it. They also dried it for later use in a gruel.

As for my friend with the cactus in his mouth and bleeding lips, I explained that the spines were there to discourage precisely what he had done.

"But how to cows get away with it?" he asked.

"They don't," I said, "they're just hungrier than you are." And only slightly dumber, I thought to myself.

from the stove. Allow this to cool and then pour it into plastic containers. Now freeze those containers. When you remove them and allow them to thaw, you'll have jelly.

"If, for some strange reason, your jelly fails to gel, the worst you'll come up with is cactus syrup. Cactus syrup is great on pancakes, waffles, or ice cream. Cactus syrup is made the same way as cactus jelly, only use one package of pectin for each quart of juice."

"To make cactus wine, add eight cups of sugar to a gallon of cooled cactus juice. Now stir in one package of yeast. Pour the juice into a gallon jug and cap it lightly. Now store the juice in a cool, dark place, like a closet. It'll be ready to drink in one month."

"Warning: if you screw the cap down tight, the jug will blow up in your closet, causing you much grief and embarrassment."

Courtesy, David L. Epperle
Arizona Cactus, 1994

Sources
Seeds: Jim Johnson,
Seedman, 3421 Bream St.,
Gautier, MS 39553, email
<seedman@seedman.com>.

Cactus purée and other products prepared from the juice or red fruit of the prickly pear: Arizona Cactus Ranch, P.O. Box 8, Green Valley, AZ 85622.

Cactus jelly and marmalade, candy and syrup: S&S Marketing, 931 S. Acora Ave., Tempe, AZ 85281, phone (800) 759-5557; email <cactushut@ssmartco.com>.

Above: Hedgehog cactus in flower, near Sedona, Arizona.
Right: Prickly pear cactus in Tonto National Forest, Arizona.

The Cactus That Ate Australia

The prickly pear was introduced in Australia in 1839 to provide natural hedges as an aid to ranchers, to control the movement of cattle without having to erect fences, expensive to put in place, costly to maintain. The plant quickly went wild in parts of Queensland and New South Wales, creating barriers over six feet tall, and by 1925, over 60 million acres of land had been bullied into submission by the hardy cactus and in half this area, no other plants would grow. How did the Aussies handle the problem? Did they take a hint from history and start eating it? No. They imported a South American caterpillar to eat it instead.

durian

Durian Ice Cream Dessert

1 quart vanilla ice cream
1 can durian
2 cups pineappele or
    orange juice

Place ice cream in the refrigerator to soften about 10 minutes while preparing the durian. Drain juice from durian and reserve. Purée the durian in a food pro-cessor, blender, or mash well with a fork. Place softened ice cream in a large bowl, add durian purée, and blend. Repack and freeze. For best flavor, use as soon as it hardens or within a day or two. Blend reserved durian juice with pineapple or orange juice and serve on top of ice cream.

Pity the poor durian, a tasty Southeast Asian fruit. Not only is it unattractive, it stinks. Many hotels won't let you take it to your room, or serve it in their restaurants. It is widely banned from taxis, buses, and ferries and Singapore Airlines will confiscate any durian brought aboard by a passenger. In Singapore's subway system, there are signs showing a durian set in a circle, with a red slash through the center, meaning just what that symbol means when it proscribes smoking, spitting, and all the other things that are taboo in that squeaky clean city-state.

It's the odor. It is, as many have said, something that tastes like heaven, smells like hell. One writer called it "the limburger cheese of fruits." Even fine chefs say it has an odor somewhere between rotten onions and stale cheese. Others have compared it to "carrion in custard" or say it's like "eating ice cream in an outhouse."

Well, maybe. The durian, which takes its name from the Malaysian word *duri*, meaning thorn, is little known outside Asia, and it does have a pungent bouquet. To smell a ripe durian is unforgettable and to walk past a street stall piled high with them in, say, Singapore, Bangkok, or Kuala Lumpur, is nearly overpowering. On a warm day, it's possible to smell a durian vendor from a block or two away. Yet, it's flavor is delicious and despite its redolence which strengthens as the fruit ripens, it commands a fine price, easily competing with more fragrant fruit.

Some say it's an acquired taste, or one you have to be born into, much as you must certainly be from the Philippines to enjoy balut, from China to savor fish maw, from Australia to fancy Vegemite. It is a fruit you either love or hate. I've eaten it many times and my reaction is that it's neither as delicious as its fans say, nor as smelly as its detractors insist. Unless it's overripe. Then I side with Singapore Airlines.

Despite all of Singapore's rules regarding where you can and can't take a durian, that city has a restaurant, the Four Seasons, that devotes an entire section of its menu to durian during the high season (May to August), while another, Durian House, located in the trendy Clarke Quay, sells only durian, offering durian pudding, durian milkshakes, durian juice, durian mousse, durian bean curd, durian sago paste, durian moon cake, durian-flavored sticky rice, durian candy, durian cake, durian puffs, durian pancakes, durian ice cream, durian noodles, and for those who wish to sneak some of the stuff onto the plane tubes of durian paste and cans of durian fruit, candy, and juice that have been "smell-free vacuum packed."

A native of Malaysia, the durian has been cultivated for hundreds of years, on trees that grow to more than a hundred feet in height, making harvest of the fruit problematic. Waiting for the fruit to fall is the easy way, but also dangerous. It varies somewhat in size and shape, but generally it is as big as a football—making it one of the largest fruits in the world. Its hard green rind is covered with sharp thorns, giving it the appearance of a medieval instrument of war, the mace, where a ball covered with metal spikes was affixed to the end of a pole and used in hand-to-hand (or, perhaps, hand-to-head) combat. Light green in color, it is not a pretty sight.

The tree may take as long as fifteen years after planting to bear fruit, compared to only three years for mangoes and other popular tropical fruits, so many farmers don't want to bother. Deforestation in Thailand, Malaysia, and Indonesia is also threatening the crop, at the same time that demand for it continues to grow. In Hong Kong, it has become a status-symbol gift among the wealthy, so much of the fruit grown on remaining plantations in countries to the south is now being exported. Cathay Pacific flies at least a hundred tons of durian from Bangkok to Hong Kong during the high season, daily! In Beijing, they may cost as much

as US$50 apiece. And in Japan, durian is marketed as the "king of fruits."

Inside the fruit, which may weigh as much as twelve pounds, are five or more oval compartments containing a cream-colored, custardy pulp with smooth, cream-colored seeds the size and shape of large Brazil nuts. Durian may be eaten raw with the fingers as is common on the streets in many Asian cities and villages, after it has been whacked open with a cleaver or sweetened with sugar and cream. It also is preserved with sugar or salt and cooked as a vegetable. In Indonesia, it's made into a fruit jelly with coconut milk. The seeds may also be eaten, boiled or roasted over an open grill like chestnuts.

In 1996 in Thailand a condom manufacturer began marketing durian-flavored condoms. The government was not amused. Saying it affronted a cherished part of Thailand's agricultural heritage and industry, the condom was banned from future sale.

There is also, among some, a belief that the durian has aphrodisiac powers, perpetuated by the folk saying, "When the durians fall, the sarongs go up." This hasn't been studied, let alone proved, but it probably doesn't hurt sales. No matter the smell.

Page 195: The spiky fruit grows directly from the woody branches.
Opposite: The fruit's unique flavor also finds its way into bonbons, paste and, with Thai imaginative flair, condoms.
This page: Durian for sale in Singapore's Bugis Street at the height of the summer season.

This page: Shoppers at the durian market in Singapore's Bugis Street sniff the spiky fruit to find the richest aroma and flavor.

leftovers

leftovers

Quite literally, "leftovers" are what remains after everyone has consumed as much as he or she can eat. This is the extra food that may be warmed up—perhaps spiced up as well—and served another day. The holidays of my childhood were memorable not only for the main feast, but also for the succeeding meals comprising the leavings of the original gorge, when, for example, a Thanksgiving banquet with all of the trimmings was followed by a couple of days of turkey soup and sandwiches.

So it is, I'm sure, in all places and was at all times. Back when humans gathered around an open fire in caves, one can be sure an entire saber-toothed tiger was not consumed at one sitting, even if shared with friends.

Similarly, this section comprises stories and recipes and other oddities that were left over when I finished the other ones. Mainly, these are dining tales and snippets of fact and fancy that didn't fit more clearly defined categories, or crossed too many boundaries to be stuck under one or another of them.

For instance, all manner of animal and vegetable matter is fermented on its way to being called a food. Fermentation plays a significant role in the world's alcohol intake, but at the same time it produces several odd foods.

As does the widespread and imaginative use of blood. Vampires are not the only ones to enjoy this ruby food.

So, too, with "fake food," a category where vegetables pretend to be meat and sugar can be duplicated with a secondary school chemistry set. If the expression "you are what you eat" has any credibility, you tell me what the hell we are.

Another chapter considers a practice that is no big deal in Asia, but in the developed world is called "barbaric" eating something that's still alive. I confess that I've done it.

Finally, there are two chapters about inorganic substances, from the top and bottom of the economic ladder: glittery precious metals and pearls, and ordinary clay and dirt.

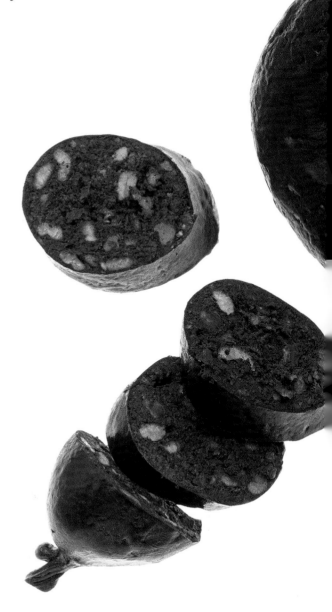

blood

**Blood and Milk,
Masai Style**

1 small onion, chopped
    (optional)
3 pints cattle blood
1/2 pint milk
4 oz. butter
Salt and pepper to taste

Separate the liquid blood
from the coagulated
lumps. Cook the onion in
half the butter until brown,
then add the combined
milk and blood, cooking
over a low heat, stirring
regularly to prevent sticking. Add more milk as
needed if the mixture
becomes too thick.
(Thicker than, say, mush-
room soup.) Add the
remaining butter, salt and
pepper, cover and simmer
for 10–12 minutes. Serve
hot over rice or in a bowl
with bread for dunking.

Various local cooks, Kenya, 1972

A photographer friend and I were accompanying a young man on a Asian shopping spree. Over the next two weeks he would spend more than two million dollars on Asian art for one of his father's fancy Hawaiian hotel developments, and the photographer and I were working on a book about the art that would be part of the decor. Our first stop was Taipei, where following the obligatory duck dinner, we went straight to Snake Alley.

This is a narrow commercial street in the city's old-est section, taking its name from small shops that offer fresh snake blood cocktails, believed by many of Taipei's residents to cure lower back pain, improve eyesight, and return sexual potency, as well as offer a nutritious protein source. All day, the young man and I had boasted how we would see who could swallow one of the powerful cocktails the fastest, a skill we both had honed years before with beer at fraternity parties in the United States.

When we came to the first shop, we saw dozens of snakes that had been caught in the mountains by pro-fessional snake-catchers, now being kept in cages behind a table set up in front of one of the shops. Nearby, hanging by their tails, were the limp, warm corpses of several snakes that had been slit and drained of their blood and bile. A thin man with a microphone stood behind the table, speaking in Chinese to a small crowd of tourists and local resi-dents. Behind him inside the shop, several old men sat peacefully at tables, popping herbal pills the size of grapes into their mouths, washing them down with glasses of warm blood. I looked at my friend and he looked at me, warily. The photographer was already taking pictures.

The salesman had a taker. The hawker extracted a snake from a cage, held it aloft for all to admire, then picked up a sharp knife and sliced the reptile from head to tail, holding it head-down over a glass on the table in front of him. Once empty, he hung the snake with the others, placed the glass full of blood on a tray with a pill, and collected some money. It was all over in about three minutes. As the man resumed his spiel, my friend and I exchanged looks again.

"Well?" I said.

"Well," he said back.

The photographer was laughing now.

There's no point dragging this out. I didn't do it. And neither did the young man from Hawaii. Maybe another time, we said.

I've still not drunk blood straight from the serpent, but since the incident in Taipei, I've eaten it many times, often while visiting a weekend market. One of my favorites is in Bac Ha, in northwestern Vietnam, not far from the China border, where a majority of the shoppers are gaily dressed Hmong hill tribe people from their nearby villages. The market covers many acres, occupying the open, paved areas around a school and along several adjacent streets. Many of the Hmong bring their goods to market on the backs of small horses, tethered in an open, grassy field, with a blacksmith in attendance should his services be need-ed.

As you enter the school yard, the first display of food is alive. Here, there are pigs, dogs, and cats, on leashes or in cages. Not far away, a variety of meat is displayed on tables; not too distant from these tables there is a woman boiling blood. It's a very efficient operation.

"Chicken, duck, buffalo, pig, dog, anything," said Duong Thi Thanh, my Hmong guide when I asked what kind of blood was being cooked. The blood was stirred and boiled in a huge wok until it congealed, then put aside to cool, when it was cut into one-inch cubes. Thanh said that it was eaten as a fortifying snack, and usually consumed with some of the local corn wine. I was surprised to find that what looked like reddish brown cubes of tofu were crunchy. And, of course, it was extremely rich, tasting like jellied organ meat.

This was a new experience for me, for which my background offered no help. The consumption of blood as I grew up in the United States, was limited to rare hamburgers. There was, in fact, in much of Euro-America a long anti-blood history. "You shall not eat flesh with its life, that is, its blood" are words I read as a youth in Genesis, the first chapter of the Old Testament in the Christian Bible. Blood was interpreted as "the life" in many other religious texts as well including Islam's Koran and therefore banned, leading butchers to bleed their animals as they slaughtered them, and many cooks to remove any blood that was left by soaking the flesh in cold water and salting it.

There was also the matter of the seventeenth century Romanian king Vlad Dracul, alias Vlad the Impaler, better known to the readers of Bram Stoker as Count Dracula. Actually, scholars think the first "vampire" was a female, a countess named Elisabeth de Bathory, a vain woman from a prominent Hungarian family who in 1604, slapped one of her servants, causing some blood to splash onto her skin. After wiping it off, she believed that her skin had been made whiter, less wrinkled. Thus, she concluded that if she could take regular baths in a virgin's blood, her fading beauty would return. Before she was done, and an act of parliament was passed for her arrest, she was thought to be responsible for the death of as many as 650 young women. Such tales have not done much to cast the subject of blood, and its consumption as a drink or food, in a positive light.

Long before Vlad Dracul and the dreaded countess appeared in the history books, and despite the religious bans, blood was accepted as a valued source of protein as well as a curative for numerous ills, a means of postponing aging, and a pre-Viagra boost to virility. For many early civilizations, fresh animal blood was consumed routinely.

In Marco Polo's vivid account of the Mongol armies, he said each of the riders had a string of eigh-teen horses and traveled "without provisions and without making a fire, living only on the blood of their horses; for every rider pierces a vein of his horse and drinks the blood." The theory was that a horse could afford to lose a pint once every ten days, enough to keep the rider going and not impair the animal's health or strength. Thus, the Mongols also were saved the trouble of finding food in a strange and barren land and did not have to gather scarce fuel for cooking fires, which would have been seen for miles, alerting their enemies. In this way, blood was not only nourishing, but also the perfect survival food.

Even before the Islamic bans, the Arabs formed patties of camel hair and blood, cooking them over an open fire. Later, in the area south of what is now called the Gulf of Aden, and farther to the south in present-day East Africa, wandering tribes survived on a diet of fresh blood and milk from their cattle, a practice the independent Masai in Kenya and Tanzania continue to this day. While others, in the upper Nile region, prefer blood boiled or coagulated, then roasted in the coals of their cook fires.

In medieval Europe, too, blood was cooked and eaten or drunk in some quarters, ignoring all religious and literary prejudice. In Ireland, a cake was made by sprinkling salt on a layer of coagulated blood, adding another layer of blood, sprinkling more salt, and so on,

A Glass of Blood

"The Marquise had gone from doctor to doctor—seeking out the celebrated and the obscure, the empirically-inclined and the homeopathic—but at every turn she had been met with a sad shake of the head. Only one of them had taken it upon himself to indicate a possible remedy: Rosaria (the Marquise's daughter) must join the ranks of consumptives who go at dawn to the abattoirs to drink the lukewarm blood freshly drawn from the calves which are bled to make veal.

"On the first few occasions, the marquise had taken it upon herself to lead the child down into the abattoirs; but the horrid odor of the blood, the warm carcases, the bellowing of the beasts as they came to be slaughtered, the carnage of the butchering...all that had caused her terrible anguish and had sickened her heart. She could not do it.

"Rosaria had been less intimidated. She had bravely swallowed the lukewarm blood, saying only, 'This red milk is a little thick for my taste.'"

Jean Lorrain
"The Glass of Blood," 1890

until a block was formed which was then cut into squares. Scandinavians still prepare a goose blood soup, calling it *swartsoppa*, or black soup. In Poland, blood from poultry, game, or pigs is eaten with rice, noodles or fried crouton, thickened with a purée of chicken livers. French cooks use blood as a thickening agent, frequently for ragouts and always in certain chicken and rabbit casseroles, where the blood is simmered briefly, then added to the dish just before serving. The latter dishes are called *en barbouille*, meaning "the smear," which describes the effect they have on the diners' lips.

Even as far back as the seventeenth century, a traveler in Ireland noted that the peasants "bleed their cows and boil the blood with some of the milk and butter that came from the same beast; and this with a mixture of savory herbs is one of their most delicious dishes." A version of this today is called *drisheen*, a kind of black pudding, or blood sausage. In Victorian England, blood was believed to prevent tuberculosis and was consumed by the glass, by women as well as men, at the neighborhood slaughterhouse.

Black pudding is one of the oldest known cooked meats, dating from ancient Greece. Today, it is served with apples and mashed potatoes, while some say that in France there are as many types of *boudin noir* (black pudding) as there are pork butchers—some blending equal portions of blood, fat, and cooked onions, others including a variety of fruits, vegetables, aromatic herbs, milk, cream, and crustless bread.

French colonialists took the dish around the world and in nineteenth century Louisiana in the United States, then known as Acadia, it became one of the great delicacies. Since the annual slaughter of pigs came during Advent, the *boudin* was usually saved for the Christmas holidays. The Cajuns, as the Acadians came to be called, slaughtered a pig, collecting the fresh blood, adding salt and stirring to prevent coagulation. Fresh pork lung, heart, and neck were cut into large pieces and simmered for three hours. After cooling, the meat was cut into small pieces and minced, returned to the cooking liquid with chopped onions, pepper and spices, and brought to a boil, when the blood was poured through a sieve. A small amount of flour was added, the whole thing was simmered for another hour, stirring frequently. The sauce was then poured over a meat entrée or added to meat and vegetables in a stew or soup.

It is in Scotland, where along with haggis, blood pudding and blood pudding sausages have attained the status of what might be called the country's unofficial, official "meat." There are records going back to the sixteenth century, when, according to *The Household Book of Lady Grisell Baillie*, there were dishes called "Scots collips wt marow and black pudings about them." Another gastronome of the period noted while writing about one of the judges of the Courts of Session that "with puddings, a great deal of anchovy toast, and plenty of good claret, his Lordship happily managed to overcome his domestic difficulties."

Interview with a Vampire?

In 1996, two Texas journalists claimed in a book titled *Something in the Blood* that there were about eight thousand "vampires" in the United States who regularly drank human blood when it was available. One of them, Cyne Presley, a thirty-eight-year-old security guard in El Paso, Texas, apparently told the writers that she drank up to a pint of blood two or three times a week, a habit she said started when she was a child, sucking the cuts and skinned knees of her friends.

"I love blood," she said when interviewed by the Los Angeles Times. "I hunger for it. I get this comfortable feeling when I drink it. It's like I'm coming home."

Where does Presley get her supply? No, not the neighborhood blood bank. Frequently, she said, she still used friends who let her puncture the fleshy part of the inside of an arm with a needle or razor. She then gently sucked the blood out. She said she rarely had trouble finding a donor, but occasionally would settle for blood from a cow, obtained from a neighborhood butcher.

Of course, there are risks. Hepatitis B and the HIV virus are transmitted by human blood. (Which is why Presley drinks only from her friends.) And once word gets out that you drink human blood, it could affect how people react and parents might not want you around their children. The Texas resident said she had received threats from people who wanted to put a stake through her heart, while others asked if she slept in a coffin.

Enough. Surely, the two journalists who wrote about Presley and the other (mostly unnamed and unverified) eight thousand "vampires" were not serious. This was a spoof, yes? No one is talking and Presley cannot be found.

Even today in Scotland they rarely skimp on the blood and up to three quarts may be mixed with raisins, sugar, assorted nuts and chestnuts (pounded), rice, oranges (including the rind), and figs, blended and baked in individual casserole dishes. Other recipes add to each quart of pig's or ox blood a half a pint of milk, a pound of shredded suet or pig fat, a large handful of oatmeal, and plenty of minced onions, pepper and salt, all of it shoveled into a length of washed intestine tied off at the ends to form the sausage, which is then cooked in the usual manner or hung from a rafter for later use.

In Poland blood soup is called *tchernina,* and in Hungary blood fritters are made by frying sliced onion in fat, adding slices of congealed goose, duck, or pig blood, seasoning with salt and paprika, serving with boiled potatoes and a salad. Germany is known for its *blutwurst,* a sausage made from pig's blood, calf's or pig's lung, and diced bacon, seasoned with cloves, mace, and marjoram.

In Asia, blood is not only cherished as an invigorating drink, but also as a hearty food. Thailand's northeastern region, called Isan, is noted for many innovative dishes, including beef noodles mixed with fresh cow's blood. Isan cooks also use pigs' blood in curries and fish maw soups, and when barbecuing spare ribs, while in the jungle in northern Thailand, elephant *mahouts* (trainers) may begin the day with a glass of wild boar's blood, congealing from the previous day's kill. While in the Philippines, a popular dish is *dinuguan,* which mixes chopped internal organs (heart, liver, and pancreas, usually from a hog) with a generous helping of blood before cooking.

Including blood in the human diet is serious business today in Brazil, where an experimental food supplement is being praised as a possible solution to the worldwide spread of malnutrition. Called Prothemol, it's primary ingredient is cow's blood. In poor regions, where government and relief agencies do not have funds to provide the needed groceries, Brazilian nutritionists in 1996 began distributing a yellowish, odor-

less, flour-like substance made from plasma, dried egg white, Vitamin A, and flour. This is dissolved in food or in sweetened beverages.

"Our children needed proteins containing the essential amino acids that the human body does not produce, but are necessary for development and growth," said Dr. Naide Teodosio, a professor of physiology at the Federal University of Perambuco. "We had plenty of it at no cost and we were wasting it."

At a *Sa dah dah eu* ceremony to honor ancestral spirits in an Akha hill-tribe village in Thailand, pigs and chickens are slaughtered and laid out, with their reserved blood, as offerings to the spirits. The Akha, always pragmatic in matters concerning food, will consume everything themselves once the spirits have had sufficient time to take note of the sacrifice. The blood is drunk and also used as a condiment.

live & almost live

"What's the strangest thing you ever ate?" is a question I get asked all the time. I'm inclined to say peanut butter, because it looks like you-know-what and sticks to the roof of your mouth. But I know that isn't what the curious are looking for. They want a story.

The tale I tell is about a food that is not so much "strange" as it was "difficult." I have mentioned elsewhere my refusal to drink a glass of freshly drained serpent's blood in Taipei and my reluctance to bite into a steamed waterbug in Bangkok, the latter finally overcome. Of all the other things I've tried, the hardest to swallow or, rather, to put in my mouth at all was a live and writhing shrimp.

It happened in Honolulu many years ago when I accompanied a friend to a sushi bar. This was back when Japanese imports—even cars and television sets—were not so commonplace, before Toyota and Sony became epithets in the offices of Ford and RCA. My friend had been to Japan many times and he spoke "fluent sushi," meaning he knew the Japanese words for eel, sea urchin, roe, various species of tuna, and other vaguely identifiable protein slices placed artfully on thumb-sized lumps of rice flavored with vinegar. Nearly a third of the Hawaii population was of Japanese heritage and the islands were a favorite holiday destination for residents of Japan, so the fiftieth American state represented a sort of beachhead in the sushi invasion that followed those of the appliance and vehicle manufacturers.

My friend and I had been working our way through the sushi menu, tossing down those thimble-sized cups of hot sake that make you think you aren't really drinking very much, when he announced it was time for the Ultimate Sushi. He said something to the sushi chef, who grinned at me and then reached into an aquarium that was on a shelf nearby, extracting two small, live shrimp.

His movement was economical and swift. He put two finely formed lumps of rice in front of him, deftly peeled the live crustaceans, placed them atop the rice, then squeezed a little lime juice over each, causing the little creatures to wriggle and thrash about in what I presumed was extreme displeasure. My friend picked up his tiny treat and popped it into his mouth, chewing delightedly. In a demonstration of courage divined in rice wine, I did the same. The difference is I don't think I chewed, I swallowed.

In the last ten years or so, eating live protein—mainly seafood, although not exclusively, as we shall see—has become almost fashionable, not only in China, Korea, and Japan, where it seems to be most popular, but in selected restaurants in major cities well scattered across the planet. The argument is: if fresh is good, can anything be better than "live"?

The idea surely is barbarian and cruel, if we are to listen to animal rights activists. (Has anyone yet taken up the cause of the sushi shrimp?) I remember seeing a movie where to prove one's manhood a live lobster was placed on a table, then whacked in half with a cleaver. The man who was being tested was expected to grab the front part of the lobster that was still scrambling to escape and dig out its flesh and eat it.

Logic demands that we ask: is it any more humane to kill the food in another room before serving it? And is it more humane to cook it first?

Of course, this is nothing new. Eating surely arrived in the history of civilization before cooking did and likely some of the early meals were so fresh as to be still breathing, flipping, or wriggling. For hundreds of thousands of years, the evolving human ate his or her food raw, before the first deliberate use of fire and it is reasonable to assume that some of the just-speared fish, for example, became lunch before they had gasped their last.

More recently, in the 1920s, there was in the United States a fad where male college students demonstrated their manliness by swallowing live goldfish. (In the syndicated cartoon by Robert Ripley, *Believe It or Not!*, it was reported that Phil Turco of Madison, Wisconsin, swallowed 339 goldfish in two hours! Believe it or not.) But this is not what we're talking about here. Today, there is a more widespread fashion, where people go to fancy restaurants and pay substantial amounts of money to eat something that hasn't been cooked. This is a boon for the restaurants. They don't have to hire a chef, only someone who knows how to fillet a fish without killing it, so that it may be served while still flopping on the plate, but boneless.

In a recent issue of *China Youth Daily* it was reported that in both commercial establishments and at home on special occasions, "consuming living animals is the latest fad to flaunt affluence and the belief that living creatures are healthier than those already slaughtered." The description provided by a subsequent report from United Press International needs no embellishment: "A healthy, three-year-old monkey was recommended, placed in a cage with its head protruding from an opening. The cook skillfully cuts the hairs, washes the head clean and then uses a sharp knife to slice a circle around the crown of the monkey's head. Tap the skull lightly with a hammer and lift up the crown just like picking up a lid from a pot. The diner then can enjoy the brains while the animal is desperately but silently struggling."

The report went on to tell about a dish called Three Screams, a incredible tale that I later had confirmed by a friend from China. For this, several newborn mice were washed, rolled wet in spicy condiments, and served in some sort of basket from which they couldn't escape. "Pick up a wiggling mouse and dip it into some flavoring, when it will emit the first cry. Stab it with a knife or fork and it will scream again. Bite into it and the little thing will give its third cry as it says farewell to the world."

The reporter further said that skinned, live pigeons, sparrows, and quail were also served, but no description was given. The writer had thrown up his hands and perhaps his lunch by then.

Whatever the response to eating live food, the custom cannot be ignored. Throughout much of the world, even today, a variety of insects, both adults and in the larvae stage, are consumed soon after being captured, described elsewhere in this book. In Thailand, where I now live, I have watched people snatch water spiders from the surface of a pond, popping them into their mouths for a snack. Even the *U.S. Army Survival Manual* recommends the just-caught, uncooked larvae of locusts, ants, and termites as a nutritious, high-protein survival food. Millions in the so-called Third World agree.

Bivalves and sea squirt offered as a raw seaside snack on South Korea's Cheju Island.

Richard Lair, an American who lived in the jungles of Southeast Asia with elephant *mahouts* (trainers) for years at a time, says the experience changed his eating habits in a major way: there is nothing, save perhaps for elephant, that he says he won't now eat. When I asked him what the oddest food was that he'd ever encountered, he told me about a couple of Chinese dishes (others subsequently insisted they were Japanese) that used rather common ingredients; it was the manner of preparation that was unusual.

"You put a pot of water on the fire or stove and once the water is hot, you dump in some cubes of tofu and a couple of dozen live baby frogs," he said. "The frogs will swim to the tofu and cling to it because it's cooler than the water. They die still holding on to the tofu and after both tofu and frog are cooked, you extract them from the water carefully and serve them with vegetables."

This introduces the "almost live" or, as Mr. Lair puts it, the "very recently deceased" category of food. There are several similar stories, again placed in Asia, the part of the world's geography where most who live elsewhere probably believe people will eat anything. In one story, tiny live fish were dumped into a pot of hot water along with vegetables with internal chambers that had been cut to expose the cavities, such as lotus root, small green peppers or water convulvalus. The fish swim into the holes seeking the same relief sought by the frogs on the tofu, where they, too, will be cooked, ready for the chopsticks to follow. With a nice chili dipping sauce.

Another variation on the same theme called for adding live baby eels to boiling water with larger blocks of tofu. The eels wriggle into the tofu, where they are cooked, after which the tofu blocks are removed and chopped before serving.

Eating Live Seafood Banned

SYDNEY (Associated Press)—A diner who watched in horror as people at a nearby restaurant table tore pieces from a live crayfish and ate them will soon be spared such sights by a new law against eating live seafood.

Cyrina Holland, 18, was out for a celebratory meal with her boyfriend. Confused by an item on the menu which offered diners the chance to "check the cray dance," she asked her boyfriend to explain.

"He pointed to the table behind me and there was a crayfish cut in half and walking around the table," she said. "It was alive, and it was getting stuck with chopsticks." She said the crayfish's tail had been stuffed with rice and noodles, but the body was still alive and the diners were breaking off its legs. "That was a complete turnoff. There were a lot of people in there and they were watching that table very strangely."

The couple left the restaurant in disgust shortly afterwards. Holland contacted the Society for the Prevention of Cruelty to Animals, but found that crustaceans were not covered by animal welfare laws. In Australia, the state of New South Wales passed legislation this year providing a sentence of up to two years' jail for anybody serving live fish or seafood.

July 31, 1997

This page: Live lobster sashimi, called *odori-gui* in Japanese, from the words "to dance" and "to eat." In its preparation, the unfortunate creature is re-assembled artfully at great speed, so that it will still be moving when it reaches the diners' table. Part of the tail is inverted and replaced as a kind of tray for the flesh, which has first been removed and sliced.

fermented food

Bill Peterson traveled widely and willingly went along with many of my suggestions about foods to order, but he was not a gastronomical experimenter at heart, and now he was complaining.

"I just don't understand," he said, "how the same process can produce so many good things to drink—beer, wine, and whisky—and also so much bad food."

An American who had tried sausage in Germany and ostrich fillets in Australia, was talking about fermentation. I laughed and asked which ones he'd tried. "After all," I said, "if it weren't for fermentation, we wouldn't have bread and cheese."

"Alright, okay, but I'm talking about some of those things you eat in Asia—the fermented fish sauce, the hundred-year-old eggs, kim chee, stuff like that. I have to admit it, I don't even like yogurt or sauerkraut."

My friend is not alone. There are many who think the only thing to do after mistakenly putting a fermented food in their mouths is to wash out their mouths with...well, something fermented.

Fermented food and drink are solids and liquids that are prepared so that micro-organisms or enzymes (a natural part of the food or added, like yeasts) change the properties of the food. The goals include a better taste or texture and an increased shelf life for the product of the biochemical change. For example, all the different types of cultured milk have evolved from the fact that fresh milk rapidly deteriorates, and a controlled fermentation with lactic acid bacteria provides the time to get it distributed widely and safely without losing nutrition or taste.

Some, like my friend, say the process doesn't just alter the taste and texture, it twists it, damaging the food's original appeal, figuratively as well as literally. Many visitors to the region where I live, Southeast Asia, will try the fermented fish sauce that is so essential to local cooking, but then make a face and call it "rotten."

In a way, they're correct, of course. In Thailand it is called *nam pla*, whose innocent-sounding translation means "fish water" and in Vietnam, *nuoc mam*, in Laos, *nam pa*, in Cambodia, *tuk trey*, in Burma, *ngan-pya-ye*, and so on. All these neighboring countries whose leaders bicker at other levels as well boast that their brands are best, although it is Thailand that exports the translucent, brown sauce in the largest quantity. All are produced by packing fish—sometimes shrimp—into barrels with salt, leaving the food to ferment for at least a month, after which the liquid is collected and bottled. (Some insist the fermenting process should last several months and Pichai Fish-Sauce Co. Ltd., Thailand's sales champ both inside and outside the country, keeps the stuff in deterioration for a full year.) Few Southeast Asian meals are considered complete without it. It takes the place of salt and is, in a way, what soy sauce is the Chinese and Japanese. But more pungent.

It is the outsider, like my friend, who thinks fish

Food and Drink

Fermentation serves us in many ways. Besides increasing the variety of our menus along with the shelf life of foods without using chemical preservatives—an important point for many—fermented food offers a high level of living enzymes. During the process of fermentation, complex proteins, starches, and fats are broken up into simple compounds which are easily assimilated by the body with minimal digestive effort.

Research also shows it can inhibit certain bacteria that cause diarrhea, which kills one out of every ten children in developing countries (through dehydration), a key factor behind a World Health Organization program to use fermentation as a technique for the preparation and storage of infant food.

As for the unusual or pungent taste and smell? One thing may be assumed by all—that many of these fermented foods go down well with a distilled, alcoholic beverage made from a fermented mash of various ingredients including grains and other plants. Whisky, gin, vodka and rum are among the most popular. Others include, in alphabetical order, aquavit, *arrack* (made from sugar cane in Sri Lanka and other tropical countries), bourbon, brandy, malt liquor, mescal (the Mexican favorite), *okolehao* (more sugar cane, from Hawaii), scotch whisky, and tequila.

Add to the list ale, lager, wine and champagne, beverages created by feeding sugars and nutrients in solution to yeast, which return the favor by producing carbon dioxide gas and alcohol.

sauce difficult. A Jesuit missionary in the eighteenth century, Nicolas Gervaise, noted in his journal that *Thai kapi*, as it was then called, "has such a pungent smell that it nauseates anyone not accustomed to it." Even as recently as 1997, Annabel Jackson-Doling noted in *The Food of Vietnam* that *nuoc mam* "in its purest form has a strong smell and incredibly salty flavor which renders it an acquired taste for non-Vietnamese. Vietnamese rarely expect a foreigner to enjoy the taste, but are delighted when one does."

There also are some solid fermented foods in Asia that command attention. In Laos, *padek* can best be described as fish sauce with chunks of the fermented fish still in it, along with some rice "dust" and husks. *Padek* has an odor so pungent that the large pottery jar holding a family's supply usually is kept out on the verandah. Phia Sing, writing in *Traditional Recipes of Laos* (1981), said that most padek was homemade: "The real thing is not available in the west, but jars of fermented fish from the Philippines are one acceptable substitute. And I was once told that the Lao bride of an Englishman, on being offered canned anchovies for the first time, exclaimed: "But this is padek—rather salty padek, but good!"

In Thailand, again, there is a dish called *pla ra*, the second word meaning "mold" or "fungus," which should give the diner a clue. In the words of David Scott and Kristiaan Inwood, authors of a small book about Thai food called *A Taste of Thailand* (1986), this is a fermented fish dish that recalls the "accumulated stench of putrefying corpses, abandoned kennels, dirty feet, stagnant bilges, and fly-blown offal," an exaggeration, certainly, but not much of one, at least to many Euro-Americans. It is made by packing gutted and scaled freshwater fish into sealed earthenware jars with salt, adding a fine powder made from fried rice in a few days, after the fish have begun to "rot." It is ready to eat in a week, although, once more, connoisseurs prefer a longer fermentation time.

As key as such foods and sauces are to their respective countries, it is possible to cook Southeast

Asian cuisine without using them. Not so in Korea, where *kim chee* (*or kimchi*) has attained the status of "national dish" and is impossible to avoid or turn away, as it served along with just about everything and not to eat it is regarded as a gross insult. A general term given to a group of fermented vegetable foods, kim chee is characterized by its sweet-and-sour carbonated taste, quite different from sauerkraut and other fermented vegetables found in Europe and North America. It was devised to keep vegetables edible through the long, cold winters in the northern part of the Korean peninsula, yet even with the modern development of greenhouse agriculture and a year-round supply of imported vegetables, the dish remains a part of nearly every meal. Although there are about 150 different kinds of kim chee, the most popular involves salting chopped Chinese cabbages and/or radishes, then washing them, adding spices and seasonings (powdered red pepper, chopped garlic and ginger, sliced green onion, salt and sugar), and letting it all sit

While all Southeast Asian countries include fermented fish sauce in their cuisines, the Lao prefer a still more pungent ingredient. Stored in large pottery jars, usually outside the house because of its strong smell, *padek* is a sauce with the fermenting fish still in it. The partially decomposed fish are lifted out and used in cooking a variety of dishes.

in a cool place for a few days to ferment. It should be served at room temperature or slightly chilled with rice and meat dishes.

Another Korean delicacy, salt-fermented oysters, dates back six hundred years and is believed not only to relieve fatigue and treat anemia, but also to contain

the spirit and wisdom of one's ancestors. In Hong Kong, fermented tofu is a common specialty found on street corners. A solid, fermented soy bean "cake" called *tempe* or *tempeh* is widely consumed as a meat substitute in Indonesia. In the Philippines, a variety of dishes are made from salted and fermented anchovies and tiny shrimps, called *bagoong*.

Asia has no exclusive on fermented foods. They are found anywhere and, in fact, can be made from nearly anything. In Alaska, the Inupiat and Kobuk Eskimos traditionally catch sheefish with hooks made from bear teeth and ivory through holes in the ice in winter, or sein for them in the summer when they swim upriver to spawn. The rich, oily flesh and roe of the twenty- to thirty-pound females (who may drop as many as 350,000 eggs each!) are preferred over the smaller males, but whatever the catch brings is buried, ungutted, in a leaf-lined pit, where it ferments (decays) in its own natural juices for several weeks. It should come as no surprise that the aromatic result is known, colloquially, as "stinkfish," which usually is eaten raw.

A similar dish, called *lutefisk*, or lye fish, is prepared in Norway and served in December at the height of the culinary calendar. This tradition dates at least to the fourteenth century, when white freshwater fish were caught in mountain lakes in August and

---

Sunflower Seed Cheese

Method: In the evening, put about one pound (depending on how much you wish to make) of raw, shelled sunflower seeds in a large bowl and cover with pure water. Any raw seed or nut may be substituted, including pumpkin, pine seeds, walnuts, pecans, and almonds, or combination thereof. Add enough extra water to cover the seeds by at least one inch. Do not use chlorinated water, for it will destroy the enzymes and prevent fermentation. Leave the seeds to soak overnight.

Next morning, drain the seeds through a colander. In a blender or food processor, put one cup of soaked seeds plus one cup of pure (unchlorinated) water, and blend well. Pour the purée into a large bowl. Purée the rest of the seeds the same way, adding one cup of water per cup of soaked seeds, and pouring the purée into the same large bowl.

Leave the bowl of puréed seeds uncovered on a table or counter in the kitchen to ferment naturally. Depending on weather, this takes 4–7 hours. The hotter and more humid it is, the shorter the fermentation time. When ready, the surface will become a bit puffy, and the "whey" (water) will have separated from the "curd" (purée) on the bottom of the bowl. There will also be a slightly sour smell, something like yogurt.

Line a large colander or sieve with a piece of cheesecloth (or any sturdy but porous cotton cloth). Pour the fermented purée into the cloth, and let it drain over a bowl by itself for about 30–45 minutes. Then, pull the corners of the cloth together and twist the pure inside the cloth, squeezing out as much additional water as possible. Scoop the drained, fermented purée into a plastic container, cover tightly with a lid, and store in the refrigerator. It will keep about one week.

To serve: Scoop out as much as you wish to use into a bowl. About 1/2 cup is sufficient for one person. Add: good quality sea salt, ground black pepper or cayenne, 5–6 finely chopped green onions (scallions), 3 tbs. extra virgin olive oil. You may also experiment with other seasonings, such as garlic, and various spices, but the combination given above is our favorite.

Blend well with a spoon or fork, then scoop into a smaller bowl for serving. It may be used as a spread for bread of toast, as a dip for chips or vegetable sticks, as a stuffing for halved avocados or tomatoes, or eaten straight with a spoon. You may also form it into small balls, then cover them with cooked brown rice and squeeze in your palms to form larger rice balls, heat briefly in the oven and serve.

The seeds are soaked and fermented, thereby "predigesting" all of the proteins, fats and carbohydrates, rending all nutrients easy to digest and assimilate. The fermentation process also produces very high concentrations of amino acids, B vitamins, and active enzymes, making this a completely balanced whole food. It is also very adaptable to various seasonings and culinary uses.

Dan Reid, *The Tao of Health, Sex, and Longevity* (1989)

September, then wrapped in birch bark and buried. The fish remained underground until the first snow, when they were dug up, rubbed with salt and packed tightly belly up in covered wooden containers. Today, the fish are stored in a similar fashion above-ground for about three months, then rehydrated in a strong alkaline solution for several days until the fish is soft enough for a finger to be pressed through without meeting resistance. Caustic soda generally is used, but documents dating back to the Middle Ages tell that the original solution was made from the ashes of the same tree used for wrapping, birch. After soaking, the fish is rinsed for several days in running cold water before preparation is completed by either steaming or poaching. The result is a translucent, golden fillet with a stiff-jelly consistency. Oddly, the taste is surprisingly bland and usually is brightened with a choice of sauces.

In Russia, southwestern Asia and eastern Europe, *kefir* dates back many centuries to the shepherds of the Caucasus Mountains who discovered that fresh milk carried in leather pouches fermented into an effervescent beverage. In Germany, sauerkraut made from shredded, fermented cabbage, is served with pork knuckle or sausages, as important to the German diet as potatoes and beer. In the United States and elsewhere, fermented cider is served as a slightly alcoholic drink. Yogurt, a fermented milk product that originated in Turkey, is now produced in numerous brands and flavors, and when plain often sweetened with sugar to disguise its sour bite. So far as my friend Bill is concerned, just about all of this food stinks.

Opposite: In a village in Vietnam's Phu Kanh province, *nuoc mam*—fermented fish sauce—is still made in the traditional way and allowed to mature in wooden barrels.
This page: Working on the sidewalk in the winter sunshine, a South Korean cook prepares *kimchi* in large quantities to last until spring. She chops a variety of vegetables which will be allowed to ferment while refrigerating with chilis and copious quantities of garlic. November is the month when kimchi is traditionally made, a process that involves the whole family and community.

fake food

During a recent trip to Singapore, I went to a vegetarian restaurant in the Geylang district, traditionally the home of the city's Malay, Arab, and Indonesian communities. The restaurant was, as expected, a clean and well-lighted place, with cheap lace tablecloths under round slabs of Plexiglas. The Plexiglas should have been my first clue about how "real" the food would be.

Of course, it wasn't my first visit to a vegetarian restaurant—the Good Earths in my past cannot be counted on the fingers of my hands—but it was the first time I deliberately ordered and ate fake meat. I'd seen "vegetarian chicken" and "vegetarian beef" on what were called "health food restaurant" menus before, but I always selected a fresh salad, or perhaps a vegetable curry instead.

Why, I wondered, did vegetarians do this? Were these dishes created for the converts, the former meat-eaters who now ate only veggies? However deep their current conviction, did they still miss the taste of flesh? (Just as some reformed smokers chew nicotine gum.) I also wondered what the ersatz meat tasted like? Did it really taste like meat (or chicken)? Was it good for you? I ordered a dish of all-vegetable chicken legs.

Guess what? It tasted like chicken—a phrase that runs like a tide through this book, I fear—but it didn't feel like chicken. I don't care how you cook or flavor what is called in the trade "textured vegetable protein," it only approaches what is being copied, and for me is never convincing. Yet, there is a market for this stuff, in specialty stores, by mail, even in traditional groceries and supermarkets. One mail order catalog recently offered a new product, "all-vegetarian smoky bits, ready to eat as is. Great for salads, dips, soups, omelettes, or anywhere you want a bacon flavor without using animal products." A pound of the stuff cost US$9.95, five pounds for just a little over double that.

Many such meat substitutes are made from the soya bean, a plant that is used all over the world to produce oil and flour and as a foodstuff in various forms for both livestock and humans. Tofu, a staple in Asian cooking that dates back to as early as the second century in China, is prepared from beans that have been soaked, reduced to a purée, then boiled and sieved, and, finally, jellified by the addition of a coagulant. As early as the sixth century in Japan, it was called the "meat vegetable" because of its high protein content.

The motives for vegetarianism seem, in sum, to be rooted in a search for good health or good karma. This assumes that you believe that flesh and fat are best eliminated from your diet, for dietary or philosophical reasons. So that a bowl of vegetarian "chicken" broth can satisfy your need to revisit your non-vegetarian past and savor the taste of chicken without threatening your health or belief system. Vegetarians argue that not only are animal fats no good for the human, but also that too much natural forest is being destroyed to create pasture land for grazing animals.

I have no disagreement with this philosophy. Still, I am puzzled by the ardent fervor for that which is fabricated from artificial or bogus ingredients. In an advertising campaign aimed at slowing sales of Pepsi-Cola, Coca-Cola called itself The Real Thing. The food I'm talking about now is the opposite. The Not Real Thing. The Kitchen Counterfeits. Strange food, indeed.

Not all imitation meat is made from soy, as were the "chicken legs" I ate in Singapore. Gluten, described by one mail-order source as a "low-fat, easy-to-use meat substitute," is a protein derived from wheat, popular for centuries in Asia and sometimes called *seitan*, the Japanese word for cooked gluten: "Unlike textured vegetarian protein, which comes pre-shaped in various sizes, you can shape gluten into whatever shape or size you need for your favorite recipes, even giant roasts or mock turkey!"

Pass the gluten and cranberry sauce.

Meat-like flavors and alternatives are not alone in the fake food industry. When some dieticians and health experts decided butter was dangerously high in cholesterol, manufacturers of margarine and other butter proxies prospered. So, too, manufacturers of all the low-fat spreads now standing side-by-side on market shelves with mayonnaise (thought to contain too much cholesterol-rich egg yolk), made from liquid safflower and soybean oil, food starch, cellulose gel and other thickeners and emulsifiers.

What of all the synthetic casings for sausage that've replaced sheep's or pig's intestine? What of mock turtle soup, which is made from the meat from a boiled calf's head? How about all the "crab-like" crab, that is made entirely of fish scraps that are jelled and streaked with a red dye? How far from reality do the many modern additives take a food—the coloring agents, preservatives, permitted antioxidants, flavorings, mineral hydrocarbons, emulsifiers, and stabilizers?

The concept of fake, or "alternative," foods is not new. During the Napoleonic wars in the early 1800s, when the British blockade of continental ports cut off supplies of cane sugar from the West Indies and Southeast Asia, the sugar beet began to take its place. That was, of course, real food, just another real source for real sugar. Yet it seemed to point the way to the near future.

In 1860, a food technologist named Hippolyte Mege-Mouries was commissioned by the French navy to find a cheap replacement for butter, a substitute that contained beef suet, minced sheep's stomach, chopped cow's udder (I'm not making this up!) and a little warm milk, steeped in warm, alkaline water. Voila! So pleased was Napoleon III, he gave the inventor his own factory and soon enough a taste and market for what was called "butterine" soon spread to America, where it was regarded as a way to turn organs normally discarded by slaughterhouses into profit. By 1876, the U.S. was exporting more than a million pounds of butterine to the UK.

Over the years, of course, the recipe changed along with the name to margarine as manufacturers learned how to "cream" the artificial product, how to mature it with micro-organisms similar to those used in making real butter, and how to utilize vegetable oils, and add vitamin concentrates. The manufacturers of real butter fought back, predictably, and are still fighting. But even strong advertising campaigns failed to stem the synthetic tide, as margarine, once made from animal fat, now could be manufactured from a single vegetable oil or a blend of a number of oils, such as sunflower, safflower, and soya bean.

Time marched (and stomachs grumbled) inevitably on and there were similar developments in the sugar industry. Sugar once was a luxury only the rich could afford, in Persia and ancient Arabia. Western Europe didn't even know about sugar until the ninth century when it was introduced by the conquering Moors. At that time, it came in large loaves or blocks that were broken apart and ground into a powder in a mortar. In time, of course, all that changed. When too many people decided they were consuming too much of it, some began looking for substitutes.

One of the first artificial sweeteners actually was discovered by accident in Baltimore in the 1880s by Johns Hopkins University scientists, developed in their lab something they called "saccharin," which was said to be three hundred times sweeter than sugar and soon, with the addition of an "e" at the end would enter the popular vocabulary as anything "cloyingly sweet or sentimental." Later still, some said that although it offered the advantage of containing only eight calories per teaspoon, it gave foods a bitter aftertaste when cooked, and, oh yes, it might be carcinogenic.

In the late 1960s, German scientists formulated something called Acesulfame-k, or Ace-k, approved by the FDA in America in 1988; it was claimed to be two hundred times sweeter than sugar and it had no unpleasant aftertaste. It was composed of carbon, nitrogen, oxygen, hydrogen, sulfur, and potassium atoms.

This is food?

Solid argument can be made in support of some

Sources

For assorted meat "style" vegetarian broth mixes and "textured vegetable protein" by mail: The Mail Order Catalog, P.O. Box 99, Summertown, TN 38483, phone (800) 695-2241.

ersatz food and drink, explained by scarcity or other pragmatic reasons, as when sugar beets took the place of sugar cane, and during World War Two, when shipping lines were interrupted in the Atlantic between South and North America, cutting the supply of coffee beans, and the somewhat bitter chicory plant found a new market. Nor was it practical to transport real eggs to the military in a battlefield situation (think of the breakage!), thus when I was in the U.S. Army, anyway, we were fed a powdered egg substitute called Starlac that only slightly resembled eggs in appearance and taste.

As humans began circling the earth in rockets, space itself became another factor dictating a variety of food substitutes. Space capsules are cramped by weight limitations, so there is not much room for food storage. The solution? Make food smaller by dehydrating it, cutting the weight in half by removing the water. Water used to rehydrate the food comes from the capsule's fuel cells, which mix hydrogen and oxygen with electricity.

In the early days, space food was not very palatable and astronauts in the Mercury program were given bite-sized, freeze-dried cubes and semi-liquids in aluminum toothpaste-type tubes. They found the food unappetizing, had trouble rehydrating the freeze-dried foods, disliked squeezing the tubes, and had to chase crumbs from the bite-sized cubes to prevent them from fouling instruments.

In time, things improved. In the Gemini launches, the bite-sized chunks were covered with an edible gelatin to reduce crumbling and rehydration was improved when water was injected into the food packs through a nozzle with a water gun and the contents were kneaded until moist, then squeezed through a tube into the astronaut's mouth. However, it still seemed largely fake.

The Apollo program introduced hot water, which made the food far more attractive, if still short of delicious, and the Skylab with its hugely increased space actually gave the space jockeys a table and chairs equipped with foot and thigh restraints that let them "sit down" in space to eat. Now the astronauts ate off metal trays with built-in warming units and used utensils held magnetically to the trays. They also had sufficient storage space to accommodate a freezer for steaks and a refrigerator for chilling fruit and beverages.

In a way, the Space Shuttle program represents a step back at meal time. Because storage is at a premium, it's back to injecting water through a large-gauge hollow needle inserted in an opening in the bag containing the dehydrated dishes. However, the food choices have multiplied. Even in the days of Gemini, astronauts got shrimp cocktail, chicken, vegetables, butterscotch pudding, and applesauce. Now that menu includes more than a hundred food items and fifty different drinks. But it's still all rehydratable and thermostabilized, the latter process using heat to destroy all microorganisms.

Contrary to what some people think, food in pill forms have not been given the astronauts. However, many say this is the path to the future, that with the earth's expanding population and land usable for agriculture and grazing shrinking, we all may soon sit down to a nourishing plate of pills.

Pass two of the blues and, oh...let me try one of the oranges.

Meanwhile, back on planet earth, Robert Kok, an agricultural engineer at McGill University in Montreal, Canada, said in 1994 that he wanted to build a factory to raise insects in "true industrial quantities" ten thousand tons a day for processing into familiar forms, like simulated hamburger or chicken breast. Kok said that in the crowded, hungry planet of the future, a hundred

The Ultimate Fake Food

The idea behind fake food is to create something that both looks and tastes like the real thing. There is one other "food" in this category that looks real, but is never eaten: the three-dimensional models of Japanese dishes displayed in restaurant windows to entice passers-by. Originally carved by skilled artisans from wax, most now are manufactured largely from plastic.

factories could supply much of the world's protein, replacing mammal livestock. To demonstrate what could be done, he prepared and served the press a meal that included a tent-caterpillar meat loaf and some flour-beetle hot dogs. He described the hot dogs as being "every bit as bad as the real ones."

Most startling of all are two developments in 1998, when the U.S. Food and Drug Administration approved two new "food" products for sale to the American public, and soon, of course, to the world. Johnson & Johnson began marketing a new, no-calorie brand of artificial sweetener that tastes like sugar, is six hundred times sweeter, yet passes right through the body without leaving any telltale fat or cellulite. How is that possible? Scientists changed sugar's molecules to make the sweetness more intense, but not allow it to be absorbed. Sucralose, as the product is called, can be used in almost every kind of processed food, from soft drinks and ice cream to baked goods, jellies, and the tabletop sugar bowl. It was also ruled safe for diabetics, to whom a significant number of low-sugar "specialty foods" are marketed.

Also in 1998, Procter and Gamble, the American company that owns Frito-Lay, introduced something called olestra, using the brand name Olean (pronounced oh-LEEN), in corn and potato chips. What the hell is Olean? Fake fat, that's what. It tastes like fat, and it cooks like fat. Yet, the body can digest it, so it, too, passes right through the intestinal tract, leaving no ugly calories behind. A snack-sized bag of potato chips with olestra had fifty-five calories (about the same as a rice cake) instead of the usual one-hundred and ten, and all fifty-five were from the potato.

Now all we need is a fake potato. Stay tuned.

Plastic Chewing Gum?

Will someone tell me what a "non-dairy creamer" is? The ingredients listed on the packets vary from place to place, but all seem to contain glucose syrup, "edible vegetable fat,"approved emulsifiers" and a variety of sodium, potassium and phosphate this-and-thats. Is coffee made from dried and roasted chicory or dandelion root still coffee?

When you take all the fat out of milk, is it still milk? Are Cheez Whiz and Velveeta really cheese? Even chewing gum, originally made from *chicle*, the sap of a Central American tree, is now being made with PVA (polyvinyl acetate, a plastic) plus artificial flavors, colors, and sweeteners.

This page: Kappa-bashi in Tokyo is the center of the wholesale trade for the food industry, and the location of shops specializing in the peculiar product of plastic food, used for restaurant window displays.

Opposite: With the appearance of quail eggs in tiny nests, these *luk chub* are in fact a sugary Thai confection, made with the same attention to detail that characterises fruit and vegetable carving.

gold, silver, & pearls

Gold has been the symbol of power and wealth for thousands of years, associated with the sun god Ra in ancient Egypt because of its sunlike color, with the throne in the time of China's first emperors, with victory in early Greece, with art and personal ornamentation in all these places and times in history, as well as in pre-Columbian Mexico and Peru.

More recently, it became the most readily accepted medium of exchange for goods and services, and starting in the nineteenth century was used as security for much of the world's paper currency, leading to an international gold standard. The passion for this rare metal did not diminish, even when the gold standard was abandoned. Although some twenty percent of the world's production is put to industrial use (gold conducts electricity and is used in microchips and satellites have been layered with gold foil to keep off excessive heat from the sun), a whopping eighty percent is still used either for art and jewelry, or hoarded as a personal safeguard against hard times.

With so much value attached, is it any wonder, then, that gold and its less expensive but still "precious" cousin silver found their way onto the gourmand's dinner plate or suspended in what are believed to be health-giving drinks?

During Japan's economic boom, in the late 1980s and early 1990s, when that country's rich delighted in finding new ways to spend a small fortune on a meal, the newest fad was food garnished with real gold. Mainly in Tokyo and other large cities, restaurants began sprinkling or wrapping gold leaf around all sorts of delicacies to excite the Japanese palate, serving omelettes and curries and ice cream with tiny flecks of gold mixed in. One establishment offered "longevity noodles" made of Korean ginseng soup, noodles, and gold flakes. The flakes or thin wafers of gold leaf also were used to brighten up traditional dishes like sushi, using the gold instead of dry seaweed to wrap the rice. Washed down with gold sake, of course.

"This fad was initiated by restaurant owners who found out that gold flakes are a convenient means to enhance the value of their food and drink," a manufacturer told a Reuters reporter in 1992. "Restaurant owners felt they could draw potential customers' attention at a relatively low cost, since gold flake appears to have more volume than its actual weight." How is this possible? First, bars of gold are mechanically pressed into strips about one ten-thousandth of an inch thick and cut into pieces measuring one-quarter by one-half inch. These pieces are then placed on translucent paper and stored in an ox-hide pouch to preserve the heat so important for the beating to follow. Locked into place with strips of bamboo, these pouches are then hammered by strong young men using heavy metal sledges. After up to six hours of pummeling, the leaf will have increased twelve times in size and is now so thin as to almost tear if you look at it.

The flimsy pieces of gold are then turned over to young women, who cut them into small squares or strips with knives made of bamboo. Metal scissors cannot be used because the gold will stick to metal. The rooms must be sealed to keep away wind, and no air conditioning is permitted because the gold will shrink in cool temperatures. At last, the small pieces are packed in thin paper and sent to the restaurants (or, more commonly, to temples and shrines in Buddhist countries, where they are rubbed onto images for luck).

"Gold flake is so thin, we had problems wrapping

Stronger than Dirt!

Because silver is said to be antibacterial, at least one manufacturer suggests using it for washing windows, mirrors, TV and computer screens, wood furniture and chrome fixtures; as a hair spray and body moisturizer; as a cleanser for everything from carpets to contact lenses; as an antiseptic for the mouth and a gargle; and as a stain-remover for clothing and upholstery. According to one company, it even adds life to house plants and cut flowers.

the sushi in it when we started" said Seiichi Ohmura, owner of a restaurant in Chiba near Tokyo, whose menu in 1992 included a wide range of gold-garnished foods, "but we've got the knack now." He said he sold three or four dishes of gold sushi a day at 5,000 yen, then worth about US$40 a plate.

If the Japanese taste for gold weakened along with the national economy in the late 1990s, there is now a growing market for both gold and silver as a "cure" for everything from asthma to depression to cancer and many consume it daily. Jim Powell reported in the magazine *Science Digest* in 1978 in an article titled "Our Mightiest Germ Fighter" that "thanks to eye-opening research, silver is emerging as a wonder of modern medicine. An antibiotic kills perhaps a half-dozen different disease organisms, but silver kills some 650. Resistant strains fail to develop. Moreover, silver is virtually non-toxic."

Technically, such products are not true foods, but categorized as "food supplements," the all-purpose euphemism for products that are reputed to be healthy, without government approval, and most are marketed in alternative "health food" distribution systems and by mail. Dozens of companies in the United States now sell gold and silver, either separately or in combination, in colloidal form, that is, ionically suspended in distilled water.

The first colloidal gold was produced in 1857 by Michael Faraday, the famous English scientist better known for developing the first laboratory model of an electric generator and inventing the electric motor. Today, some manufacturers blend the gold and silver with rhodium, iridium, and platinum, or package it as a gel with aloe vera, the plant whose sticky interior frequently is used to treat burns.

None of this is cheap. A four-ounce bottle of colloidal silver and gold, equal to about a third of a can of soda, usually costs more than US$20; the same amount of the mixture that also contains the other metals costs almost three times as much. As a money-saving service to customers, some companies market Colloidal Silver Generators for home manufacture. They sell for US$99 and up.

If self-medication is not your strong suit, like many others I usually content myself with aspirin and alcohol—not necessarily in that order—perhaps it is better to mix these precious metals in the food. The use of silver leaf in India is fairly common, although understandably it's an extravagance. In the more prosperous cities, such as Mumbai and New Delhi, the best thing for a hot summer's day is ice cream with silver flakes.

Not even Baskin-Robbins or Ben and Jerry offer this one.

There also is a full-bodied liqueur called Goldwasser, flavored with caraway seed, orange peel, and spices. Its name, which translates from German as "gold water," comes from the fact that it has minuscule flecks of gold leaf suspended in it. A similar drink, called Goldschlager, is sold in parts of the U.S. Looking for something for the kids? A firm in the United States markets lollipops with gold leaf inside.

Finally, a recipe published in 1995 in *Gourmet*, the American magazine, may offer more appeal. This was for Gold-Dusted Bourbon Pecan Balls, calling for unsweetened cocoa butter, confectioner's sugar, vanilla-wafer crumbs, roasted and finely chopped pecans, honey, and bourbon, along with the gold powder.

The Ore-ganic Harvest?

Scientists at Massey University in Palmerston North, New Zealand, in 1998 in an article in *Nature* magazine, said they had found a way to make plants soak up gold from ore. Although they were suggesting a new way of mining the precious metal, the report of Christopher Anderson, Robert Brooks and their colleagues made it clear the discovery could, in time, spill over into kitchens and onto dinner plates.

They said the approach, called phytomining, already was used for recovering nickel and for removing pollutants like lead and mercury from the soil. In their new findings, the New Zealand team said that Indian mustard and chicory plants that grew in pots of ore for a week contained about twenty parts per million by weight, when the leaves and stalks were harvested and dried.

While this mining technique is not regarded as commercially viable when compared to more traditional recovery methods, the produce potential is obvious. The ore-ganic food fans will love it.

This page: Pearls are sold
for medicinal purposes in a
Singaporean pharmacy,
eaten after being ground to
a fine powder. Because the
more common cultivated
pearls have a large core of
freshwater mussel shell, only
natural pearls can be used —
at considerable expense.
Opposite, above: Burmese
workers in Mandalay beat
gold between thick ox-hide
to produce gold leaf.
Opposite, below left: Flakes
of gold leaf are sealed in
candy for an exotic lollipop.
Opposite, below right: A fad
that arose in Japan during
the booming economy of
the 1980s—gold-leaf sushi—
bacame an over-priced specialty of some restaurants.
Since gold is inert, in these
quantities it has no biological effect on the human
body, good or bad.

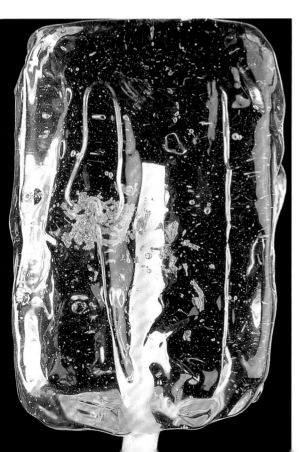

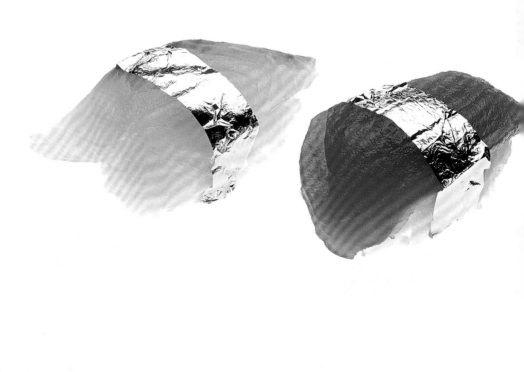

dirt

I've always thought that eating dirt would be the last resort, something you did when there wasn't even any grass left, nor leaves remaining on trees, nor even any bark. In fact, I never even considered eating dirt at all, except when I was a toddler making mud pies in the garden. So it was with great surprise that during the research of this book, I discovered that eating dirt,

the soil beneath our feet, the ground we walk on, had a long and impressive history, that it even had a scientific name: *geophagy*, meaning, literally, "eating the geography."

I always liked geography. It was my favorite subject in secondary school. For some reason, I took pride in identifying all the countries on a map of the world and naming their capitals as well as their major exports. I collected stamps and could tell anyone who wanted to know (and no one did) where the Cameroons and Cook Islands were. I loved maps, and still do. At one point, as an adult, I filled up forty or fifty small bottles with sand from beaches I sat on during my travels, and gave them to my stepson, thinking he'd love it. He didn't. In the 1960s, I participated in the then-popular "back-to-the-earth" movement, buying some property in northern California in an attempt to live off the land. I spent a lot of time studying and working that land, exulting at the end of the day that I had dirt under my fingernails and mud all over my boots. That was something my mother, who enjoyed digging in the garden, always told me: one of the greatest pleasures in life (she said) came from working in the earth.

Besides making mud pies, I knew that children commonly ate dirt when they were little because at age one to three they tend to put everything in their mouths as an aid to identification. I'd also seen photographs of people returning to their homelands after a long absence or ordeal (such as war), kneeling to kiss the ground. I knew that chickens and a number of animals ate gravel to aid digestion. And I knew that worms ate dirt. But geophagy was a new one for me.

But never, not once, did I ever consider eating it.

But geophagy is not a new concept for humankind. Now I discover that people have been doing just that for millennia, by choice! Not because they were starving and there was nothing else to eat, but because it offered them something as a legitimate food source.

The Case of the Coffin that Ended Up Inside the Man

Actually, there seem to be two kinds of dirt eaters. There are the ones with a rare medical condition called "pica." Often they are children who seem addicted to eating non-nourishing items such as dirt or clay. Doctors say the child usually starts foraging between age one and two years, sometimes because of a lack of warm parenting, or a delay in intellectual development. The same child may also be seen eating paint from the walls of the home. A medical examination is urged.

Pica is not just about eating dirt, by the way. It's about eating any non-food items, and the medical history books are full of odd cases about people—adults as well as children—eating hair, chalk, glue, even their socks. There was a case in the United States where a twenty-two-year-old woman was eating about half a sock each evening. She told doctors she'd been eating her clothing since she was a teenager. Another recent story reported that another twenty-two-year-old, this one a man in China, swallowed up to fifty stones a day from a supply used to make roads. He explained that the habit began when he was ten and experienced an epileptic seizure while tending the family's goats. To diminish the pain, he said, he swallowed peb-

bles and his discomfort went away.

There are two others who earned a strange sort of immortality by eating non-food items. The first was called "The Human Ostrich" by Robert Ripley in one of his syndicated cartoon panels, *Believe It Or Not!*, published in 1937. So named because ostriches are believed (erroneously) to eat anything, Edmond C. Nickels reportedly consumed 607 objects ranging from several dollars in pennies, nickels, dimes and quarters, to nails, screws, watch parts, chains, and streetcar tokens. He died of pneumonia in 1934, three years before Ripley made him famous.

More recently, in the 1996 edition of *The Guinness Book of Records*, under the heading Medical Extremes, Michel Lotito, a forty-six-year-old man from Grenoble, France, known as *Monsieur Mangetout* ("Mr. Eat Anything"), was said to have been eating metal and glass from the time he was nine years of age.

"Gastroenterologists have x-rayed his stomach and described his ability to consume two pounds of metal per day as unique," Guinness said. "His diet since 1966 has included ten bicycles, a supermarket cart (in four and a half days), seven TV sets, six chandeliers, a Cessna light aircraft, and a computer. He is said to have provided the only example in history of a coffin (handles an all) ending up inside a man.'

I made my discovery when researching acorns and I read in *Edible Plants and Animals* (1993) by A.D. and Helen Livingston that "...certain Indians mixed clay with acorn meal (at a ratio of about one part clay to twenty parts meal by weight). The clay was said to make the resulting bread sweet, and to make it 'rise' like yeast."

A University of Mississippi professor in the United States, Dennis Frate, who has studied dining on dirt, told a writer for the *Columbus Ledger-Enquirer* in Georgia in 1997 that the practice was first noticed around 40 B.C., when Greeks prescribed a variety of clays to combat a number of illnesses. "Almost every major population has been observed eating dirt," he said.

Frate admitted there was a downside, however. "There have been documented cases of bowel compaction caused by this," he says. "I've conducted a chemical analysis of the soil in our area and found no reason for not eating dirt, but that doesn't mean that I condone it."

Other scientists went further, actually *enthusing* over the value of eating dirt. Researchers Susan Aufreiter, a laboratory analyst at the University of Toronto in Canada, and William Mahaney, a York University geography professor, published their findings in 1997 in *New Scientist* magazine and the *International Journal of Food Sciences and Nutrition*, both published in England, saying that chemical analysis showed a light, yellowish soil used as survival food in China was rich in iron, calcium, vanadium, magnesium, manganese, and potassium, all of which would be in short supply in times of famine.

The same wide-ranging study also showed that in Zimbabwe the natives ate the red soil from termite mounds for digestive complaints; careful analysis revealed that the termite soil contained kaolinite, the principle ingredient in the popular diarrhea remedy, Kaopectate. The clay was also rich in iodine and iron, two elements whose scarcity was "responsible for a lot of (nutritional) deficiency diseases," Ms. Aufreiter said. When the termite clay was eaten, "these elements go into solution in the acids of the stomach, (improving) the odds that your body can absorb it, and that's nutritional." Another sample, taken in North Carolina in the United States, also was found to contain iron and iodine.

Looking back, Ms. Aufreiter and her colleagues noted that the Romans made medicinal tablets from soil and goats' blood, that the Germans in the nineteenth century spread fine clay on their bread instead of butter, and that in some West African countries today pellets made of termite clay are sold as a digestive remedy, a practice that spread to the United States during the days of the slave trade, remaining in some pockets of the American South today, where usually it is taken by pregnant or lactating women. According to Peter Farb and George Armelagos in "Consuming Passions: the Anthropology of Eating" (1980), this is a response to a need for calcium and other minerals.

Some Indian groups in the Amazon eat blocks of clay with their meat. It's also well known that lime–not the fruit but the white or grayish calcium oxide that is used in mortars, plasters, and cements and as a fertilizer–is an ingredient in the Mexican dish *posole*. The great Spanish explorer Cabeza de Vaca wrote in his memoirs that the Indian tribes in what is now central and south Texas and northern Mexico, processed mesquite beans for human consumption by mixing them with earth and water. So, too, in India, where the shards of earthenware vessels are crushed in sandalwood oil, made into pills called *mitti*, another form of dirt ingested by pregnant women.

At this time, their taste changes, said the agent for the Mexican manufacturer. "Ask any lady who is in the family way. They want different things to eat. Some ladies eat tamarind, others may eat non-vegetarian, even though usually they are totally vegetarian. But normally, they eat earth. That is why this product was invented. The smell of this is like the first drops of the monsoon on the hard earth."

Also in India, silt from the Ganges River is added to a cooling summer drink containing dried fruit, herbs, and water or water buffalo milk.

So, can anyone just go into the woods or garden, scoop up some dirt, and expect to derive any nourishment from ingesting it? Not likely. "You can't go around eating topsoil," Aufreiter said. Many organic food markets and restaurants around the world have adopted the name Good Earth, but that didn't mean all earth was good for you. To obtain quality clay for medicinal purposes, she suggested visiting reputable shops.

Nor is it a good idea to assume dirt-eating is widespread in the American South, a region that some outsiders said was so poor and peopled by so many ignorant people, they ate dirt. Humorist Roy Blount Jr., a Southerner, got so fed up with Yankees making such rude remarks, he began distributing fictitious recipes he swore were legitimate, for example, for "blackened red dirt," Cajun style.

For a time in the mid-1990s, it was possible to buy one-pound bags of fine red dirt in Atlanta shops. Only US$1.19. Visiting conventioneers bought lots of it.

Selected Bibliography

No newspaper stories and only a few magazine articles are credited here, although they contributed much information; they numbered in the thousands. Nor are there specific citations from various editions of the *Collier's Encyclopedia, Encyclopedia Americana, Macmillan Family Encyclopedia, New Standard Encyclopedia,* and the *World Book Encyclopedia.* Many Internet connections and television documentaries also go unmentioned, with humble apologies to all.

A

Allen, Jana; and Gin, Margret. *Innards and Other Variety Meats.* San Francisco: 101 Productions, 1974.

B

Barash, Cathy Wilkinson. *Edible Flowers: From Garden to Palate.* Golden, CO: Fulcrum Publishing, 1993.

Bates, H.W. *The Naturalist on the River Amazons.* London: John Murray, 1863.

Behnke, Frances L. *Natural History of Termites.* New York: Charles Scribner's Sons, 1977.

Blunt, Wilfrid. *The Ark in the Park: The Zoo in the Nineteenth Century.* London: Hamish Hamilton in association with The Tryon Gallery, 1976.

Brennan, Jennifer. *Thai Cooking.* London: Warner Books, 1992.

Bridgeman, Richard Thomas Orlando, Earl of Bradford. *The Eccentric Cookbook.* London: Robson Books, 1985.

Bruman, Ray. "Ray's List of Weird and Disgusting Foods." Internet: <www.andreas.com/ray/food.html>

Burkhill, I.H. *A Dictionary of the Economic Products of the Malay Peninsula, Vols. I & II.* London: Published for the Malay Government by Crown Agents, 1935.

Bushnell, G.H.S. *The First Americans.* London: Thames & Hudson, 1968.

Burton, Sir Richard. *The Hindu Art of Love.* New York: Castle Books, 1967.

---*The Perfumed Garden.* New York: Castle Books,1965.

C

Cadwallader, Sharon. *Savoring Mexico: Classic Recipes of Traditional Cuisine from All Regions of Mexico.* San Francisco: Chronicle Books, 1987.

Canby, Thomas. "The Rat: Lapdog of the Devil." *National Geographic* 152 July 1977.

Cherry, Ron. "Use of Insects by Australian Aborigines." *American Entomologist* 32: 8-13.

Conniff, Richard. "From Jaws to Laws: Now the Big, Bad Shark Needs Protection from Us." *Smithsonian* May 1993: 32-43.

Cornwall, I.W. *Prehistoric Animals and Their Hunters.* London: Faber & Faber, 1968.

Cost, Bruce. *Bruce Cost's Asian Ingredients: Buying and Cooking the Staple Foods of China, Japan and Southeast Asia.* New York: William Morrow and Company, Inc., 1988.

Courtine, Robert J., Introduction to *Larousse Gastronomique* by Prosper Montague, edited by Jennifer H. Lang. London: Paul Hamlyn, 1988.

D

DeFoliart, Gene R. "Edible Insects as Minilivestock." *Biodiversity and Conservation* 4 (1995): 306-321

---"Insects as a Source of Protein." *Bulletin of the Entomological Society of America* 21/2 1975: 161-63.

---"Insects as Human Food." *Crop Protection* 11 1992.

Densmore, Frances. *How Indians Use Wild Plants for Food, Medicine & Crafts.* New York: Dover Publications, 1974.

Detrick, Mia. *Sushi.* San Francisco: Chronicle Books, 1981.

Dorje, Rinjing. *Food in Tibetan Life.* London: Prospect Books, 1985.

Dowell, Philip, and Adrian Bailey, Elisabeth Lambert Ortiz;and Helena Radecka. *The Book of Ingredients.* London: Mermaid Books, 1983.

E

Ellis, Eleanor A., ed. *Northern Cookbook.* Ottawa: Ministry of Indian Affairs, 1998.

Eppele, David L. *On the Desert: Arizona Cactus.* Self-published on the Internet, <http://www.arizonacactus.com>, 1998.

Etkin, Nina L., ed. *Eating on the Wild Side.* Tucson and London: University of Arizona Press, 1994.

F

Fisher, M.F.K. *The Art of Eating* (includes: *Serve It Forth, Consider the Oyster, How to Cook a Wolf, The Gastronomical Me,* and *An Alphabet of Gourmets*). NewYork: Collier Books, 1990.

G

Gattey, Charles Neilson. *Excess in Food, Drink and Sex.* London: Harrap Ltd., 1986.

Groll, Jonathan. "Introduction to Cassava." Johannesburg: Department of Biology, University of Witwatersrand, 1998.

H

Headquarters, Department of the Army. *US Army Survival Manuel*: FM 21-76. New York: Dorset Press, 1994.

Holt, Vincent M. *Why Not Eat Insects.* Faringdon, Oxon., UK: E.W. Classey Ltd., 1978.

Humphries, Bronwen. "What Did Our Ancestors Eat?" Personal information file, <http:/environlink.org/arrs/essays/man_eat.html>

I

International Starch Institute. "ISI Technical Memoradum on Production of Tapioca Starch." Aarhus, Denmark: 1998.

J

Jackson-Doling, Annabel. *The Food of Vietnam.* Singapore: Periplus Editions, 1997.

Jamaican Information Service. "Jamaican Cuisine." Kingston: <jiz@jamaica-info.com>, 1998.

Jenkins, D.T. *Amanita of North America.* Eureka, CA: Mad River Press, 1986.

K

Konto, Fumihiro & Sheng-ji Pei, editors. *Proceedings of the International Symposium on Flower-Eating Culture in Asia.* Kunming, 1989.

-----& Guo, Huijin; Li , Yanhui; and Tsui, Jingyun. "Record of Ethnobotanical Investigation of Flower-eating Culture in Yunnan Province of China," 1990.

Kurlansky, Mark. "Better Red: Caviar lovers mourn the demise of communism." *Scanorama* 1994.

Kyle, Russel. *A Feast in the Wild.* Oxford: Kudu Publishing,1987.

L

Lever, Christopher. *They Dined on Eland: The Story of the Acclimatisation Societies.* London, Quiller Press, 1992.

Lincoff, G.H. *National Audubon Society Field Guide to North American Mushrooms.* New York: Alfred A. Knopf, 1981.

Livingston, A.D.; and Livingston, Helen. *Edible Plants and Animals: Unusual Foods from Aardvark to Zamia.* New York: Facts on File, 1993.

Luard, Elisabeth. *European Peasant Cooking.* NewYork: Bantam, 1988.

Lucan, Medlar; and Gray, Durian. *The Decadent Cookbook.* Sawtry, Cambs., UK: Dedalus, 1995.

M
Majupuria, Indra; and Lobsang, Diki. *Tibetan Cooking.* Lashkar, India: S. Devi, 1994

McGee, Harold. *On Food and Cooking: The Science and Lore of the Kitchen.* New York: Charles Scribner's Sons, 1984.

McKie, Robin. "The People Eaters." *New Scientist* March 14, 1998.

Miller, Richard Alan. *The Magical and Ritual Use of Aphrodisiacs.* Rochester, VT: Destiny Books, 1985 & 1993.

Morris, Sallie. *South-East Asian Cookery: The Authentic Taste of the Orient.* London: Grafton Books, 1989.

N
Nancarrow, Loren; and Janet Taylor Hogan. *The Worm Book.* Berkeley: Ten Speed Press, 1998.

Nobel, Park S. *Remarkable Agaves and Cacti.* New York: Oxford University Press, 1994.

Noh, Chin-hwa. *Traditional Korean Cooking.* Seoul: Hollym Corporation, 1985.

Novick, Alvin, M.D. "Bats Aren't All Bad." *National Geographic* (May 1973).

O
O'Hanlon, Redmond. *In Trouble Again.* London: Hamish Hamilton, 1988.

P
Palmer, Joan. *All About Cats.* London: Ward, Lock & Uitgeverij Het Spectrum, 1986.

Pan, Lynn. *Sons of the Yellow Emperor: A History of the Chinese Diaspora.* Tokyo: Kodansha International, 1990.

Pearman, Rosemary. *Even More Wild Ways with Cooking.* Linden, South Africa: KwaZulu-Natal Region of the Wildlife Society of South Africa, 1998.

Peiris, Doreen. *A Ceylon Cookery Book.* Colombo: published by the author, 1995.

Peterson, Buck. *International Roadkill Cookbook.* Berkeley: Ten Speed Press, 1994.

Ponting, Clive. *A Green History of the World: The Environment and the Collapse of Great Civilizations.* New York: Penguin, 1993.

Pope, Clifford H. *The Reptile World.* New York: Alfred A. Knopf, 1955.

R
Ross, Philip E. "Man Bites Shark." *Scientific American* June 1990.

S
Scott, David; and Inwood, Kristiaan. *A Taste of Thailand: A Practical and Atmospheric Guide to Thai Cuisine.* London: Rider, 1986.

Shreeve, James. "Infants, Cannibals, and the Pit of Bones." *Discover* January 1994.

Sing, Phia. *Traditional Recipes of Laos.* London: Prospect Books, 1981.

Smith, Joan. "People Eaters." *Granta* 52 Winter 1995: 69-84.

Smith, Leona Woodring. *The Forgotten Art of Flower Cookery.* Gretna, LA: Pelican Publishing Co., 1990.

Sterling, Richard, ed. *Travelers' Tales: Food–A Taste of the Road.* San Francisco: Travelers Tales, Inc., 1996.

Stewart, Matthew. *The Incredible Edible Wild: A Rare Collection of Wilderness Recipes.* Milan, IN: Stewart Associates, 1998

Stobart, Tom. *The Cook's Encyclopedia.* New York: Harper and Row, 1981.

Stolzenburg, William. "Hunting Dragons: On Safari for the Big Game of the Insect World." *Nature Conservancy* May/June 1994.

T
Tannahil, Reay. *Food in History.* London: Penguin, 1973.

U
Unger, Lana. "Bugfood III: Insects Snacks from Around the World." Cooperative Extension Service, Universty of Kentucky, 1998.

University of Hawaii Sea Grant College. "Ono Hawaiian Shark Recipes." Honolulu: May 1979.

US Department of the Interior. "American Alligator." Washington: US Fish and Wildlife Service, 1995.

V
Van Der Post, Laurens. *First Catch Your Eland.* Leicester: Ulverscroft, 1982.

Ventura, Emma. "Dinner with a Twist." *Heritage* Marach/April 1998.

Vietmeyer, Noel D. "The Preposterous Puffer." *National Geographic* August 1984.

———"The Puffer–World's Deadliest Delicacy." *Reader's Digest* June 1985.

W
Warren, William. *The Food of Thailand.* Singapore: Periplus Editions, 1995.

Whitaker, Zai. "Winning the Rat Race in India." *International Wildlife* November/December 1992.

Wiseman, John. *The SAS Survival Handbook.* New York: HarperCollins, 1995.

Y
Young, Mark C., ed. *The Guinesss Book of Records.* New York: Bantam, by arrangement with Guinness Publishing, Ltd., 1977.

acknowledgments

The bibliography acknowledges only a relative handful of the published sources—of which there were thousands—and does not credit the hundred or so individuals who provided information and told stories. During the book's three-year-long cooking process, I found no easier way to get a lively discussion going than to mention the title of my book. Others responded quickly with envelopes of literature and informative e-mail messages, as well as referrals to other sources.

When I told a mutual friend, Richard Lair (who contributed several stories about the years he lived in the jungle with elephant trainers in Thailand), about the book, he introduced me to Michael Freeman the next time the photographer passed through Bangkok. We were pleasantly surprised to learn that we shared an interest in odd foods. For the next year, he took photographs while traveling on three continents, to add to his already extensive library on the subject, as I completed the text. Of the many others who contributed: Dee Aldrich, *Condé Nast Traveler,* New York; Karl Amman, primatologist at <kamman@form-net.com>; Mrs. Vanda Balbir, Bangkok; Thng Wee Chong, Global Ostrich Holdings Pte. Ltd., Singapore; Charles Daly and Simone Jordan, Australian Ostrich Co. Ltd.; Gene DeFoliart and present staff, *The Food and Insect Newsletter,* University of Wisconsin, Madison, WI; Duong Thi Thanh, Sapa, Vietnam; Iowa State University, Department of Entomology; Japan Whaling Association; Ian Lloyd, Singapore; Tom McRae, University of Queensland, Australia; Nittaya Phanthachat, Ban Bung, Thailand; archive department, Ripley s Believe It or Not!, Orlando, FL; Rodrigo Rodriquez, maker of insect and gold leaf lollipops, The Woodlands, TX; Harry Rolnick, New York; Anthony Rose of the Biosynergy Institute, Hermosa Beach, CA; the Sweetwater Jaycees, promoters of the Rattlesnake Round-Up, Sweetwater, TX; Roger Tomlinson, London Zoological Society; Finally, my publishers, Eric Oey and Christina Ong in Singapore, and my editor, Sharon Silva in San Francisco, for sustained support, gentle guidance, and a shared taste for the subject.

Photo Credits
All photos copyright Michael Freeman except:

Pages iv-v, ix, 9, 65, 67, 228-229
Mary Evans Picture Library, London

Pages 184-185
Mary Evans Picture Library/Arthur Rackham Collection

Page 123
Michael Jensen/Auscape International Photo Library, Australia

Page 151
Reg Morrison/Auscape International Photo Library, Australia

Pages 32-5
Karl Ammann
Web site: www.agpix.com/kamman.shtul

The publisher has made every effort to credit content sources where applicable. Erroneous credits will be revised in a timely fashion in subsequent printings.

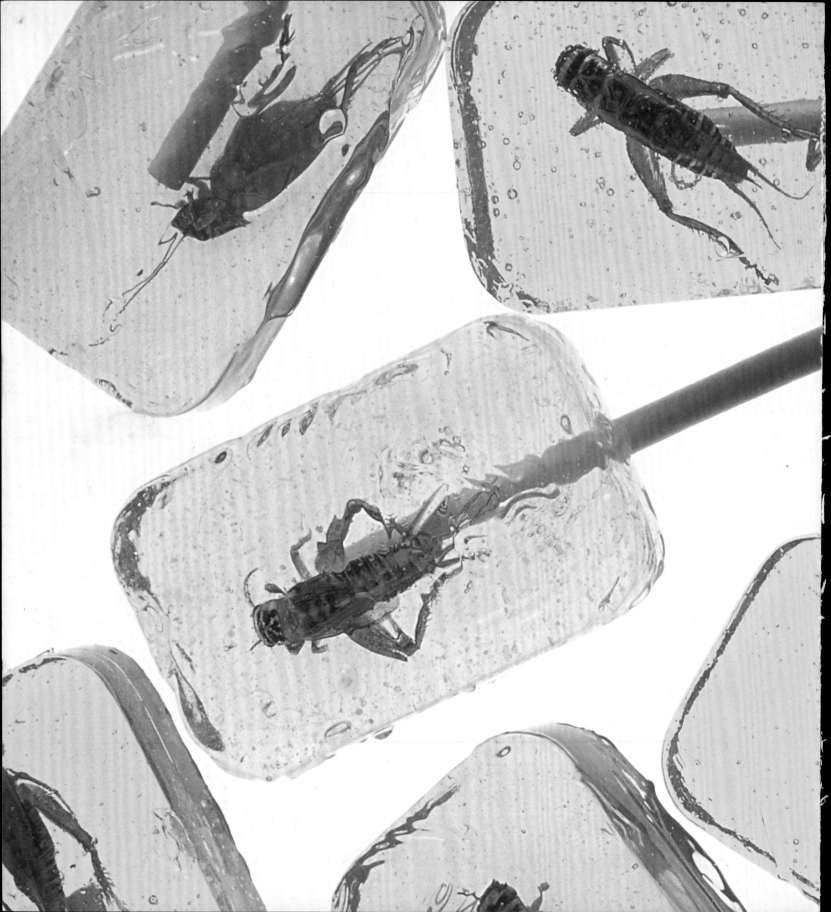